Reading the New Testament

Also by Christopher Tuckett from SPCK:

The Messianic Secret (ed.) 1983

Reading the New Testament

Methods of Interpretation

❖

Christopher Tuckett

First published in Great Britain 1987
SPCK
Holy Trinity Church
Marylebone Road
London NW1 4DU

British Library Cataloguing in Publication Data

Tuckett, C.M.
Reading the New Testament:
methods of interpretation.
1. Bible. N.T.—Criticism, interpretation, etc.
I. Title
225.6 BS2350

ISBN 0–281–04259–4

Printed in Great Britain by
Richard Clay Ltd, Bungay, Suffolk

Contents

Acknowledgements

Many people have helped me in the writing of this book. The publishers first kindly suggested to me the idea of writing a book about methods of biblical criticism, and I am very grateful to them for their continual support for the project throughout the time of writing. Students and colleagues at Manchester University have contributed perhaps more than they realize to this book, though I have no doubt that few will agree with all the ideas expressed here. My wife read more than one draft of each chapter and laboured long and hard to try to adapt tortuous first drafts into something approaching readable English, as well as making several incisive comments about the substance of the book. It is to her above all that I owe a very great debt of gratitude.

Introductio

Any biblical text can be approached in a numb
Take, for example, one of the Gospels. A Gospel can be
source to enable us to find out about the historical events it de-
scribes; it can be used to shed light on the primitive Christian communities which preserved the traditions incorporated in it; it can be used to give insight into the situation and ideas of its author; it can be used as a literary text in its own right, abstracted from its original context and worthy of attention in the same way as any other piece of literature.

The purpose of this book is to offer some discussion of the many ways in which the New Testament can be interpreted. It is therefore a book about *methods.* It is not primarily about results which arise from applying those methods. Although some 'results' will be mentioned in passing to illustrate the various methods, any brief arguments given here do not claim to be providing full reasons for the results to which they lead. Such treatments can be found elsewhere. In any case, we shall see that very few results in biblical studies are final and unquestionable. For almost every argument there is a counter argument. However, the purpose of this book is not to establish results. It is to introduce the reader to the various methods which New Testament critics use today.

This is intended primarily as an 'introductory' book in that it aims to introduce students to the methods of critical scholarship. (It is not an 'Introduction': New Testament 'Introduction' is a rather more specialized discipline, as we shall see.) Yet it is also hoped that this book will itself share in the critical endeavour. We shall be looking at methods in a critical, as well as a descriptive way. Being 'critical' in this context is of course not meant in the looser sense of passing only negative value judgements. I am not intending to down-play any of the approaches we shall be considering. Being 'critical' is meant here in the stricter sense of discriminating and evaluating the subject matter under discussion. So in looking at the various ways scholars have approached the New Testament, I shall be trying not only to describe the various approaches, but also to see how valuable they are, what their limitations are, where their strengths and weaknesses lie, where they break new ground, and so on.

Testament scholarship generally has a very good record ng self-critical. No 'result' can now be produced by a New ament scholar without two or three Ph.D. students descending it and tearing it to pieces to analyse it, discredit it, explain it, or efurbish it anew. This is, of course, a very healthy state of affairs for any scholarly discipline (though it leads some to accuse New Testament scholarship of never succeeding in establishing any firm results!). There is, however, sometimes rather less critical self-evaluation of the methods used by New Testament scholars. This does not apply across the board. Textual criticism, for example, has developed in such a way that scholarly discussions today often revolve almost exclusively around the question of methodology. Redaction criticism on the other hand has until recently generated relatively little critical reflection about its own methodology, despite its tremendous popularity. This book is therefore intended to fill what may be a small gap in the scholarly literature at present by looking critically at the various methods we use.

There is always a danger in biblical scholarship that discussions become so erudite that they lose contact with the subject matter they are meant to be discussing. (Cf. the remarks made by many who welcome more 'sociological' approaches to the New Testament: see pp. 136f below.) Whether this book suffers this way is for others to judge. One attempt is however made to avoid this danger. All the 'methods' we shall be looking at represent different ways of approaching the biblical *texts*. I shall therefore try to relate everything said here about methods to the actual process of applying the methods to the text. The methods will in turn be applied to one particular text, and the example chosen is the story of the healing of the man with the withered hand in Mark 3.1–6 and parallels. (In fact we cannot do this in every chapter. Considerations of genre, for example, are dealing with wider contexts of whole Gospels, not individual stories within a Gospel; but as far as possible I have tried to illustrate all the methods concerned by reference to this test passage.)

Most of the approaches discussed here are part of the so-called 'historical-critical method'. This is in fact scarcely a single 'method' but rather encompasses a number of different methods. The basis of this approach is that the New Testament texts are 'historical', not necessarily in the sense that they recount history but in the sense that they stem from a particular historical context. Thus in order to understand them we have to try to find out something about that context.

In the last two chapters we shall venture into areas where the value of the historical-critical approach is questioned, and more account is taken of the text as an entity independent of its original historical context. For many who have become accustomed to the traditional historical approach, such new ways of looking at the New Testament texts often appear rather strange. I shall be arguing that such approaches can never jettison the historical-critical approach completely and that this remains of fundamental importance for any responsible interpretation of the New Testament.

Others who are more versed in these methods may find what is said here somewhat simplistic. Very few will probably agree with all the critical comments made in this book. However, scholarship should thrive on criticism, and if this book provokes further critical reflection on the subject of methodology, and also more clarification of some of the methods used, it will have served some useful purpose.

Some important areas of discussion have deliberately not been included here. I have not, for example, included any discussion of various philosophical problems associated with the attempt to understand a text from a culture very different from our own. The problem of whether we can understand anything which comes from a different culture, the so-called problem of 'cultural relativity', has been deliberately bypassed here. I have assumed that at least some such understanding is possible, though I am aware of the problems involved.[1]

I have also avoided discussion of several important philosophical questions about what might or might not have happened as events in history. For example, I have not discussed the problem of whether 'miracles' occurred. Rather, I have tried to confine attention to the more 'literary' problems of understanding the *texts*. Some may feel that this constitutes a deficiency in the book. In self-defence I would plead that a full discussion of problems like this really needs another book in its own right.

I am also aware that the discussion in the final two chapters is by no means a complete treatment of all the issues implicitly raised there. I have not tried to give a comprehensive discussion of the vast 'hermeneutical' problem of how one moves from 'what a text meant originally' to 'what a text means today'. In these chapters I have simply considered some approaches which appear to bracket off the historical question of 'what a text meant', and I have argued that such bracketing off cannot be total. The scope of these chapters is therefore relatively limited. This book does not claim to offer a full treatment of hermeneutics in the sense that that word is usually understood today. (It is however perhaps a book about hermeneutics in an older sense of the word; 'hermeneutics' was at one time the study of methods in criticism, as opposed to 'exegesis' which was the application of those methods.)

Despite this disclaimer, this book does hopefully show some awareness of hermeneutical issues. I have fully recognized that the New Testament texts occupy a very special position within the Christian Church, and that for many Christians the New Testament texts are not only of antiquarian interest. The fact that the New Testament forms part of canonical Scripture for the Christian Church means that many Christians believe that these texts do 'mean' something for Christians today. I have tried to look at some aspects of this issue in the first chapter, and I have given there one suggestion for how the New Testament might still be given a unique position within Christianity in the light of modern research. This view does lead to some freedom in correlating 'what a text meant' with 'what it means'. We may decide that a text 'meant' one thing originally but 'means' precious little to us now. However, my argument will be that we can never completely give up the historical approach to discovering the meaning of a text, even when our primary concern is to discern what contemporary significance these texts might have within the context of Christian commitment.

As this is intended to be an introductory book for students starting academic study of the Bible, footnotes have been kept to a minimum. Suggestions for further reading will be found at the end of the book, but again no attempt has been made to provide anything like full documentation. Those who need more help will no doubt get it from their teachers; those who notice deficiencies here probably do not need this book at all!

Notes

1. For a strong statement of the problem, see D. E. Nineham, *The Use and Abuse of the Bible* (London 1976). For a very fair discussion, see J. Barton, 'Reflections on Cultural Relativism', *Theology* 82 (1979), pp. 103–9 and 191–9.

1
Scripture and Canon

This book is about methods, in particular methods of studying the New Testament. But why do we study the New Testament at all? Why do we have books about studying the New Testament? Certainly many people do study it and many people write books about it. The volume of secondary literature – books about the New Testament and books about books about the New Testament – is now vast and quite daunting even to professional New Testament scholars who have (some) time to devote to this literature. This book may perhaps occupy one small extra space on some library shelves which are already groaning under the weight of vast numbers of books about the New Testament, and the literary output of New Testament students shows no sign of abating. Why then do we devote so much time and energy to studying the New Testament? Should we be doing so? In this first chapter we shall try to explore at least one of the reasons why the New Testament arouses so much interest today.

One of the most important reasons is undoubtedly the fact that the New Testament texts occupy a very special position within the Christian Church. 'The New Testament' consists of a fixed body of precisely twenty-seven assorted documents.[1] Further, this collection is not made for reasons of scholarly convenience. Nor are the limits arbitrary. The fact is that these texts constitute a part of the canon of Scripture for the Christian Church. Now both the words 'Scripture' and 'canon' raise a number of important issues, and it is these we shall try to examine in this chapter. However, in order to avoid confusion, we should perhaps first clarify what we mean by these terms.

As I shall use the words here, 'Scripture' will be taken to mean a body of literature which a community accepts as in some sense authoritative for its existence; 'canon' will be taken to mean a well-defined list of scriptural texts. With these definitions, it is worth noting that the whole idea of a canon presupposes the existence of Scripture: one can only put limits round something that is already there. In order to have a canon, one must therefore have some Scripture. In this chapter we shall be considering some aspects of the claim that the New Testament is canonical Scripture, and in what sense such a claim might be maintained today in the light of critical scholarship. However, in order to put that discussion into focus, we shall glance very briefly at the historical development which led to the New Testament documents being regarded as canonical in the first place.

History of the Canon

This is not the place to give a full-scale history of the canon. Such a history can be found elsewhere.[2] The process by which the individual documents of the New Testament were collected together and given the status of canonical Scripture was a very long and complicated one. Moreover, much of that history is hidden from us; there are several stages in the development of the canon about which we are ignorant and where we have to resort to intelligent guesswork. This is particularly the case for the crucial period of the second century.

In the initial period of the Christian Church, there was clearly no 'New Testament' at all. The first Christians certainly had their 'Scripture': they simply appropriated all the Scriptures of Judaism. When Paul says in Romans 15.4 that 'whatever was written in former days was written for our instruction', he is quite typical of all the New Testament writers. Paul is referring here to the Jewish Scriptures (later to be called the 'old' Testament by the Christian Church), and these Jewish Scriptures are assumed without question to be Scripture for the Christian Church as well.

(Whether Jewish Scripture at this time was clearly defined by the limits of a 'canon' is a much-debated issue. Probably this was not the case. Judaism may not have set well-defined limits around its body of sacred literature, its 'Scripture', until about AD 100. Thus first-century Judaism had a Scripture whose limits may have been rather fuzzy at its edges, so to speak. We can see this fuzziness reflected in Christian writings where, for example, the author of Jude quite happily quotes 1 Enoch (Jude 14–15) in a way that suggests that the latter was 'scriptural' for him, even though it was not included eventually in a Jewish canon of Scripture.)

However, Christianity did not always accept Jewish Scripture uncritically. Various figures within the new Christian movement felt free to criticize the Jewish law in various ways. In Matthew's Gospel, for example, Jesus sets his own assertions against those of the Jewish law in the great antitheses of the Sermon on the Mount (Matt. 5.21–48); and Paul can say that, in some sense at least, 'Christ is the end of the law' (Rom. 10.4).

Further, the basis for being able to make such critiques was clearly the authority claimed by individuals within the Church; it was not the authority of another written text alongside the Old Testament. In the Gospels, Jesus claims at times to set aside the Old Testament law on the basis of his own authority, not by appealing to further written texts. The same is true of Paul's letters. These letters undoubtedly carried authority and were clearly regarded as having some status in all the Pauline communities (cf. p. 72 below). However, the authority in question was that of Paul himself: the letters did not have authority by virtue of being part of a 'scriptural' body of sacred writings.

In relation to the writings themselves, early Christians evidently assumed a great freedom. Matthew felt at liberty to rewrite Mark's written text, changing it considerably at times. Matthew evidently did not regard Mark's text as part of a sacred Scripture. No doubt Matthew thought that Mark's stories about Jesus had some authority, but the authority was almost certainly that of Jesus himself, not of the written text of Mark's Gospel.

Gradually, the books which we now call 'the New Testament' were collected together and came to be regarded as Scripture, on a par with the books of the 'Old Testament'. The process was a slow one, and many of the stages are no longer visible to us. For example, we have no direct evidence about the process whereby Paul's letters were collected together to form a single corpus. Various theories have been proposed, but in the end we have to admit ignorance. However, the author of 2 Peter (probably writing in the early second century) appears to presuppose such a collection and to view it as comparable with other Scriptures, warning his readers about various people who twist Paul's letters 'as they do the other scriptures' (2 Pet. 3.16). Whatever the precise reference, it is clear that Paul's letters have become important texts which people are interpreting as the basis for their own beliefs and practices. One only bothers to interpret texts that matter! Moreover, the writer of 2 Peter quite naturally refers to Paul's letters and 'the other scriptures/writings' (the translation is disputed) in parallel. This may not be fully conscious, but it does reveal tendencies at work.

Similar phenomena can be seen in other texts from the same period. For example, the writer of the homily known as 2 Clement at one point quotes Isaiah 54.1 and then has ' and another scripture says', followed by the saying of Jesus, 'I came not to call the righteous, but sinners' (2 Clem. 2.4; cf. Matt. 9.13). A little later Justin Martyr records that the 'memoirs of the apostles' (= the Gospels?) were being read as part of the Christian liturgy alongside the writings of the prophets (*First Apology*, 67). These examples, of which more could be given, show that gradually the traditions about Jesus, Paul and others were revered and cited alongside the words of the Old Testament and were used in similar contexts.

In this development, a great change seems to have occurred by the end of the second century. Above all in the writings of Irenaeus (*c.* AD 180), there are discussions about documents themselves, and about which documents are to be considered reliable and appropriate to be used by Christians. We also start to get at this period clear lists of documents with decisions about which texts can be read and used in churches and which cannot. The precise reason for this shift of emphasis is not entirely clear. One very attractive theory is that the change was due to the influence of the work of Marcion. Marcion was an influential Christian leader in the middle of the second century who believed that the God of the Old Testament could have nothing to do with the God of Jesus. He thus drove a sharp wedge between Christianity and Judaism. His hero was Paul, but he believed that some of Paul's letters had been adulterated by subsequent Judaizing additions. (For example Paul's positive attitude to the Old Testament in Romans 15.4 was probably eliminated by Marcion as a later corruption of the 'true' Paul.) He thus adopted a 'canon' of Paul's letters and one Gospel, Luke, both duly purged of Judaizing tendencies. It may well be that the later Church's insistence on the *four*fold Gospel canon is in part a reaction against Marcion's influence. If so, then the real impetus to the formation of a 'canon', by setting strict limits around a body of sacred literature, is the work of Marcion and the reaction he provoked.[3]

Such a theory cannot be easily proved or disproved, simply because we have so little clear evidence of the period concerned. Marcion may not have been the first to form collections of written texts: the author of 2 Peter, for example, seems to be presupposing the existence of such a collection of Paul's letters. Nevertheless, the attempt to define the limits of such collections very precisely cannot easily be dated prior to Marcion.

By the end of the second century, the idea of a body of texts to be regarded as sacred Scripture seems to have been well established. Moreover, there was broad agreement about what should be included. The four Gospels, Acts and the Pauline corpus occupied an unquestioned position. The remaining texts provoked some discussion. Hebrews was regarded with a certain suspicion in the West, Revelation in the East. 2 Peter is rarely mentioned in the early lists of canonical writings. The remaining history of the canon is thus concerned with the 'mopping-up' operation, sorting out what the precise limits of the canon should be.

What criteria were applied in this process? It is rather difficult to provide a neat answer to this question. Different people seem to have used different criteria, and were not always consistent either. Moreover, we may suspect that many of the so-called criteria which were used were often only *ad hoc* rationalizations to justify the existing state of affairs.

'Apostolicity' in the sense of apostolic authorship is often thought to have been extremely important. It is however doubtful if this was ever a very significant factor. Undoubtedly antiquity was important: more recent texts, however edifying in themselves, could not be considered in the same class as texts from the start of the Christian movement.[4] But within the class of ancient texts, it is not certain whether the identity of the author as an apostle was ever very important.

Irenaeus devotes some space to defending the status of the four Gospels, but as von Campenhausen has shown, what was important for Irenaeus was not their apostolic authorship as such but their historical reliability.[5] Similarly Eusebius records a story about a bishop, Serapion, and one of his congregations which was using the Gospel of Peter.[6] Serapion's attitude was to allow this at first; but when he saw the text itself, he was appalled by its contents and so banned its usage. (The Gospel of Peter suggests that the true Christ never really suffered on the cross.) At no time was it suggested that the Gospel of Peter might be a 'forgery' and banned for that reason. The authorship question never arose. What was important was simply the contents of the text.

The same is probably the case for Hebrews. Doubts about its Pauline authorship were expressed continuously. But the suspicion which it aroused was probably due much more to its statements which appeared to rule out the possibility of a second repentance after apostasy (cf. Heb. 6.4–6). These statements were used in a very rigorous way by Montanists in the second century, and it is this which probably led to the uncertain position of Hebrews in the canon, rather than any questions about its authorship.

Much more important than the question of apostolic authorship seems to have been the universal practice of the Church for determining what was canonical. For someone like Origen (early third century AD) it was of supreme importance that a text was universally recognized throughout the Church, and this factor outweighed any problems about authorship. Other texts were disputed, but in cases like that, it was ecclesiastical usage which settled the issue. Eusebius' language later (fourth century AD) also seems to reflect the same idea: he talks of books that are 'accepted' and others which are 'disputed'. Many of the lists of canonical texts which emerge from this period, including Athanasius' famous festal letter of AD 367 which is often thought to mark the definitive closing of the canon, may thus be simply reflecting current practice which had evolved gradually over a number of years. Further, this notion of universal practice may provide us with some help when we turn to consider the question of the status of the New Testament today.

The Canon Today

What value do the concepts of Scripture and canon have today as applied to the books of the New Testament? It is sometimes thought that the whole approach of biblical criticism has swept away the status of the New Testament as canonical Scripture. Do the results of biblical criticism then allow any special position for the New Testament texts?

One point must be made clear initially. The terms 'Scripture' and 'canon' are fundamentally confessional terms. They relate to the activities and beliefs of a confessing community, a 'Church'. Scripture is by definition a body of literature accepted by a Church as in some sense authoritative. Whilst it may be possible to have a 'Church' without 'Scripture', we cannot have a body of 'Scripture' without a 'Church' to acknowledge it as such.[7] Further, we have already seen that the whole idea of a 'canon' presupposes the existence of a Scripture (see p. 5 above). Thus the ideas of Scripture and canon only have meaning in relation to a Church which accepts them. How valid or important then are these twin concepts for the interpretation of the New Testament today?

It is clear that at one level, these concepts can be ignored entirely. The New Testament texts are pieces of literature stemming from the ancient world; as such they can be studied in their own right independently of the status they have acquired within Christianity. Primitive Christianity and its literature can be seen simply as a part of ancient history and can be studied at that level. We do not have to be Christians ourselves in order to study ancient Christian history. Moreover, when we do study at that level, many of us will ignore the limits of the Christian canon completely (though see ch. 11 below). We may decide that information about Jesus can be found in the Gospel of Thomas as well as in the Gospel of Mark; the fact that Mark is in the canon and Thomas is not will not make a scrap of difference to those who are trying to recover reliable information about Jesus. Similarly, we may decide that the use of the term 'Son of Man' in the Gospels is similar to the use of the term in Daniel or in 1 Enoch; the legitimacy of appealing to either text as possible background for illuminating the Gospels is generally regarded as quite independent of the fact that Daniel is canonical whilst 1 Enoch is not. So too, an historical investigation of Christianity at the end of the first century will potentially gain as much from looking at the uncanonical texts of the Didache and 1 Clement as at the canonical texts of 1 Timothy and 2 Peter. In terms of the historical study of early Christianity and its literature, we can and do ignore the limits imposed by the canon.[8]

Nevertheless, it is also the case that the texts of the New Testament have engendered far more interest and study than other Christian texts of the same period. Within the last twenty years, at least four full-scale English commentaries on 2 Peter have been published. (There may well be more.) As far as I am aware, there are no recent English commentaries on the Epistle to Diognetus which, many would argue, is of about the same date as 2 Peter and of considerably greater theological value. Clearly the fact that 2 Peter is in the New Testament, whereas the Epistle to Diognetus is not, has led to such a disparity in the amount of interest shown in the two works. Again, we can recognize and accept this fact of canonicity without ourselves subscribing to the belief system for which these texts form a canon. We do not have to be Christians to acknowledge the fact that 2 Peter and other texts do form a canon for the Christian Church. Further, the very fact that these texts have been canonized means that they have influenced Christianity decisively in ways that non-canonical texts have not. Moreover, the dominant place which Christianity has occupied in western culture means that the New Testament texts have influenced our culture very deeply in many ways, for example in art, secular literature and ethics. It is therefore in one way quite justified to give the texts of the New Testament a special position within academic study. Given the fact of the Bible's wide-ranging influence on contemporary society (this may be less overt today but it is still present), study of the biblical texts will continue to be undertaken by a large number of people; and this can be done irrespective of individual belief or lack of belief.

It is, however, also the case that the greater proportion of biblical study is undertaken by those who are believing Christians. Even within secular institutions such as English universities, the fact remains that the majority of those who study the Bible have some Christian commitment. (There are, of course, notable exceptions: but they are exceptions.) Can we then say anything about the status of the Bible at the level of contemporary Christian commitment? In what sense can the New Testament still be accepted as Scripture, and the limits set around the canon in the fourth century still be accepted in the twentieth? The issue has been raised sharply in recent years by a number of writers who have questioned whether the decisions of past councils about the precise limits of the canon should be accepted today; or, more drastically, whether the whole idea of a 'holy Scripture' is not foreign to the essence of Christianity.[9]

One thing is clear in this discussion: many of the arguments used in the past to justify specific decisions about the limits of the New Testament canon cannot be applied in the same way today to produce the same decisions.

If apostolic authorship is considered to be an important test, then not all the books of the New Testament would pass such a test.[10] Modern critical scholarship has cast severe doubts on whether the apostle Peter wrote 2 Peter, and whether Paul wrote the Pastoral epistles, to name but two examples.

If antiquity is regarded as a decisive factor, again it is doubtful how far such a criterion would produce precisely our New Testament. Some books of the New Testament are probably comparatively late (2 Peter probably dates from the second century); other Christian texts which are not in the New Testament are at least as early as these late canonical texts. (1 Clement dates from the AD 90s, which is a period where many would place several of the New Testament texts.)

A criterion of historical reliability for canonicity would also present problems today. Many would argue that the historical books of the New Testament, the Gospels and Acts, are not accurate eyewitness accounts of the events concerned. They may be none the worse for that, but if they have to be historically accurate to be accepted as canonical, they might well fail the test.

Finally, any suggestion that texts be accepted on the basis of their content and their 'orthodoxy' would also lead to problems today in the light of modern research. If there is one thing that modern study of the New Testament has shown, it is that there is a great diversity within the New Testament.[11] It may be that this is a 'diversity in unity', but if so, it is the unity which needs demonstration today. This diversity goes beyond the level of terminology used. In the areas of eschatology, attitudes to the Jewish law, Christology, attitudes to material possessions, there are enormous differences between various New Testament writers. It is not easy to find a central core of belief which unites the texts of the New Testament. Even if we could, it is difficult to see how such a core could serve to give the New Testament texts alone a privileged position within Christianity. For if we make the core fairly general (and we would have to in order to encompass the whole New

Testament) then a whole range of Christian literature from all ages would come into consideration. In order to produce just our New Testament we would have to couple this with appeals to antiquity or something similar, and then we would be faced with all the problems which we have already encountered.

The upshot of all this is that many of the arguments which were used in the past to justify the present New Testament canon can no longer be used with the same results in the light of modern scholarship. Is it then still justifiable for Christianity to cling on to the same canon of Scripture?

Many have argued not. Some have suggested that the canon ought to be restricted to something smaller than our present canon, arguing for a 'canon within the canon'. Thus some have argued that the real norm for Christian faith should not be the New Testament as such, but the Pauline doctrine of justification by faith maybe, or the teaching of Jesus. Others have argued that the canon could be extended almost without limit (which is virtually another way of abolishing it altogether). Can we not learn, it is argued, just as much about the Christian faith from the writings of Augustine, Bonhoeffer and T. S. Eliot as from Jude and Hebrews?

Such arguments have some force. It is certainly the case that most Christians work with a rather restricted New Testament canon for many practical purposes. Most preachers avoid considerable parts of the New Testament in choosing texts for sermons. Many also find little spiritual value in a writing such as Hebrews, or Jude, or in the bizarre imagery of Revelation. So too, given the great diversity in the New Testament, people pick out different themes as the assumed centre to which the rest of the New Testament is to be subordinated. Such a procedure is absolutely inevitable and quite right and proper, given the range of different viewpoints represented in the New Testament. However, as J. Barr points out, such a 'centre' within the New Testament is not a 'canon' in the same sense that the twenty-seven books of the New Testament form a 'canon'.[12] These books form a 'canon' in the sense that they form a prescribed list of scriptural books. To talk about justification by faith, say, as a 'canon' within the New Testament 'canon' is to use that word in two quite different ways, and this probably only creates confusion.

We are still left with the question of whether there is any justification for the idea of a canon of Scripture within Christianity, and if there is, whether its limits should be preserved or changed. Has modern critical scholarship undermined all the reasons which gave the New Testament their special status in the past? One criterion that we referred to in discussing the history of the canon has not yet been mentioned here. This is the fact that often texts were accepted as canonical simply because they had established themselves throughout the Christian Church. This may help in providing us with a viable view about the canon which will still allow us to accept all the insights of modern biblical studies.

We have seen that part of the modern difficulty about the canon concerns the diversity within the New Testament. But the diversity of the New Testament is in some ways simply a microcosm of the diversity of Christianity itself.[13] If it is difficult to define what the central core of the New Testament is, it is even worse trying to define what Christianity is. Or, to put it the other way round, it is difficult to define what can *not* count as Christianity. Christianity is so broad that it is often problematic to know when a pattern of belief goes beyond the limits of what can be accepted as 'Christian'. However, most would agree that anything that would claim to be Christian should satisfy at least two minimal requirements: firstly, it must give a central place to the person of Jesus; and secondly, it must show at least some continuity with what has been claimed to be Christian in the past.[14] A Christianity with no place for the person of Jesus seems a self-contradiction; and something that is totally new, bearing no relationship to Christian tradition at all, cannot really claim to be Christian. If we accept this, it may enable us to see how we can continue to give the New Testament documents some kind of a normative role today.

We considered earlier the problems of applying a sort of 'criterion of antiquity' to establish what should be regarded as canonical. Now despite the problems raised here, it is still the case that the New Testament documents provide us with the earliest and most reliable records about Jesus. Although we now recognize that the synoptic evangelists have pressed their own stamp on the material (cf. ch. 8 below), few would go so far as to say that the figure of the pre-Easter Jesus has become totally invisible to us. If we want to discover information about Jesus, we can and do still turn to the New Testament to provide it. Further, it is unlikely that we shall find much reliable information elsewhere. Some traditions about Jesus may have been preserved outside the New Testament (e.g. in the Gospel of Thomas), though it is unlikely that these will substantially alter our picture of Jesus gained from the New Testament itself. The New Testament thus retains its value as our primary source of information about the man Jesus of Nazareth. If we then agree that an indispensable requirement of any Christian viewpoint is that it gives a central place to the person of Jesus, then we shall have to return continually to the New Testament to find out who Jesus was and to check whether our picture of Jesus corresponds with the historical facts insofar as we can discover them.

However, the previous paragraph might suggest at most a canon of the Gospels alone. Other Christian writers in the New Testament, for whatever reason, very rarely refer to the person of Jesus in such a way as to give us further historical information about the sort of man Jesus was, what he said and what he did. Rather, they represent responses to the whole event of Jesus' life, death and resurrection, dwelling on particular aspects to bring out salient points for their own situation. For example, Paul and the author of Hebrews are concerned above all with the meaning and significance of Jesus' death and resurrection. What Jesus did before Good Friday receives less attention. However, the fact that we receive relatively little direct information about Jesus here does not mean that these parts of the New Testament have no place within a canon of Scripture today. We suggested that the centrality of Jesus was only one of the basic criteria for what should count as genuinely Christian. The other was that Christianity must preserve continuity with its traditions, at least in part. It is here that the rest of the New Testament plays a vital role, for the whole New Testament really represents the starting point and origin of all subsequent Christian tradition, as we shall now try to show.

Despite the fact that some parts of the New Testament are of quite a late date, the bulk of the New Testament gives us the earliest evidence of Christian tradition available to us, where Christians are beginning to articulate their responses to the events of Jesus' life, death and resurrection. Paul's letters are to be dated within thirty years of the crucifixion of Jesus; and virtually all the New Testament documents are to be dated before the end of the first century AD, hence within sixty or seventy years of Jesus' death. However early some of the non-canonical Christian texts which we now possess may be, it is unlikely that they can be dated significantly earlier than the bulk of the New Testament writings themselves. The New Testament documents thus provide the earliest access point which we have to enable us to see the developing Christian tradition.

This is not to say that the tradition actually started with Paul himself. Far from it. As we shall see, several parts of Paul's letters may represent traditions which are even earlier than Paul, and we can see from the various disputes which Paul had in his communities that rival interpretations about aspects of the Christian faith were already current in this early period. Nevertheless it is still the case that the earliest Christian traditions which we have are contained in the New Testament.

Insofar as the New Testament then enables us to see the earliest parts of the tradition which are available to us, it provides an indispensable reference point for contemporary Christian reflection. However, the New Testament also contains later traditions as well as earlier ones, as we have seen. Does this affect our view of the canon, and what does it say about the normativeness of Scripture?

One fact which we must also bear in mind is that the New Testament has, from a very early period, always occupied a normative role. The fact is almost trite when stated baldly like this, but it is important in this context. However much we may wish to question just how, and in what way, the New Testament should be normative in the present, we can still accept as a fact of history that the New Testament has been Scripture and canon for the Church. The 'tradition' which the Christian Church has referred to has always been based, directly or indirectly, on the Bible.

Two results of the New Testament documents' being regarded as 'scriptural' were that, firstly, other contemporary writings tended not to be preserved, and secondly, the New Testament received the particular role whereby all subsequent Christian tradition referred back to it.[15] Sometimes this reference has been direct, when some Christians seek to justify their positions as direct interpretations of the Bible.[16] At other times the reference has been less direct: A refers back to B in Christian tradition for support, B has referred to C, C to D and so on. There may be many stages in this chain, but ultimately the reference will be back to the text of the Bible or to individuals represented in the biblical text. We can think, for example, of modern Lutherans justifying their present beliefs by reference to Martin Luther; and Luther himself may have appealed to Paul for support.

The New Testament texts thus have a unique position within the Christian Church simply by virtue of the fact that they have occupied the position of a canon of Scripture. Their universal usage, which we saw was an important factor in their being accepted as canonical in the first place, gives them a quite special place today.[17]

There is too a sense in which we can say that the role which these texts play is a normative one. It may well be normative in a rather different way from the way in which this was understood in the past. We are now far more aware of the fact that the texts of the New Testament were written in an age, and for situations, very different from our own. The New Testament does not supply us with lists of timeless maxims of universal and eternal validity.

It does not even address many of the severe problems which face modern men and women in their contemporary situations. The presuppositions of New Testament writers are at times rather different from our own.

All this is of course quite familiar to many of us; indeed the whole purpose of much biblical study which we shall be looking at in this book is to enable us to bridge the gap between our day and the first century in a responsible way and to interpret the words of the New Testament writers sympathetically and with care. In the light of this knowledge we cannot simply transfer the words of a first-century writer and apply them without more ado to solve twentieth-century problems. This is, I will assume, quite obvious and needs no further elaboration here. We cannot therefore adopt the position of many Christians in the past and use the Bible as a source of 'proof-texts'. The Bible cannot be normative in this sense.

It can still however be normative in a looser sense. If we accept that the canon provides the basis, the starting point and origin, for all subsequent Christian tradition, then we can recognize that the biblical texts can and should continue to occupy this position for all further Christian reflection. This does not mean, however, that we have to accept uncritically everything that the Bible says. Nor do we need to demand that all contemporary Christian reflecton must take the form of directly referring to the Bible. All that we are suggesting is that the Bible continues to occupy the position of being the starting point of Christian reflection and hence providing the initial point in the tradition from which all else flows.

Such a view gives the Bible a normative role in the Christian life; but it also enables us to be critical about individual parts of the Bible. On this view, it really does not matter very much whether all the ascriptions of authorship are true or not. Whether Paul wrote the Pastorals, or whether Peter wrote 2 Peter, becomes irrelevant for the question of the status of the Bible today. The simple fact that the Pastorals and 2 Peter have always formed part of the New Testament is enough to justify their special position as I have tried to define it here.

We can recognize too, with this model of scriptural normativeness, that some things may no longer be valid or acceptable for us today in exactly the same form as they appear in the Bible. The attitude of the New Testament to slavery, whereby slavery as an institution is rarely if every questioned at the concrete social level, is a case in point. Again this would cause no problem for the model I have suggested. We could accept that attitudes to slavery in the New Testament were worked out when the social realities of the situation were very different from what pertained later, for example in America. Slaves in the first century were often better off materially than many freedmen. But a changed social situation led Christians to further reflection, bringing in insights from elsewhere in the New Testament and in the Christian tradition, and this has led to a widely held view that slavery as an institution is fundamentally un-Christian.

Scripture is thus the primary *source* for all subsequent reflection that claims to be Christian. If we accept this, then we are ascribing some sort of normative role to the New Testament. We are not saying that the New Testament is always right; we are not saying that the New Testament is always self-consistent. All that we are saying is that all subsequent Christian reflection and development, if it is to be recognizably Christian, must relate to the New Testament witness in some way or other. It cannot ignore it.

I have tried in this chapter to outline one possible way in which the New Testament can be accepted as canonical Scripture and be assigned some kind of 'normative' role within contemporary Christianity. This is of course not the only way in which the New Testament can be regarded as normative.[18] Many will regard the view suggested here as giving Scripture too 'low' a position. This view does however have the advantage that it can take full note of, and accept, many of the results of critical biblical scholarship without in any way prejudicing the status of the New Testament. In the past, the authority of the New Testament texts has sometimes been tied up with the question of authorship, so that a pseudonymous work has been thought to be less authoritative than a 'genuine' text. With the model of normativeness outlined above, such worries about authenticity do not matter so much. (For further on this question, see pp. 56ff below.)

The view of the status of the New Testament given here will certainly not satisfy everyone and may not satisfy anyone. In one sense that does not matter. This book is intended to be about methods used in interpreting the New Testament and the reasons why we start the enterprise of interpretation at all will be many and varied. All that this chapter has attempted to do is to indicate one possible way in which critical scholarship need not be seen as a threat to a 'religious' use of the New Testament. We can, I believe, still accept that the New Testament texts rightly occupy a unique position within Christianity, and also fully welcome the insights which critical scholarship brings. To regard, and accept, the New Testament as canon need not mean that we suspend our critical faculties. The experience of many is that only when we use those faculties to the full does the New Testament come alive and speak to us in the present. That for many is why New Testament scholarship remains so exciting and worthwhile an endeavour.

Notes

1. The situation is of course rather different in the case of the Old Testament: Protestant Bibles classify a number of writings as part of the so-called 'Apocrypha' which is separated from the Old Testament; Roman Catholic Bibles include these writings as part of the Old Testament itself.
2. See for example H. von Campenhausen, *The Formation of the Christian Bible* (ET, London 1972); also the relevant sections in various standard Introductions to the New Testament (e.g. W. G. Kümmel's).
3. See von Campenhausen and others.
4. This is asserted by the Muratorian canon in relation to the Shepherd of Hermas: see von Campenhausen, *Formation*, pp. 257–8.
5. ibid., pp. 195ff.
6. Eusebius, *E.H.* 6.12.
7. See D. H. Kelsey, *The Uses of Scripture in Recent Theology* (London 1975), pp. 89ff.
8. The *locus classicus* for such an approach to the New Testament documents is that of W. Wrede: see his essay 'The Tasks and Methods of "New Testament Theology"', translated in Robert Morgan (ed.), *The Nature of New Testament Theology* (London 1973), pp. 68ff., together with Morgan's own introduction.
9. See C. F. Evans, *Is 'Holy Scripture' Christian?* (London 1971).
10. We might even have difficulty in deciding who is an 'apostle'. Even amongst the New Testament writers themselves, there is not always agreement. See C. K. Barrett, *The Signs of an Apostle* (London 1970).
11. cf. J. D. G. Dunn, *Unity and Diversity in the New Testament* (London 1977).
12. J. Barr, *Holy Scripture. Canon, Authority, Criticism* (Oxford 1983), pp. 70–3.
13. See the well-known essay of E. Käsemann, 'The Canon of the New Testament and the Unity of the Church', in his *Essays on New Testament Themes* (ET, London 1964), pp. 95ff.
14. See Robert Morgan, 'Expansion and Criticism in the Christian Tradition', in M. Pye & Robert Morgan (eds.), *The Cardinal Meaning* (The Hague 1973), pp. 59–101, esp. pp. 69, 71.
15. cf. J. Barr, *The Bible in the Modern World* (London 1973), pp. 116–17.
16. The classic example in the modern era is of course R. Bultmann: Bultmann presents his own theology in the form of an interpretation of the theology of Paul and John. See the discussion in Morgan, *Nature*, pp. 33ff.

17. The view of the authority of the Bible presented here is intended to be closely related to that of Barr (see his *Bible in the Modern World*, esp. pp. 117–18; also his essay 'Has the Bible any Authority?', in *Explorations in Theology 7* (London 1980), pp. 52ff.) and Kelsey (*Uses of Scripture*, esp. pp. 164ff.), though probably without being fully identical with either.
18. See Kelsey, *Uses of Scripture*, *passim*.

2
Textual Criticism

However we approach a New Testament text and apply our various skills to it, we have to know what 'it' is. All study of the New Testament presupposes a text, and hence a vital initial problem must be to determine what precisely is the wording of the text to be interpreted. This is certainly not a trivial task and can sometimes be an extremely complex one. The branch of study devoted to this problem is known as textual criticism.

No original copy survives of any of the New Testament documents. Nearly all the books of the New Testament were written by the end of the first century. Yet the earliest surviving manuscript containing any substantial quantity of the text of part of the New Testament dates from around AD 200; and the bulk of the manuscript evidence which we possess for the New Testament dates from the fourth century and later. Ideally, of course, we would like to have the original manuscripts of the books of the New Testament. Instead we only have later copies which may be several stages removed from the autographs themselves.

Moreover one must remember that the first few hundred years of the Christian Church were still a millennium away from the era of printing. Thus all copying had to be done by hand, and the process of copying inevitably led to alterations being introduced into the text by scribes at work. Some alterations were doubtless completely accidental, as, for example, when the scribe's eye would jump a line by mistake and omit something from the text he was copying. Other alterations may have been deliberate if the scribe thought that he could 'improve' the text in some way. Some alterations may have been a cross between the two – semi-conscious changes which were introduced for a variety of reasons. Still, whatever the reasons, alterations did occur. The result is that no two manuscripts of the New Testament are identical in their wording. The general aim of textual criticism is to try to recover from these 'altered' texts the 'original' form of the text.

Now the study of any text of antiquity involves some textual criticism. Yet textual criticism applied to the New Testament is far more complicated than in the case of other texts. This is due simply to the fact that the Bible has always been an extremely popular book. Even today, Bibles sell very well, and the situation was no different in earlier times. Not only was the New Testament copied, it was copied very frequently. Thus there is an enormous number of manuscripts available to the New Testament textual critic, as well as a great deal of other relevant evidence. The number of manuscripts which we now possess of the Greek New Testament (or parts of it) runs into thousands. Further, the New Testament was soon translated into other languages (e.g. Syriac, Coptic, Latin) and there are large numbers of manuscripts available in these languages too. The New Testament was also used in lectionaries, and it was frequently quoted, or alluded to, by the Church Fathers. All these instances provide secondary evidence for the state of the text of the New Testament at the points where it was used.

The sheer volume of evidence available to the New Testament textual critic contrasts strikingly with the amount of evidence available for the text of other important classical works. Part of Tacitus' *Annals* is available to us via only one ninth-century manuscript;[1] the original Greek of large parts of Irenaeus' work *Against the Heresies* has not survived at all and we depend on Latin translations. By contrast, we now possess about 100 papyrus texts, nearly 300 uncial manuscripts, and nearly 3,000 minuscule manuscripts of the Greek text of the New Testament alone;[2] and to these must be added the vast number of manuscripts of the New Testament text in other languages, as well as the evidence from lectionaries and patristic citations. The enormous quantity of manuscript evidence available thus makes New Testament textual criticism infinitely more complex than textual criticism applied to other classical texts. How then does one go about seeking to bring order to the apparent chaos which the manuscript evidence provides?

One of the classic studies of textual criticism of the New Testament is the edition of the Greek New Testament published by Westcott and Hort in 1881;[3] although they were by no means the first textual critics, and although some of their work has now been superseded, their discussion set the agenda for all future textual criticism so that it is appropriate to start with them.

One of Hort's fundamental principles, which most scholars would still accept today as important (though see p. 32 below), was that 'knowledge of documents should precede final judgement upon readings'.[4] In other words, in order to be able to assess the value of an individual reading in a manuscript one should know something about the manuscript in which it occurs. To take an extreme example, a reading of a third-century papyrus would probably command greater respect as possibly preserving the original text than a reading which occurs in a fourteenth-century minuscule manuscript, all things being equal. Today most textual critics would accept Hort's dictum, at least in general terms, and would base decisions about individual texts on some theories about the nature of the manuscripts.

One of the most important factors to bear in mind about the manuscripts is that they are not all independent of one another. As manuscripts were transcribed, it is highly likely that the older manuscript and its copy would have broadly similar forms of the text. Any 'mistake' or peculiar reading in one manuscript would be perpetuated as further manuscripts were copied from it and were in turn used to copy from themselves.

In the case of the New Testament manuscripts, it is possible to collect together large numbers of individual manuscripts into a much smaller number of groupings where the manuscripts within any one grouping have a broadly similar text form. Today the New Testament manuscripts are frequently divided into three groups: (i) the 'Alexandrian' group, consisting of manuscripts such as p^{75} ℵ B C L 33, etc.; (ii) the 'Western' group, consisting of D F G 614 old Latin, old Syriac, etc.; (iii) the 'Byzantine' group consisting of most of the later uncials and the vast majority of minuscule manuscripts.[5] Whether the names 'Alexandrian' and 'Western' are appropriate or not (see p. 24 below), such classification of the mass of manuscripts into a small number of groups helps the work of textual criticism enormously.

One should, however, beware of thinking that, even within one group, it is possible to identify direct lines of descent involving extant manuscripts. Only very rarely has this been possible. All that we can say is that manuscripts within one grouping have text forms which are closely related to each other. One should also beware of assuming that one manuscript can always be assigned to one and only one grouping. For example, codex A has a Byzantine form of the text in the Gospels but is close to the Alexandrian form of the text elsewhere in the New Testament. Such mixture can even occur within a single book: codex ℵ appears to have a Western text for John 1–8 but an Alexandrian text for the rest of John.[6] Life is never simple for the New Testament textual critic!

Ever since Hort's day a great deal of work has been done in trying to refine the groupings of manuscripts, to identify smaller sub-groups within the larger groupings, and so on. One famous example was the attempt to isolate another main grouping of texts, the so-called 'Caesarean' text.[7] And although this attempt may have turned out to be unsuccessful, the discussion which the issue provokes involves a number of very important methodological points.

The case for the existence of a Caesarean text form was made most strongly by B. H. Streeter in his famous book of 1924, *The Four Gospels.* Streeter argued that a definite grouping could be identified in the manuscripts W (at least in the latter half of Mark's Gospel) Θ 565 700 fam 1 and fam 13.[8] Streeter also tried to show that this text form could be assigned to a very precise geographical location. He analysed the biblical citations of Origen and sought to show that a change in the text form of Origen's quotations could be detected at just the moment when Origen moved from Alexandria to Caesarea: after his move, his citations appeared to agree with the new text form proposed. Streeter thus coined the description 'Caesarean' for this text form. It also led him to suggest that all the major text forms could be assigned to specific geographical areas, or major centres, in the early Church: the 'Alexandrian' text emanated from Alexandria, the 'Western' text from the west of the empire, and so on.

Such a theory of 'local texts' seems eminently reasonable at first sight and very attractive. Presumably texts with similar text forms must have come from the same geographical area at some stage. However, it is doubtful whether the state of the manuscript evidence as we have it today can support such a theory. More detailed work on Origen's citations has shown that Origen used a 'Caesarean' text form before, as well as after, his move to Caesarea, and that he used an 'Alexandrian' text for a time whilst he was at Caesarea. Thus Streeter's new text form could not be localized so specifically on the basis of the evidence we now have. Similarly, the so-called 'Western' text was far more widespread than the name 'Western' might imply. Such a text form is attested, for example, by such geographically diverse witnesses as the old Syriac versions, Egyptian papyri such as $\mathfrak{p}^{38}$, and citations by Justin Martyr of Rome and Irenaeus of Lyons. With the more recent discoveries of papyri manuscripts during the twentieth century, it has become clear that, at almost the earliest date in the manuscript tradition to which we have access, some of the major text forms had a very wide geographical circulation in the early Church.

If there are doubts about whether the grouping isolated by Streeter constitutes a 'Caesarean' text, there are now also more doubts about whether it constitutes a real grouping at all. The publication of the Chester Beatty papyrus $\mathfrak{p}^{45}$ (which dates from the third century) in the 1930s was thought at first to be a great vindication of the theory, since $\mathfrak{p}^{45}$ seemed to represent a Caesarean form of the text in existence at a very early date. However, subsequent study has shown that such enthusiasm was probably premature.

In part, this has been due to a more refined methodology in classifying manuscripts into groupings. Older studies tended to classify texts on the basis of a list of differences from one standard text. (The standard was usually taken to be the so-called Textus Receptus (TR), the Greek text which became standard in the later Middle Ages and which underlies the English Authorized Version. But the same methodological problems arise whatever text is used as the basis for comparison.) To take a very simplified example, suppose that in a given test passage, an unknown manuscript X differed from the text of the TR at ten points; suppose too that in nine of these instances the text of X agreed with that of codex B. It would be tempting to conclude that the texts of X and B were closely related to each other, showing a 90 per cent agreement. However, if B had a further ninety variations from the TR in the same passage, the agreement between X and B would not be nine out of ten (90 per cent) but nine out of 100 (9 per cent).

In more recent study it has therefore been proposed that larger numbers of manuscripts should be compared in pairs to test passages, listing what agreements there are at all the points where there is variation between the manuscripts. Then, in order to be able to establish a common text type, the agreement between manuscripts should be at least 70 per cent in the passages examined.[9]

When this more refined method is applied to the manuscripts of the so-called Caesarean group, the results are somewhat negative. Earlier studies had already suggested that the Caesarean text was not a unity: there was an earlier 'pre-Caesarean' form of the text, represented by $\mathfrak{p}^{45}$ W fam 1 fam 13 28, and a late Caesarean text proper represented by Θ 565 700.[10] However, more recent study has cast serious doubts on the existence of any link at all between the 'pre-Caesarean' and 'Caesarean' texts.[11] It is thus doubtful if the existence of a Caesarean text form can be established with any certainty as a major grouping of early manuscripts.

So far we have looked at some of the problems in classifying New Testament manuscripts into a smaller number of groupings. But how does this classifying help the work of textual criticism in practice?

One immediate consequence of the fact that manuscripts can be grouped together is that the number of individual manuscripts supporting a given reading is not necessarily the most important factor in assessing the evidence. Suppose that one reading is given by nine manuscripts, and another reading by one manuscript. This looks at first sight like a 9—1 majority in favour of the first reading. But if the nine manuscripts are all from the same group, and have all been copied from the same ancestor, the real 'score' should be a 1—1 draw between the single ancestor (of the nine surviving manuscripts) and the tenth manuscript. The classification of manuscripts into groupings thus means that in assessing the strength of support for any given reading we cannot just make a numerical head-count of the number of individual manuscripts supporting a reading; rather, we must see if the reading is attested in different groupings in different strands of the textual tradition as well.

It was above all Hort who appealed to the 'genealogies' of manuscripts in order to discount the simple numerical support for any given reading, and he called this the 'genealogical method'.[12] In dealing with classical texts, where very often only a few manuscripts have survived, it is sometimes possible to construct a genealogical tree of relationships between the manuscripts, showing how one was copied from another and so on. Hort tried to do the same sort of thing in very general terms with reference to *groups* of manuscripts. This has attracted a lot of quite harsh criticism, since it is doubtful how legitimate the whole enterprise is when one is not dealing with actual manuscripts being copied.[13] However, in defence of Hort, one could say that despite his own enthusiasm for the 'genealogical method', his actual procedure only used such a method in a very general way.[14]

Primarily, Hort used such considerations to discount the value of the Byzantine text despite its numerical support in the vast majority of manuscripts. However, he appealed to other considerations as well in seeking to show that the Byzantine text was generally secondary. He pointed to the fact that often the Byzantine text gave a 'conflated' reading, i.e. where two competing readings were current, the Byzantine text gave both. For example, at Mark 9.49, Alexandrian texts read 'For every one will be salted with fire'; Western texts read 'For every sacrifice will be salted with salt.' The Byzantine text runs both together and has 'For every one will be salted with fire and every sacrifice will be salted with salt.' Hort also showed that the Byzantine text form is not quoted by any Church Father prior to the fourth century. Further, in many places the Byzantine text is grammatically smoother and free of the difficulties which occur in other texts (cf. p. 28 below). In view of all these factors Hort argued that the Byzantine form of the text only came into being in about the fourth century as a result of a deliberate revision (the technical word is 'recension'), and thereafter it gradually dominated the textual tradition. It thus appears in the vast majority of surviving manuscripts, but is not of great value in the process of rediscovering the earliest form of the text.

In many respects Hort's theories about the Byzantine text have been accepted. However, the genealogical method clearly breaks down at the point where one has just two divergent streams of tradition, e.g. the Alexandrian and Western forms of the text. Given two readings A and B, neither of which is clearly dependent on the other, one must apply other criteria to determine which is more likely to have been the original reading. Now in practice, textual critics implicitly use a large number of different kinds of arguments and criteria to determine which reading is likely to be nearer the original. These can be classified in various ways and different scholars give differing relative weight to each consideration.

In very broad general terms, most textual critics work with a rough rule of thumb that 'the reading which most easily explains the existence of other readings is to be preferred'. Thus, if we are faced with two readings A and B in different manuscripts, and if one can see how a scribe might well have written B when copying A, but not vice versa, then A is probably more original. To a certain extent this involves getting into the mind of the scribes themselves, but this is not always impossible.

Scribes often had a tendency to expand a text, especially if they felt that something was lacking. For example, the story of the Ethiopian eunuch in Acts 8 was clearly felt to be deficient in that the eunuch was baptized without making any profession of the Christian faith. Thus many later manuscripts add, after the eunuch's question in Acts 8.36 'What is to prevent my being baptized?', an extra verse 37: 'And Philip said, "If you believe with all your heart you may." And he replied, "I believe that Jesus Christ is the Son of God."' This addition (in the Byzantine text) was clearly a secondary expansion of the text, added to supply what was felt to be a lack in the original text. It is no part of the original text of Acts (and hence modern versions of the text have no v. 37 in Acts 8).

Sometimes, however, it is clear that a shorter text has arisen by accident, by a scribe's eye slipping from one word to a similar word (or collection of letters) later. For example, the scribe copying codex א has omitted one verse in Luke's parable of the Good Samaritan, i.e. Luke 10.32. Both verses 31 and 32 end with the Greek verb for 'passed by on the other side'. Clearly the scribe's eye slipped from one occurrence to the other so that the whole of v. 32 (and all mention of the Levite) was accidentally omitted. In these cases it is quite easy to see how the change in the text has arisen.

Scribes also had a tendency to make a 'hard' text 'easier'. Several passages in the New Testament clearly cause difficulties at a number of levels. For example at Mark 7.31 Alexandrian and Western texts say that Jesus 'left Tyre and came through Sidon to the Sea of Galilee'. This itinerary appears to presuppose that Sidon is between Tyre and the Sea of Galilee, whereas in fact it lies forty miles further north of Tyre. Several later (Byzantine) manuscripts thus ease the difficulty by reading 'Jesus left Tyre and Sidon and came to the Sea of Galilee.' Again it is relatively easy to see how an original difficult reading has been made easier by a scribe.

We must remember too that scribes were probably all Christians. Thus in copying texts which were close in wording to other texts, scribes had a tendency to conform the text they were copying to the version they knew well from other contexts. Especially this occurred in the case of the Gospels, where the text of Matthew was clearly well known. Scribes copying Mark and Luke tended at times to let the well-known text of Matthew influence their work. For example, in the Lucan version of the Lord's Prayer (Luke 11.2–4) several later manuscripts have the longer, fuller version to be found in Matthew's Gospel, with the long address, 'Our Father who art in heaven' instead of the simple 'Father', and including the clauses 'Thy will be done, on earth as in heaven' and 'Deliver us from the evil one'. These are not present in many of the earliest manuscripts of Luke, and their presence in other manuscripts is almost certainly due to scribes' 'remembering' the version of the Lord's Prayer which they knew well from Matthew, and which they were accustomed to use in prayer, and writing it into the text of Luke. A similar instance is 1 Corinthians 15.55. Paul's cry, 'O death, where is thy victory? O death, where is thy sting?' is a citation from Hosea 13.14. However, the Septuagint version (the Greek translation of the Hebrew text) has 'Hades' instead of the second 'death' in Hosea 13.14. Several manuscripts of 1 Corinthians have this reading too, and clearly scribes have conformed Paul's quotation to the version of the Old Testament which they knew.

Other criteria which can be used are sometimes more delicate to apply. One such is the suggestion that a reading which best fits the author's style, or his theology, is to be preferred. As an example, consider the opening verse of Mark's Gospel. Some manuscripts read 'The beginning of the gospel of Jesus Christ.' Others add the words 'the Son of God' at the end. The division of manuscripts supporting each reading cuts across the standard groupings and there is good, early support for each reading. In this case one could very reasonably appeal to the fact that the phrase 'Son of God' is of fundamental importance for Mark's Christology (it occurs at key points in his Gospel: cf. 1.11; 3.11; 9.7; 14.61–62; 15.39). It would thus fit in extremely well, and make very good Marcan sense, if the phrase also occurred in the title verse of the Gospel.

The difficulties with such an argument are however twofold. First, there is the problem of possible circularity: a writer's style or theology are deduced from the text, but then this criterion makes the text determined in part by the writer's style or theology. Such circularity is inevitable and we shall meet it again at a number of different levels. In the case of Mark 1.1, the problem is not too great, since the importance of the phrase 'Son of God' for Mark's Christology can be deduced from verses in Mark where there is no doubt at all about the text. In practice, therefore, the problem of circularity is not insuperable.

The second difficulty arises from the fact that a rigid application of such a criterion would make an author's text extremely monochrome. If one author introduces a variation in his language or style, and a later scribe changes it back to the author's normal usage (perhaps precisely under that influence) one will be faced with two variants, one of which is the writer's 'norm', the other being his own variation. A rigid application of this criterion would in fact decide that the later scribe's version is original! Maybe this only shows that textual critics must always be flexible.

A final criterion which should be mentioned here is that which argues that the reading which conforms to the style and language of 'Koine' (common) Greek is to be preferred. Scribes may have had a tendency to conform the text to the standards of Attic Greek which saw a strong revival in the post-biblical period. Hence, a reading which does not conform to these standards is more likely to be original than one which does. This criterion has been advocated most powerfully in contemporary scholarship by G. D. Kilpatrick and J. K. Elliott.[15] However, such a criterion is not without its difficulties. We do not know for certain that later scribes conformed their texts only to the standards of Attic purists. Other tendencies may have been equally strong, e.g. to conform to the style of the Septuagint, or to conform to the text of parallel versions elsewhere in the New Testament or to liturgical usage (cf. p. 28 above). Again, a one-sided application of such a criterion is probably dangerous.

It will be clear that, in individual cases, the various criteria may point in different directions. A 'hard' reading may be 'hard' precisely because it does not fit with what a writer says elsewhere in his text. Does one then accept the harder reading, or the reading which fits the author's text best? Take, for example, the text of Acts 12.25. Most manuscripts say that 'Barnabas and Saul returned from Jerusalem' (i.e. to Antioch). The manuscripts ℵ and B, which are generally thought to be very good ones, say that Barnabas and Saul returned 'to Jerusalem'. The geographical context demands a reading 'from'. (At the end of Acts 11 the two apostles are in Jerusalem; Acts 12 is about other matters; Acts 13 takes up the story of the two in Antioch.) The ℵB reading makes little sense geographically. Does one say that it is the 'harder' reading and hence original? Or does one say that Luke's context demands a reading 'from' and hence the ℵB text is wrong? Clearly the decision could go (and has gone!) either way.

Textual critics inevitably differ in the ways in which they give value to the various criteria, whether consciously or sub-consciously. One of the criticisms brought against Westcott and Hort has been that they probably had an innate preference for the Alexandrian text, especially the text of ℵ and B, as against the Western text. They believed that the best means of access to the original form of the text was via ℵ and B and they called this form of the text, somewhat tendentiously, the Neutral text. They also believed that subsequently this text had been slightly revised in Alexandria. By contrast, the Western text was believed by Westcott and Hort to be generally secondary. It is often more wordy, more given to paraphrase, to harmonization with parallel passages and so on. It is especially in the book of Acts that the Western text is often strikingly different from the Alexandrian text. Much discussion has taken place about the origin of such different text forms, though it cannot be said that there is any unanimity about this today.

There is one small group of readings in the Western text which has led to a lot of discussion and where Hort's influence can still be seen in some of the language used. The Western text is almost always longer than the Alexandrian text. However, in a few instances, many of which occur in Luke's passion narrative, the Western text is shorter. Clearly, either the Western text has cut something out, or the Alexandrian text has added something. Westcott and Hort decided that the general feature of the Western text being longer could be used as a criterion to judge other readings: the tendency of the Western text was always to expand, not to abbreviate. Thus in cases where the Western text was shorter, Westcott and Hort decided that this could not be due to the Western text's omitting material (as this would be counter to its general tendency). Thus in these cases the Western text was original and it was the Alexandrian text which had added, or 'interpolated', extra material. Westcott and Hort, however, appeared to have an almost unshakeable faith in the reliability of the ℵB text and they could not bring themselves to admit that the 'neutral' text was wrong. They therefore refused to call these texts 'neutral additions' or 'neutral interpolations'. Instead they coined the clumsy phrase 'Western non-interpolations' and, despite its awkwardness, the phrase has stuck in the scholarly vocabulary ever since.

The most famous of these Western non-interpolations occurs in the words of institution at the Last Supper in Luke's Gospel. In the Western text, Jesus takes bread and says simply 'This is my body' (Luke 22.19a). Missing from the Western text are the words which follow in most manuscripts: '"which is given for you. Do this in remembrance of me." And likewise the cup after supper, saying, "This cup which is poured out for you is the new covenant in my blood"' (Luke 22.19b–20). Other notable Western non-interpolations include the note about Peter running to the tomb on the first Easter morning (Luke 24.12) and the reference to the ascension on the first Easter day in Luke 24.51.

More recent scholarship has tended to be less enthusiastic about the value of these Western readings. Some may be simply accidental omissions. Others may be to avoid difficulties in the longer text. In Luke's version of the Last Supper, the longer text mentions two cups, one in v. 17 and another in v. 20. The shorter Western text may have been produced to avoid this duplication of cups. Similarly the omission of the reference to the ascension in Luke 24.51 may have been to avoid the embarrassing parallel in Acts 1, where Jesus ascends again forty days after Easter.[16] It is probably fair to say that modern textual critics would be more cautious in deciding that a shorter Western reading is *ipso facto* original. Each case must be decided on its own merits. Still, some of these texts are of great interest, and, for example, it cannot be said that Luke 22.19b–20 has yielded up all its secrets yet.

It is clear that Westcott and Hort's general method was very firmly based on assumptions about the nature of the manuscripts in which individual readings occur. All other things being equal (which they rarely are!) the neutral text was to be preferred to the Western text. (Although it should be pointed out that this was not a decision made by Hort out of the blue: it represented the result of what was regarded as the cumulative evidence of a large number of individual readings, analysed on the basis of such internal criteria as we have already discussed.)

Now such a 'cult' of the 'best' manuscripts has come under

attack in more recent textual studies. Part of the reason for this has been due to the discovery this century of various papyri, none of which was available in Hort's day. One of the corollaries which was swiftly drawn from the work of Westcott and Hort (though not explicitly by Hort himself) was that the 'Alexandrian' text represented a recension, or edition, of the text, produced by skilled editors during the fourth century in the school of Alexandria where the expertise and evidence necessary for such an enterprise would have been readily available.[17]

Such a theory about the origin of the Alexandrian text thus carried with it implications about its value: its very manner of production suggested that it was probably extremely reliable. All this was thrown into question by the discovery of some of the papyri, particularly $\mathfrak{p}^{75}$. $\mathfrak{p}^{75}$ is a papyrus dating from the beginning of the third century. Its interest lies in the fact that its text form is almost identical to that of codex B. This shows that the text of B is certainly very old. But it is then *not* the result of a fourth century scholarly recension in Alexandria: rather, its existence can be traced back into the second century in Egypt. However, the Western text can also be traced back to this early period. Thus the $\mathfrak{p}^{75}$B text was by no means the only early form of the text. It was simply one of a great number of text forms, *all* of which can be traced back to this early period. The origin of the B text is thus no longer any guarantee of its reliability. It does not represent the result of critical editing by Alexandrian scholars, and we can no longer place quite as much confidence in it as Westcott and Hort did.

Some textual critics have in fact gone to the other extreme and have argued that Westcott and Hort were quite wrong to place such confidence in *any* one manuscript or group of manuscripts. Rather, these critics would argue that it is quite possible for primitive readings to be preserved in late manuscripts. One notable champion of such a view is G. D. Kilpatrick, who says: 'No readings can be condemned categorically because they are characteristic of certain manuscripts or groups of manuscripts. We have to pursue a consistent eclecticism.'[18] 'Eclecticism' is the name by which this method has come to be known, and it effectively means the rejection of Hort's initial dictum that 'knowledge of documents should precede final judgement upon readings' (cf. p. 22 above).

Certainly it is the case that most textual critics are happy to accept that primitive readings may be preserved in textual traditions other than the Alexandrian one. G. Zuntz, for example, has argued that many readings which had been rejected as Western and/or Byzantine have now turned up in $\mathfrak{p}^{46}$: they are thus early and several may be adjudged on internal grounds to be original.[19] Whether one is prepared to go as far as Kilpatrick and rely at times on the witness of a few (sometimes even only one) very late minuscule manuscripts is another matter. Kilpatrick himself is certainly prepared to do this. He argues for the primacy of the criterion of Attic/Koine Greek, so that if a variant occurs in Koine Greek, even if it is attested very weakly, it should be accepted.

Strictly speaking, it is doubtful if this can really be called an 'eclectic' method.[20] It represents a rather one-sided approach, placing exclusive weight on internal considerations, and sometimes on only one such consideration, viz. the criterion of Attic/Koine Greek. It effectively precludes the possibility of reconstructing anything of the history of the transmission of the text, and such an ahistorical approach to what is, after all, basically a historical subject must remain somewhat dangerous. Thus it is probably true to say that the majority of textual critics today would follow a 'reasoned eclecticism'.[21] This would involve paying some attention to the nature of the manuscripts in which variant readings occur, but also taking note of internal considerations as well.

The days of Westcott and Hort, when the ℵB text reigned supreme, are gone. We must take seriously the possibility of primitive readings being preserved in other textual traditions, possibly only surfacing relatively late. But one must pay some attention to the place where a variant reading occurs. If, for example, a variant occurs only in one late manuscript which is known to have been written very carelessly elsewhere with a large number of sheer mistakes, this fact must be taken into account in assessing the value of the individual variant.

So far we have looked at some of the methods used in textual criticism: the classification of manuscripts into groups, the criteria that textual critics use, and some of the methodological problems involved. What then can we say is achieved as a result of such work?

We started with the relatively general, but also somewhat naive, statement that textual criticism seeks to reconstruct the original form of the text. Westcott and Hort seem to have believed that they had almost succeeded in doing this: they called their work *The New Testament in the* Original *Greek*. Today, most would agree that any such claim must be exaggerated. The manuscript evidence does not enable us to get back to the original text.[22] All that we can do is reconstruct the earliest form of the text which the manuscripts allow us to see. This means that between our earliest manuscripts and the actual New Testament writers themselves there is a gap which we cannot ignore. This is not to say that this gap is unbridgeable. It is rare that New Testament critics would argue that textual corruption has affected *all* available manuscripts of a particular text. However, this may be the case and the possibility should not be completely discounted in individual cases.

One example may be John 21, which many have argued is a secondary appendix to the rest of the Gospel, written by someone other than the author of John 1–20 (cf. p. 84 below). However, there is no manuscript support for a text of John's Gospel which ends at John 20. A textual critic can thus only say that, at the earliest period which available manuscripts enable us to see, John 21 was an integral part of John's Gospel. To settle the question of whether the chapter was originally part of the Gospel or not, one will have to appeal to other evidence. But it is certainly not impossible that John 21 was secondarily added to the rest of the Gospel after the writing of John 1–20, and that this addition was made sufficiently early to influence all known manuscripts of the Gospel.

Another, perhaps more controversial, instance of the same phenomenon may be the text of Matthew 26.68, where the mockers at the Sanhedrin trial of Jesus ask him, 'Who is it that struck you?' This is one of the most famous of the 'minor agreements' of Matthew and Luke against Mark and constitutes a difficulty for the standard theory of synoptic interrelationships.[23] Streeter's explanation was that a primitive corruption of the text of Matthew had occurred, so that the question 'Who is it that struck you?' had been added to Matthew's text under influence from the Lucan parallel; this had affected all extant manuscripts of Matthew but was not part of Matthew's original text. Support for the suggestion might be added by the observation that the mocking question makes perfect sense in Luke's narrative where Jesus is blindfolded, but precious little sense in Matthew's where Jesus is not.[24]

Such an argument can be easily ridiculed as a case of special pleading to avoid a major difficulty for the theory of Marcan priority. However, one should note that textual criticism involves study of part of the whole history of the tradition which culminates in the present New Testament text. Source criticism (cf. ch. 6 below) involves study of another part of the history of the same tradition. It may be that, in a few instances, the parts of the history covered by each discipline overlap. Thus in some instances textual criticism and source criticism may have to interact with each other.

However, it must also be said that the two instances given above are the exception rather than the rule. Most critics today would be instinctively wary about conjecturing an 'original' form of a text for which there was no manuscript support at all. (Such 'conjectural emendation' of all existing manuscripts is more common in Old Testament studies.) However, these examples should perhaps serve as a warning that textual criticism can never be a hermetically sealed discipline, cut off from the rest of New Testament study. Nor should one expect the textual critic to be able to produce a definitive form of the 'original' text of each book of the New Testament on which one can then operate with other critical methods. The actual state of the available evidence makes that simply impossible.

How important is the discipline of textual criticism for the New Testament student who is not a specialist textual critic? Do decisions made by textual critics have a substantial effect on the text? Certainly it is the case that in the past some textual decisions have made a real difference in substance to the meaning of the text.

One variant reading where the 'original text' is not in doubt comes at the end of Mark's Gospel. In some English translations, the final chapter of Mark has twenty verses. It is almost universally agreed today that only the first eight verses were written by the author of the rest of the Gospel; vv. 9–20 are a secondary appendix added later in the textual tradition. (The verses are omitted by ℵB and others, and are indicated as secondary, by asterisks and other marks, in several other manuscripts.)

The text of the evangelist Mark as we have it ends at Mark 16.8 with the note about the women running away from the empty tomb and saying nothing to anyone. There is thus no account of a resurrection appearance of Jesus and the ending is regarded by many as very abrupt, both grammatically (Mark 16.8 ends with a preposition) and thematically. Whether it is impossibly abrupt is another matter.

Did Mark intend to end at Mark 16.8? Was Mark prevented from finishing his Gospel (e.g. by arrest or illness)? Was an ending written by Mark but subsequently lost, or deliberately suppressed? We cannot deal with that particular issue here, but it is clear that the textual decision about the inauthenticity of vv. 9–20 raises many issues for the interpretation of Mark's Gospel as a whole.

One instance where the original text is more doubtful, but where again the reading chosen has important consequences, is the text of Luke's account of the words of institution by Jesus at the Last Supper (Luke 22.19b–20). This has already been noted as one of the most famous of the 'Western non-interpolations'. The shorter, Western, text omits the words which interpret the bread and the cup in sacrificial terms (the bread 'given *for you*' and the cup 'poured out *for you*') as well as the reference to the inauguration of a new covenant relationship. Given the fact that Luke may well be preserving a tradition independent of Mark, there may be important issues raised at this point regarding Jesus' intentions at the Last Supper as well as Luke's ideas about the meaning of Jesus' death. Some of these will be significantly affected depending on which text is adopted.

Another instance where the reading chosen may alter the sense is the text of Romans 8.28. Most manuscripts read 'All things work together for good for those who love God'. A very few manuscripts (including $\mathfrak{p}^{46}$ A B) make God the subject of the clause (though also having a rather clumsy repetition of 'God'): 'God works for good for those who love God' (cf. RSV, NEB, GNB, JB). The first reading could be taken as implying some kind of innate benevolence within the natural order; the second reading is far more theocentric (and for that reason, it could be argued, fits better into the argument of Romans 8 as a whole, even if it is very weakly attested).

Such instances, where there is genuine doubt about the original text and where the textual decision entails a drastic change in meaning, are not however very frequent in the New Testament. In a large number of cases, there is still doubt about the original reading, but the competing variants are relatively close in meaning. Nevertheless, such cases are also of great importance at other levels. They may affect our judgement about the Greek style of an author (whether he has written a narrative in the present tense or the past, whether he has written cultured Attic Greek or a less refined Koine Greek or a heavily Semitic Greek); they may affect source-critical questions (whether one writer's Greek agrees precisely with the Greek of another text). Thus in any detailed study of the New Testament, we have to take account of textual criticism and be aware of the contribution it can make to the overall discussion.

It is true that many variant readings are not of great interest to the person who is not a specialist textual critic. In several instances it is quite clear which readings are secondary; in others, the various textual possibilities do not involve any great difference in meaning. Further, the text of the New Testament as established by modern textual criticism may be regarded as reasonably secure. It is unlikely that debates amongst textual critics will produce any enormous changes in a standard text of the Greek New Testament such as the twenty-sixth edition of the Nestle–Aland text. (This is not to say that there will not always be doubt about individual cases.) Even so, the New Testament student who is not a specialist textual critic should be aware of the importance of the discipline, of the provisional nature of the text established by modern textual criticism, and of some of the sorts of argument that are used in the contemporary debate.

Mark 3.1–6 and Parallels

The three versions of the story of the man with the withered hand do not provide very many important textual difficulties. In general there is no serious doubt about the text of the three versions. The inevitable process of harmonization between the versions has occurred (cf. the bulk of the variants noted in Aland's *Synopsis*), and the vast majority of other variants do not affect the sense of the passage in any significant way.

One small detail, which may appear very trivial, occurs in Mark 3.1. Almost all manuscripts read 'Jesus entered *the* synagogue' (presumably the one previously mentioned in Mark 1.21). ℵB alone omit the definite article, and read 'Jesus entered a synagogue' (or perhaps 'Jesus went to synagogue' (so NEB), an idiom analagous to 'going to church' in modern English). Matthew and Luke both have the definite article here. If one follows the ℵB text one has a minor agreement between Matthew and Luke against Mark. If one follows the rest of the manuscript tradition, there are no such problems. Should one follow the ℵB reading because these manuscripts are 'best'? Or should one follow this reading because it is 'harder' (e.g. for the standard theory of synoptic interrelationships)? Or should one follow the other manuscripts as giving overwhelming support for reading 'the synagogue'? It may be a sign of changing attitudes that the majority of older editions followed the ℵB text (because it was 'best'?), whereas the most recent (twenty-sixth) edition of the Nestle-Aland text reads the definite article (perhaps conceding that the ℵB text no longer rules the day?).

Another variant of some intrinsic interest occurs in the Lucan version at Luke 6.10. After v. 10, codex D reads the verse which is usually printed as v. 5 of Luke 6 ('And he said to them, "The Son of man is lord of the sabbath"') as the conclusion of the previous pericope; and instead of v. 5, D has a famous extra little story about Jesus on the sabbath: 'On the same day he saw a man working on the sabbath, and he said to him "Man, if you know what you are doing you are blessed; but if you do not know, you are cursed and a transgressor of the law."' This saying has generated a lot of discussion, with some scholars arguing that it represents a genuine saying of Jesus.[25] On text-critical grounds it cannot claim to be part of the 'original' text of Luke's Gospel. But it is perhaps a good example of a primitive tradition (possibly dominical) resurfacing relatively late in the textual tradition in an isolated place. It thus provides a good illustration of the principle that old traditions may have been preserved in later manuscripts (even though in this case there is no question that the tradition ever formed part of Luke's Gospel prior to its inclusion in the text of Luke 6 by codex D).

Notes

1. cf. B. M. Metzger, *The Text of the New Testament* (Oxford 1964), p. 34.
2. Papyrus was the writing material used in the very earliest period, and hence texts written on papyrus are generally very old. However, we have very few substantial parts of the New Testament text on papyri: most of the papyri which have survived contain only scraps. After about the fourth century AD, parchment was used as the basis for writing. In the early period, writing was all in Greek capital letters, called 'uncials': hence manuscripts written in this way are called uncial manuscripts. Around the ninth century, the style of writing gradually changed to using small Greek letters, called minuscules. Clearly most of the minuscule manuscripts are relatively late and of less value to the textual critic in the search for the most original form of the text. However, one cannot simply assume that an early manuscript is necessarily a reliable one. Some very early papyrus texts are written extremely carelessly with bad mistakes in them; conversely, later manuscripts sometimes preserve much earlier traditions.

   The New Testament manuscripts are referred to in a number of different systems. One which has become widespread is to refer to papyri by a $\mathfrak{p}$ and a superscript number ($\mathfrak{p}^{45}$ $\mathfrak{p}^{72}$ etc.), the most important uncials by capital Roman letters (with the exception of one important uncial, Codex Sinaiticus, which is referred to by the first letter of the Hebrew alphabet א), and minuscules by numbers (1 33 614 etc.). Full lists of the most important manuscripts can be found in any standard textbook, e.g. Lake or Metzger.
3. B. F. Westcott & F. J. A. Hort (ed.), *The New Testament in the Original Greek* (Cambridge & London 1881). This appeared in two volumes, the first volume giving the actual text, the second (written mostly by Hort rather than Westcott) giving a full discussion of the principles used in constructing the text.
4. ibid., p. 31.
5. Such a division goes back at least as far in time as Griesbach (100 years before Hort) if not further, to Semler and Bengel. In fact Hort proposed a fourfold division: what is called the 'Alexandrian' text above was sub-divided into a 'Neutral' and an 'Alexandrian' com-

ponent. But on Hort's own admission the difference between these two was not large.

6. See G. D. Fee, 'Codex Sinaiticus in the Gospel of John: A Contribution to Methology in Establishing Textual Relationships', *NTS* 15 (1968), pp. 23–44.
7. For a full discussion of research on the Caesarean text, see B. M. Metzger, 'The Caesarean Text of the Gospels', *JBL* 64 (1945), pp. 457–89, reprinted in his *Chapters in the History of New Testament Textual Criticism* (Leiden 1962), ch. 2.
8. 'Family 1' and 'family 13' are two small 'families' of minuscule texts very closely related to each other and containing the minuscule manuscripts 1 and 13 respectively.
9. See the important essays of E. C. Colwell, collected in his *Studies in Methodology in Textual Criticism of the New Testament* (Leiden 1969).
10. See Metzger, *Chapters*, pp. 63–4, referring to the work of T. Ayuso, 'Texto cesariense o precesariense?', *Biblica* 16 (1935), pp. 369–415.
11. p^{45} and W are closely related, but, for example, W and Θ are not really related at all and in fact the Western text of codex D sometimes shows a greater measure of agreement with both W and Θ than W and Θ have between themselves. Thus whilst p^{45} and W (and possibly fam 13) may constitute an important smaller grouping, it is difficult to relate these at all to the manuscripts usually known as 'Caesarean'. See E. J. Epp, 'The Twentieth Century Interlude in New Testament Textual Criticism', *JBL* 93 (1974), pp. 386–414, on pp. 394–5.
12. Hort, *Original Greek*, pp. 90ff.
13. See, for example, the severe criticisms of Colwell, *Studies*.
14. See Colwell, *Studies*; also E. J. Epp, 'The Eclectic Method in New Testament Textual Criticism: Solution or Symptom?' *HTR* 69 (1976), pp. 211–57, on pp. 236–9.
15. cf. G. D. Kilpatrick, 'Atticism and the Text of the Greek New Testament', *Neutestamentliche Aufsätze* (FS for J. Schmid. Regensburg 1963), pp. 125–37; J. K. Elliott, 'Can We Recover the Original New Testament?', *Theology* 77 (1974), pp. 338–53.
16. For a fuller discussion of these Western non-interpolations, see J. Jeremias, *The Eucharistic Words of Jesus* (London 1966), pp. 145ff.; K. Snodgrass, 'Western Non-Interpolations', *JBL* 91 (1972), pp. 369–79.
17. cf. Metzger, *Text*, p. 215, with other references.
18. G. D. Kilpatrick, 'The Greek New Testament of Today and the *Textus Receptus*', in H. Anderson & W. Barclay (eds.), *The New Testament in Historical and Contemporary Perspective. In Memory of G. H. C. MacGregor* (Oxford 1965), pp. 189–208, on p. 205.
19. See G. Zuntz, *Text of the Epistles* (London 1953).
20. See Epp, 'Eclectic Method', pp. 248ff.
21. See G. D. Fee, 'Rigorous or Reasoned Eclecticism – Which?', in J. K. Elliott (ed.), *Studies in New Testament Language and Text* (Essays in Honour of G. D. Kilpatrick. Leiden 1976), pp. 174–97.
22. See the critical remarks of E. J. Epp, 'A Continuing Interlude in New

Testament Textual Criticism?', *HTR* 73 (1980), pp. 131–51, on pp. 149–50, in relation to the claims of K. Aland, 'The Twentieth-Century Interlude in New Testament Textual Criticism', in E. Best & R. McL. Wilson (eds.), *Text and Interpretation* (FS for M. Black. Cambridge 1979), pp. 1–14.

23. It is widely believed that Matthew and Luke independently used Mark's Gospel as a source in writing their own Gospels (cf. pp. 79ff below). In a few instances, however, Matthew and Luke agree against Mark, and hence, on the standard theory, must have independently altered Mark in an identical way. Such coincidences provide an embarrassment for the theory of Marcan priority since one would normally assume that two independent writers would not change their common source in exactly the same way. It is these texts which are known as the 'minor agreements'.
24. B. H. Streeter, *The Four Gospels* (London 1924), pp. 325–8.
25. cf. J. Jeremias, *Unknown Sayings of Jesus* (London 1957), pp. 49ff.

3

Problems of Introduction – I

One of the difficulties with the 'in-language' of any discipline is that a word may not mean the same as it does in ordinary usage. One such word is probably 'introduction'. There are a number of books entitled *Introduction to the New Testament*, and any reader who is not aware of the in-language of biblical studies might well be forgiven for assuming that such books are beginners' guides to New Testament studies. Nothing could be further from the truth. One 'Introduction' which has become a standard work is that of W. G. Kümmel; but any beginner starting biblical studies by trying to read Kümmel's *Introduction* from cover to cover would probably give up in despair rapidly! For 'New Testament Introduction' involves a very specific way of studying the New Testament documents; and this can be done at both an elementary and an advanced level. (In this respect Kümmel's work is one of the most in-depth treatments available today.)

The subject of New Testament Introduction really arises from the nature of the historical-critical method. This method recognizes that the New Testament texts stem from a particular point within history, and as such they are open to historical investigation. These texts were written by authors in a period of past history, writing for audiences who also belonged to that history. Thus in order to understand what the authors were saying, we have to try to place ourselves as far as possible in the position of the people for whom the texts were written. This involves a measure of creative imagination on our part as twentieth-century readers. We do not live in the first century, and yet we have to try to imagine ourselves in such a setting. But such 'imagination', if it is to be responsible, must be as well-informed as possible, and it is here that the discipline of 'New Testament Introduction' tries to provide the necessary background information for us.

This information can be at a number of different levels. At a relatively general level, we shall have to know something about the language in which the New Testament texts were written if we are to have a hope of understanding them properly. We shall have to know something of the social background, and of the religious environment, if we are to make proper sense of some of the words and ideas which the New Testament writers use. They, after all, do not provide detailed footnotes to explain what for us are difficult words! What for us may be strange and unusual could have been taken as common knowledge by the New Testament writers and their readership.

At a more specific level, in relation to a particular text, we may need to know something of the particular circumstances which lay behind the writing of a text: Who wrote this text? When and where was it written? To whom was it written? In practice the discipline of 'New Testament Introduction' is often thought to be primarily concerned with these more specific questions related to individual texts, although in terms of method the more general questions about the linguistic, social and religious background belong here too. The aim of all such work is to enable the modern reader to be in as similar position as possible to that of the people for whom the text was first written, so that the author's text can be heard in its original setting.

The subject of New Testament Introduction (at least as I have defined it) is thus an extremely large one. In order to keep the discussion within manageable limits it will be necessary to break the subject down into smaller parts. Therefore in this chapter we will look at some of the issues raised by the study of the general background of the New Testament, and in the next chapter we will look at the problems raised by the specific background of individual texts.

Language is probably the most fundamental area where we need to have some knowledge of the background. Clearly there is the obvious problem of the fact that the New Testament was not written originally in modern English! It was written in Greek and hence we have to know something of that language in order to understand what the writers were saying. Now many students of the New Testament do not have the time, inclination or ability (or a combination of these!) to learn Greek. In itself this is not disastrous by any manner of means. There are a number of good English translations of the New Testament available today; and many students can get a great deal out of New Testament study without knowing the Greek language as such. Yet even without knowledge of Greek, it is still worthwhile to be aware of some of the problems of language in general, and of New Testament Greek in particular.

What has become accepted in modern study of language is that the meaning of any 'text', be it a word or a phrase or a longer unit, is dependent on its context. For example, many words or phrases are ambiguous. Words can have different meanings or shades of meaning in different contexts. To take a very obvious and naive example, consider the word 'pound'. I can talk of 'a pound coin', 'a pound of apples', and 'to pound my fist on the table'. In each case the slightly wider context of the phrase determines the meaning of the single word 'pound' fairly precisely. Such ambiguity in the meaning of individual words is of course the basis of many cryptic clues to crossword puzzles: the crossword compiler plays on the multiple meanings of individual words.

In other instances words can have different shades of meaning in different places and settings. The word 'poorly' tends to mean 'slightly off-colour' in the South of England, whereas it means 'seriously ill' in the North of England. In order to interpret the statement 'X is poorly', one needs to know at least which part of England the speaker comes from before one decides whether one can rush brightly in to see X or whether one should tread rather more warily. 'Starving' means 'hungry' in the South; I am told that it means 'cold' in the North. Again, if we are told that 'Gran is starving', we must know where the speaker comes from to know whether poor Gran needs a solid meal or an electric blanket. Similarly, the word 'introduction', as we have already seen, means one thing for biblical scholars and something slightly different for non-specialists.

Sometimes too the identity of the speaker will make a difference to the interpretation of the actual words used. 'We must obey the law' could be said by a High Court judge or by a Jewish rabbi, and would mean different things in each case. 'We must arm ourselves for the coming struggle' could be said by an army commander prior to a military war, by a politician prior to a general election, or by a leader of a pacifist organization prior to a big campaign. Again, the same words would mean different things depending on who is the speaker.

Another factor which must also be borne in mind is that language is a part of a culture and, as the culture changes, so too does its language. In the course of time some words become obsolete and drop out of current usage; other words are retained in normal usage but change their meanings. This phenomenon will be well known to anyone who has tried to read an English text written 400 years ago, such as the Authorized Version of the Bible. There one sees words used in ways which are rather different from their usage in modern English. The word 'conversation' today means only verbal communication; in the seventeenth century the word meant all conduct. Thus the wording of Hebrews 13.5 in the AV, 'Let your conversation be without covetousness', would be interpreted too narrowly if the word 'conversation' is given its modern meaning. There are still documents in archaic English emanating from bishops which start 'I, X, by divine oversight Bishop of . . .' What is perfectly normal usage in an older form of English conjures up strange images of slight divine incompetence if the same words are taken as modern English.

All these considerations are particularly relevant in interpreting the New Testament text. There is in New Testament Greek, just as in English, the phenomenon of homonyms, i.e. words which though spelt and pronounced the same, bear different meanings in different contexts. We looked at the English word 'pound' above. A more biblical example might be the Greek word *pneuma* which can mean both 'wind' and 'spirit'; and 'spirit' itself can be man's spirit (in a loose sense) or God's Spirit. The text of John 3.8 ('the *pneuma* blows where it wills') is clearly playing deliberately on the ambiguity in the word *pneuma*. Sometimes there may have been no deliberate ambiguity intended originally, but the words are ambiguous for us. For example, in Acts 18.25 it is said that Apollos was 'glowing with/in *pneuma*'. Does this mean that he was 'aglow in his spirit', a very fiery individual, or that he was 'aglow with God's Holy Spirit'? The words are ambiguous but the decision here has a number of important corollaries in the study of Acts.

There is also the fact which we have mentioned above that languages change and develop, and hence we must know just what is the proper linguistic background of the New Testament writers. It has been recognized for a very long time that the form of Greek used by New Testament writers is very different from classical Greek. At one time it was thought that New Testament Greek was a special sort of Greek. (This view was reflected in many older English translations of the Bible; it was felt appropriate to use a special kind of English to reflect the special Greek of the New Testament. Thus many older English translations deliberately set out to produce a version in old-fashioned English; the Revised Version is a good example of this.)

Such a view was discounted almost completely as a result of the wealth of discoveries of papyrus texts by A. Deissmann and others around the turn of the century.[1] A vast number of papyrus scraps were discovered in Egypt during this period, many of them giving us insights into the ordinary life of people around the time the New Testament was written. (So often the literary remains of a society reflect the extraordinary features of that society. First-century Christianity may also have been no exception in this respect!)

At the linguistic level, these finds gave evidence of the language of ordinary people, with their bills, accounts, and everyday letters. Further, it became clear that the form of Greek used here coincided to a remarkable degree with that of the New Testament. The New Testament writers were thus not using a special form of Greek, but were simply using the ordinary form of Greek (the 'Koine') of their period. (This result has also had its effect on English translations of the New Testament. Ever since the discovery of the papyri, almost every English translation has attempted to translate the Bible into ordinary everyday English.) Thus in order to understand the Greek language as it is used by New Testament writers, we must be aware of the meaning that Greek words and idioms had in the surrounding culture of the first-century Roman Empire, quite as much as the meanings they may have had in classical Greek.

However, the 'surrounding culture' of the New Testament writers was not monochrome. New Testament Greek was also affected by the origins of Christianity in Judaism. All the New Testament writers had a close contact with the religion of Judaism (whether they themselves were Jews or not). It is therefore not surprising that the Greek language used by New Testament writers was affected by the language of Greek-speaking Judaism, especially by the Greek form of the Jewish Bible, the Septuagint (LXX), with ideas from the Hebrew Old Testament lying one stage further back.

Paul's use of the word which we usually translate as 'righteousness' (Greek *dikaiosune*) in Romans 3.21 is an example of this. Non-Jewish usage of the word does not really provide a parallel to the idea of righteousness as a saving activity (by God or anyone else); rather, what we find reflected in Paul are probably ideas associated with the Hebrew word *tsedaqah* (e.g. in Isa. 46.13) which is used to refer to God's intervention to rescue Israel.

Other words do make sense against a non-Jewish background, but the sense is radically altered when the word is set against a Jewish background. Take, for example, the Greek word *hilasterion* and related words from the same root (cf. Rom. 3.25; 1 John 2.2). In non-Jewish usage, this root is used to convey the idea of 'propitiation', of appeasing the anger of a person (divine or human); in Septuagintal Greek, it almost always conveys the idea of 'expiation', i.e. of nullifying the effects of (impersonal) sin. The small change in the initial syllable in English constitutes a very great change in meaning. Expiation has nothing to do with God's anger; propitiation necessarily implies that God is angry. Most would argue that the New Testament usage is regularly that of Septuagintal Greek, not secular Greek.[2] Clearly then, knowledge of the linguistic background is of vital importance in finding out the meaning of individual words or phrases.

Exactly the same considerations apply if we extend the horizon slightly beyond the purely linguistic area. Knowledge of the social and religious background is also indispensable for the correct historical interpretation of New Testament concepts. (In a sense this overlaps with what has been said already about language, since concepts in the New Testament are expressed precisely through language.)

For example, Jesus' preaching about the Kingdom of God as something which is to come in the future is really only fully intelligible in the light of Jewish eschatological beliefs in the first century. Some Jews looked forward to a great intervention by God into the historical framework to establish his kingly rule, and it is this that Jesus probably had in mind.[3] Thus any attempts to interpret the Kingdom as, for example, something 'growing in the hearts of men' does not really do justice to what Jesus probably meant in his preaching about the Kingdom.

Similarly, a background of Jewish eschatological belief is essential to understand what the New Testament writers are claiming when they talk of the 'resurrection' of Jesus. Even to use the word 'resurrection' is to place the events of Easter within a very specific framework of thought: many Jews believed that the events of the end-time would include the resurrection of the dead to appear before God, either all the dead to be rewarded or punished, or only the righteous to be rewarded. (In part such a belief was the result of the bitter experience of apparently unrewarded faithfulness to God in situations of persecution: if the faithful had not been rewarded in this life, then the hope grew that they would be rewarded in a future life.) Thus any claims that the events of Easter were a 'resurrection' carried with them the implicit claim that the events of the end-time had already started. (This is indeed Paul's argument in 1 Corinthians 15.20ff.) Without the framework of Jewish eschatology, New Testament talk about Jesus' resurrection is liable to be misinterpreted.[4]

Respect for the background is also essential for the proper interpretation of the language of the New Testament about Jesus as the 'Son of God'. Here there is no clearly 'right' answer. But one should certainly beware of interpreting such language through the spectacles of later Christian orthodoxy, whereby Jesus *qua* Son of God is the second person of a fully divine Trinity. First-century Jews could talk about a 'son of God' without in any way implying that they were talking about a divine being. The king could be called God's son (cf. Ps. 2.7; 2 Sam. 7.14), as could a righteous sufferer (cf. Wisd. 2.18; 5.5). The precise background for each writer's use of the term 'Son of God' as applied to Jesus in the New Testament is debatable; but certainly some consideration of the background evidence is essential if we are to understand what the New Testament writers are trying to say when they refer to Jesus as 'Son of God'.

So far we have looked at the background in Judaism to illuminate the New Testament texts. Appeals have also frequently been made to the non-Jewish environment in the first-century Hellenistic world to provide the necessary background against which the New Testament texts should be interpreted. Some have claimed that the frequent references to Jesus as 'Lord' (Greek *Kurios*) in the New Testament should be seen against the background of Hellenistic mystery cults where the deities were frequently called 'lords'. Some of Paul's language about the Christian dying and rising with Christ in baptism (Rom. 6.1–4) has been seen as closely parallel to the language associated with the mystery cults which also talk of the initiates dying and rising with the cult deities. The approach which looks for such parallels is sometimes called the 'history of religions' approach, and has in the past been associated with the work of such famous scholars as R. Reitzenstein, W. Bousset, R. Bultmann and others in the early part of this century, and their work is often considered together as that of a 'history of religions school'.

Such appeals to the parallel material in the ancient world can raise methodological problems. There is, for example, the fact that 'the background' is not a monolithic, unchanging entity. The world to which the New Testament writers belonged had many different facets. It was also a changing world. In the past, scholars have taken full account of this at the level of language, in their insistence that New Testament Greek is not the same as classical Greek.

It is at least questionable how far some scholars have paid more than lip-service to this at the level of concepts used. The history of religions school can perhaps be accused of not taking full account of chronological differences in the dates of various materials cited as relevant 'background' for interpreting the New Testament. Scholars in this school tended to cite texts from a wide range of periods of history and produced a composite picture which was then proposed as 'an idea' serving to provide 'the background' for the New Testament. The possibility that ideas may have developed in the non-Christian background as well as in Christianity, and that the same words might be expressing radically different concepts in different contexts, tended to be forgotten. So too there may have been a tendency to assume too quickly that parallel vocabulary provides evidence for the *source* of the New Testament language, as if, for example, Paul's talk of the union of the Christian believer with Christ was *derived* from the language of the mystery cults.[5]

Now all this is not intended to be a criticism of the basic method of the history of religions approach.[6] The fundamental procedure, taking full note of the world in which the New Testament language was coined, is admirable. What may have been questionable in the past was the failure by some to apply the same historical sensitivity to the background material as one (rightly) expects in the study of the New Testament texts themselves.

Nevertheless, even when all the problems of dating are fully considered, there are still some delicate methodological problems. Take, for example, the problem of whether Gnosticism provides a possible background for interpreting the New Testament. Various forms of religion which we now call Gnosticism are known to have existed from the second century AD onwards. This type of religion laid great stress on the alienation of man in the world. Man's true destiny is to be reunited with the Deity from whom he has been separated as a result of a cosmic catastrophe. This resulted in the fragmentation and scattering of the divine being and in the disastrous act of the creation of the world. Man in the world is lost, and ignorant of his true nature. What can redeem man is the knowledge (Greek *gnosis*) of who he is, where he came from, and how he can return to the heavenly realm. In some forms of Gnostic mythology, the saving knowledge is brought from the heavenly realm by a divine figure who comes down into the world to rescue the saved remnant by revealing to them their true identity. This is the so-called Gnostic 'redeemer myth'. Such a model is clearly not dissimilar to the classic claims of Christianity about Jesus, especially, for example, in the fourth Gospel. The question then arises of how far Gnosticism forms part of the background of the New Testament.

For some it is legitimate and proper to assume a Gnostic background for interpreting the New Testament (or parts of it). Others, however, have pointed out that none of the evidence we have about Gnosticism is of a pre-Christian date; further, most of the Gnostic texts which we have are clearly Christian, and much of our information about Gnosticism comes from the Church Fathers of the second century or later writing against Gnostics. Hence, many would argue that Gnosticism is a purely Christian phenomenon and represents a development of the Christian religion subsequent to the New Testament period.

The whole debate has become much more urgent as a result of the evidence which is now available from the Nag Hammadi texts. These texts were first discovered in 1945 but, due to various delays in their publication, much work on them still needs to be done.[7] They consist of a number of writings, most of which are Gnostic (though some are not). They are all written in Coptic, a dialect of the Egyptian language, but it is generally thought that they are all translation of originals in other languages, probably Greek. Moreover, the Coptic manuscripts themselves can be pinpointed fairly precisely to a date around the middle of the fourth century AD. Several of them are clearly Christian Gnostic texts, but others appear to provide clear evidence of non-Christian Gnosticism. The consensus of scholarly opinion now seems to be that Gnosticism is not simply an offshoot of Christianity, but has its roots outside Christianity in Judaism and elsewhere. The evidence from Nag Hammadi opens up again the possibility that Gnosticism may have provided part of the background for some of the New Testament writers.

There is still however the problem of dates. The Nag Hammadi evidence has shown that Gnosticism may well be a *non*-Christian phenomenon. Is it also *pre*-Christian? Strictly, of course, we have to say that we just do not know, given the available evidence. It is still the case that all our extant pieces of evidence, including the Nag Hammadi texts, date from a period well after the time of the New Testament. The Nag Hammadi library still does not provide direct evidence for pre-Christian Gnosticism.

For many, the date of the evidence is enough to settle the question: these fourth-century texts should not be used to illustrate the thought-world of the first century. On the other hand, one could apply exactly the same considerations to the New Testament texts themselves. The bulk of the manuscript evidence for the New Testament dates from no earlier than the fourth century. There are a few exceptions in papyri: some papyrus texts of parts of the New Testament from the early third century are available to us. But equally, a few of the Nag Hammadi texts are available to us via Greek papyri from the second and third century.[8] Most people are happy to accept that there is a gap of 200 years or so between the actual writing of a New Testament text and the earliest manuscript which includes it, so that manuscript evidence from the third and fourth centuries can be used to give information about the first century. Should we perhaps not allow the same possibility for the Nag Hammadi texts?

The whole problem of relative datings means that the same evidence can be interpreted in diametrically opposite ways. For example, a close parallel between a Pauline passage and a Nag Hammadi text can be used to show that either (a) Paul is presupposing non-Christian Gnostic ideas as evidenced from Nag

Hammadi, or (b) the Nag Hammadi text is clearly a Christian development based on Paul![9] Unless and until the Nag Hammadi texts can be dated more precisely, this kind of ambiguity will inevitably remain in such discussions.

Other methodological problems are raised if we look at the question of the precise relationship of the New Testament to its background. Clearly, the whole presupposition behind everything that we have discussed so far in this chapter is that the New Testament is part of its background. But one can look at the problem the other way round: how far is it legitimate to use the New Testament itself as evidence for illuminating, or giving information about, the background?

At one level, of course, there is no reason at all why this should not be done. If the New Testament is part of the first-century religious world, then that world can be illuminated by Christian as well as non-Christian writings. Methodological problems arise, however, if we now go back to our original aim of seeking to interpret the New Testament. Can we use the New Testament as evidence to reconstruct an underlying thought-world, and then use this reconstructed thought-world to illuminate the New Testament? Such a procedure is sometimes advocated.

For example, take the vexed problem of the New Testament use of the term 'Son of Man'. There is no space here to go into this tremendously difficult question. However, some of the Son of Man sayings in the Gospels appear to presuppose that the term 'Son of Man' implies a well-known idea of a figure who was expected to come at the end-time and to play an active part in the final judgement (e.g. Mark 8.38; Luke 12.8). But it is agreed by all that there is no pre-Christian evidence in non-Christian sources for such an idea. Is it then legitimate to use the Gospel sayings themselves as evidence for the existence of an underlying belief about a 'Son of Man' figure, and then use this belief to interpret the Gospel sayings?[10] Such a procedure is circular, and as such is clearly rather dangerous. In general, New Testament scholars have been wary about arguments in this form and have tried to restrict attention to sources other than the text under consideration when trying to find the background of a particular text or series of texts.

At one level this is right and proper. Circularity in arguments should if possible be avoided. Nevertheless one could argue that such a procedure makes New Testament scholarship rather parasitic. The New Testament scholar takes what he wants from the cultural world of the first century to illuminate his texts, since he argues that the New Testament is part of that world; but he does not allow the New Testament itself to contribute to that world. The New Testament is thus in danger of being both a part, and not a part, of its environment.

One could also argue that refusing to allow a text to provide the evidence of its own background may be making some pretty hefty implicit assumptions about the sufficiency of our knowledge of 'the background'. If we say that the only background which we will accept is one which is attested independently of the text itself, we may be in danger of assuming that the information we have at present about the first century is all-encompassing; of assuming that the fact that we know nothing about a thing therefore implies that it never existed. Such an assumption about the ancient world is clearly dangerous. Even within Christianity itself, we know of several gaps in our information. (How did Christianity reach Rome? What was the nature of early Alexandrian Christianity? What was in lost writings like the Gospel of the Hebrews?)

Now all this is not meant to be an incitement to forget about our available extant evidence of the first-century world. Far from it. The whole thrust of this chapter has been to stress the importance of seeing the New Testament texts as part of their first-century environment. But problems do arise where non-Christian sources do not exist, or where they appear to conflict with the Christian evidence. At these points it is at least worth reflecting on the methodological problem of how far the New Testament is to be taken as part of its environment, and how far the New Testament can be used as evidence for its own background.

Enough has hopefully been said to show that knowledge of the background is a vital element in the interpretation of the New Testament. Insofar as it enables modern readers to be in as similar a position as possible to that of the first readers of the text, this aspect of study belongs methodologically within the whole area of 'New Testament Introduction'. However, as we have already noted, the discipline of New Testament Introduction is often in practice a little more restricted in scope, dealing with the particular questions about the individual books of the New Testament. And it is to this aspect of New Testament study that we shall turn in the next chapter.

Notes

1. Many of these may conveniently be found in A. Deissmann, *Light from the Ancient East* (ET, London 1927).
2. I am aware that this is disputed, but see the seminal essay of C. H.

Dodd, 'Atonement', in his *The Bible and the Greeks* (London 1935), pp. 82–95.

3. See N. Perrin, *Rediscovering the Teaching of Jesus* (London 1967), pp. 54ff., and the discussion of various views in B. D. Chilton (ed.), *The Kingdom of God* (London 1984).
4. cf. C. F. Evans, *Resurrection and the New Testament* (London 1970).
5. See the valuable first chapter of H. C. Kee, *Miracle in the Early Christian World* (New Haven & London 1983).
6. Kee probably goes too far in his critique. He subtitles his chapter 'The Decline *and Fall* of the History-of-Religions Methods', yet his own method is very similar. See too ch. 9 below, on the similarity between so-called 'sociological' approaches to the New Testament texts and the approach discussed here.
7. The texts are now available in translation in J. M. Robinson (ed.), *The Nag Hammadi Library* (Leiden 1977).
8. We have Greek papyrus fragments of the Gospel of Thomas and the Gospel of Mary. (The latter is not strictly one of the Nag Hammadi texts, but belongs to a codex containing three other works, two of which also appear in the Nag Hammadi library.)
9. See the discussion in my *Nag Hammadi and the Gospel Tradition* (Edinburgh 1986), p. 17 with reference to ParShem 36.2ff. and 1 Cor. 2.8.
10. This is done by C. Colpe in his influential article on the 'Son of Man' in the Kittel *Wörterbuch*.

4

Problems of Introduction – II

The New Testament documents were mostly written for specific occasions, to specific people or communities, and addressing issues of common concern. Frequently, however, all that has survived is one side of the conversation, so to speak.

For example, in most, if not all, of Paul's letters, Paul is dealing with specific situations, answering questions which have been put to him, speaking about problems that have arisen in the community, and so on. Further, there are often things that Paul knows that he can take for granted, matters which he can assume are common knowledge between himself and his readers.

We, however, only hear one side of the dialogue and have to try to piece together the common ground shared between Paul and his original readers. Sometimes it is like listening to one end of a telephone conversation which is the follow-up to three previous calls. If the speaker says, 'As I was saying yesterday . . .', the subsequent monologue may well be totally incomprehensible if we do not know what has been said before.

Examples of this can be found throughout the New Testament. When Paul writes to the Corinthian church in 2 Corinthians 10–13 about various outsiders who have come into the community, he has no need to give any detailed information, because he and his readers know exactly who he is talking about. We do not. In order to try to interpret what Paul says, we have to try to fill in that background information and discover something about the people concerned. In this case one is inevitably sucked into a circular kind of argument: the text is used to reconstruct the background and the background is then used to interpret the text. But circularity here is quite unavoidable, since there is no other source of direct information available.

The main purpose of many 'New Testament Introductions' is to try to provide some of the necessary background information about the historical situation from which the individual writings of the New Testament stem: Who wrote such and such a book? When? Where? Why? At times some of this work can appear very dull, and apparently of no further interest beyond a purely antiquarian one. For example, the question of the date of Romans – was it written in AD 55 or 58? – would not appear to be of earth-shattering importance, really, one way or the other.

However, some 'introductory' problems like this may have more far-reaching consequences. The problem of the dating of the other Pauline letters can be quite an important issue. There is, for example, a standard 'introductory' problem associated with the so-called 'captivity epistles' (i.e. Philippians, Philemon, together with Colossians and Ephesians if these are genuine). Were these written late in Paul's life during an imprisonment in Rome? Or were they written earlier in his ministry during an otherwise unknown imprisonment in Ephesus? An answer to this question may be quite important if one wishes to suggest (as some have) that Paul's thought underwent a development as his ministry progressed.[1] Such a theory is clearly heavily dependent on having the relative chronology of the letters well established.

The problem of the date of Galatians also brings in many other issues. Scholars are divided over the question of whether Galatians should be dated relatively late in Paul's career, close in time to the writing of Romans, or whether it should be dated extremely early, perhaps being the earliest Pauline letter we have.

One famous problem about Galatians concerns the number of Paul's visits to Jerusalem prior to the Apostolic Council. If the meeting described by Paul in Galatians 2.1–10 is the same as that described in Acts 15, then there is a discrepancy between Acts and Galatians: Paul himself swears vehemently that this is his second visit to the city, whereas Luke implies that it is Paul's third visit (cf. Acts 9, 11, 15). An early date for Galatians would solve some of these problems: if Galatians was written before the meeting of Acts 15, then the visit to Jerusalem described in Galatians 2 cannot be the same as that of Acts 15 and can be identified with the visit described in Acts 11.[2] If, however, Galatians is dated later, after the time of Acts 15, then there is a discrepancy between Acts and Galatians which must be explained. This may well affect one's assessment of the identity and/or the reliability of the author of Acts.

Other issues are involved as well. As is well known, the theological argument of Galatians is remarkably close to that of Romans: in both letters Paul's language is dominated by the theme of justification by faith; he appeals to the same figure of Abraham, citing the same Old Testament texts to back up his case, the line of argument is similar, and so on. These themes and arguments do not occur so prominently, if at all, in the other Pauline letters. For many people, the theology of Galatians and Romans forms the central core of Pauline theology and, many assume further, the central core of what should be a contemporary Christian theology.

Now if Galatians is a very early letter, written a number of years before Romans, it becomes rather easier to maintain that the theme of the two letters is indeed the central core of Paul's theology, since it surfaces in Paul's writings over such a wide time-span. If however Galatians was written later, very close in time to the writing of Romans, then the great similarity between the two letters could be explained by the fact that this sort of theological language was uppermost in Paul's mind at this stage of his career, but that it was not the fundamental basis of his theology. Thus the problem of the date of Galatians is by no means a trivial one and has important ramifications.

The same issue of what constitutes the centre of Paul's theology is potentially raised by another 'introductory' question. One of the standing problems of the study of the Pauline corpus is to know why Romans was written.[3] Was Romans written as a measured statement of Paul's basic theological position? Or was it written to address a specific situation in Rome?

Decisions about this may have consequences for one's evaluation of Paul's theology. For if Romans is indeed Paul's *Summa*, then one can take the teaching of Romans, especially the doctrine of justification by faith, as indeed the centre of Paul's theology. But if Romans is addressed to a specific situation in Rome, then one could argue that Paul's teaching about justification is mostly confined to Romans and Galatians, both of which are situation-oriented and (*if* Galatians is dated close to Romans) arise from a specific period in Paul's life, so that one should not necessarily make the theme of these two letters fundamental for Pauline theology. 'Introductory' problems about Romans and Galatians may thus have far-reaching effects in the study of Paul's theology.

Knowledge about the situation addressed by a writer is also a very important factor in the exegesis of individual texts. For example, most scholars agree that in 1 Corinthians Paul sometimes corrects the ideas of those to whom he is writing by first quoting their views before modifying them considerably, if not rejecting them. Thus in 1 Corinthians 8.1, Paul says 'we know that "all of us possess knowledge."' Most accept that 'all of us possess knowledge' is a Corinthian slogan which Paul proceeds to qualify radically. Hence these words are put in inverted commas in several modern English translations (RSV, JB, NEB, GNB). What though of 1 Corinthians 7.1, where Paul says 'It is well for a man not to touch a woman' (i.e. to abstain completely from sexual relationships)? Is this Paul's own opinion? Most modern English translations assume that it is and do not include any inverted commas (RSV, JB; but NEB and GNB acknowledge the ambiguity). However, it is much more likely that it was some of the Corinthians who were advocating this position and refusing to consummate marital relationships.[4] If so, then it is likely that these words represent the Corinthian view, not Paul's view. Paul's answer may be to qualify this statement very radically: he will allow such asceticism *only* if it is agreed by both parties, *only* as a temporary state, and *only* if it is not enforced on others – it is a concession not a command.[5] On this interpretation Paul's attitude to sexual relationships within marriage becomes a thoroughly positive one and quite different from the position which 1 Corinthians 7.1 taken on its own would imply.

So far we have looked at how problems of the date, purpose and situation of a New Testament text can affect its interpretation. Another issue frequently discussed under the heading of 'Introduction' is that of authorship. Clearly, knowledge of the identity of the author of a work may at times affect the interpretation of what is said. Certainly it is the case that the same words may have different meanings if used by different people. (Cf. the examples about 'the law', or 'arming for the struggle' which we looked at earlier, on p. 43.)

The phrase 'God's righteousness' is one that is used by both Matthew and Paul. In Matthew 6.33 ('But seek first his kingdom and his righteousness') it almost certainly refers to the ethical behaviour required by God of man, whereas in Romans 3.21 ('But now the righteousness of God has been manifested') Paul does not mean that the ethical pattern for us to follow has now been revealed; rather, the phrase refers to God's own saving activity in restoring the broken relationship between mankind and himself. The same words can thus mean different things when used by different people.

It is the issue of authorship which can cause concern to newcomers to biblical criticism, especially when claims are made that certain New Testament books were not in fact written by the person to whom the book is ascribed, whether in the book itself or in later tradition. (The technical word for such a writing is 'pseudonymous'.)

It is accepted by all that pseudonymous works were written in antiquity, and that some Christina writers wrote pseudonymously. There are, for example, later Christian works written in the name of a famous apostle: there is a '3 Corinthians' and a 'Letter to the Laodiceans', both allegedly written by Paul; there is a Gospel of Peter, a Gospel of Philip, and so on. Nobody denies that there is a substantial body of Christian pseudonymous literature. The question arises of how much, if any, of such literature there is in the New Testament. Few would argue that there is none. 2 Peter is almost universally accepted as pseudonymous. Most would agree that the Pastoral epistles (1 and 2 Timothy, Titus) are not by Paul himself. Similarly, Ephesians is widely regarded as non-Pauline and there are serious doubts about the authenticity of Colossians and 2 Thessalonians.

Now inauthenticity should not necessarily be equated with lack of authority. 1 Timothy does not lose anything of its power to speak to the modern reader simply because one decides that its author was not Paul himself but a later writer speaking in Paul's name and implicitly claiming Paul's stamp of approval for what he wants to say. We may at times decide that a pseudonymous writing says something which is in almost direct contradiction to what is said elsewhere by the writer in whose name the writing is written. (Indeed such features often provide a very important part of the evidence in the test of whether a writing is pseudonymous.) For example, the statement in 1 Timothy 1.8–11 to the effect that the law holds no terrors for the righteous man is somewhat at variance (to say the least) with Paul's own statements about the law as the power which enslaves all men (e.g. in Rom. 7). But if one decides (on the basis of this and other considerations) that 1 Timothy is not by Paul, this does not settle the question of who is 'right' about the law. That is a quite separate issue.[6]

The problem of how one determines the authorship of individual documents is a complex one and many different criteria are used, whether explicitly or implicitly. However, since the subject of New Testament study is qualitatively different from academic study in the material sciences or mathematics, absolute certainty is simply not possible. It is perfectly feasible, and indeed often happens, that eminent scholars will produce very learned and detailed arguments to support diametrically opposite conclusions. One scholar will argue with great learning that Colossians is a genuine Pauline letter; another will argue that it is not. Clearly both cannot be right. But it is not always so easy to see why one set of arguments is wrong. Each side will produce different arguments, laying greater stress on one set of considerations, playing down the significance of another, etc.

In this situation, it is all too easy to take up predetermined positions, to assume that one is right and to assert that the 'burden of proof' lies on the side of those who adopt different views. Given the fact that Christian pseudonymous literature was produced, it would probably be naive to say that all explicit descriptions of authorship are to be accepted unless 'proved' otherwise, and then to set the standards of 'proof' demanded so high that in practice the initial assumption of 'genuineness' is never changed. Equally, it would be quite absurd to assume that a work is pseudonymous unless proved otherwise!

The sorts of argument which people use are based on the possible existence of elements in the text under consideration which appear to be contrary to the alleged author's usage elsewhere (if indeed this is available). For example, the vocabulary and style of the Pastoral epistles are quite unlike those of the other Pauline letters. The absence of any eschatological perspective in Ephesians (and indeed the very opposite perspective in Eph. 3.21 where it seems to be assumed that the present world order will continue almost indefinitely) seems at variance with Paul's views elsewhere in his genuine letters.

Arguments like this do raise the question of how consistent one writer should be held to be; alternatively, how inconsistent is one writer allowed to be before one calls a halt and says that there must have been two writers? Mathematical proof is simply not possible and should not be expected, and decisions will have to be made on the basis of the delicate weighing and balancing of a whole host of different considerations.

In fact, the decision that a particular text is pseudonymous can often be liberating, rather than simply negative. For if a work is pseudonymous, then it is free to be interpreted on its own terms and independently of other writings of its alleged author. It is probably at this level that the question of authorship is important for exegesis. In some cases it is true that the question is quite immaterial: for example, it does not make very much difference whether the letter of James was in fact written by James (presumably the brother of Jesus is intended) or by a later writer writing in James' name. The letter has its own distinctive slant whoever wrote it.

In the case of the letters ascribed to Paul the situation is more complex. Decisions about the authenticity of, say, Ephesians may have far-reaching effects in the assessment of Pauline theology. Ephesians has its own distinctive teaching about the cosmic role of the Church, as well as being notable for its lack of any eschatological expectation. In both these respects, Ephesians is somewhat different from the other genuine Pauline letters.

If Ephesians is judged to be by Paul, then this decision will have major consequences in assessing Paul's doctrine of the Church and in interpreting other passages about the Church in Paul's other letters; it will also mean that Paul's eschatology will have to be reconsidered, and either a development postulated in Paul's thought, or a radical reassessment of Ephesians' eschatology undertaken to make it cohere with Paul's thought elsewhere.

On the other hand, if Ephesians is judged not to be by Paul, then the letter is free to be interpreted on its own merits; there is no pressure to force Ephesians into too Pauline a mould, or to force Paul into an 'Ephesians mould'. (In practice, of course, the decision about authorship cannot be separated from the issues mentioned here. For many, Ephesians is to be regarded as un-Pauline precisely because it is so unlike Paul's other letters in its eschatology and/or its ecclesiology.)

In the case of the narrative books of the New Teatament (i.e. the Gospels and Acts), the situation is not so clear cut and the issues are considerably more complex. In any case we are dealing with a rather different class of writing in that none of the Gospels makes any direct claim to be written by a particular individual: all the Gospels are anonymous. This has not prevented later tradition from ascribing names to the authors of each Gospel and indicating quite specific people by these names. Thus by tradition, Matthew's Gospel is ascribed to Matthew, the tax-collector and one of the Twelve; Mark's Gospel is ascribed to John Mark of the primitive Jerusalem church; Luke's Gospel and Acts are ascribed to Luke, the beloved physician and companion of Paul.

Each ascription must be assessed individually and on its own merits. Many believe that these ascriptions are historically 'wrong'. Again it is too simplistic to adopt an entrenched position and say that the Church's tradition must be accepted until 'proved' otherwise. This is especially so if appeal is made to the Church's memory as being somehow 'better' than our historical-critical methods. Most of the claims made by the Church Fathers may well have been nothing more than inspired guesses, partly based on an analysis of the text itself. For example, the ascription of Luke–Acts to a companion of Paul is as likely to have been a deduction from the 'we-passages' in Acts (i.e. the passages where the narrative slips into the first person plural) as due to any well-preserved accurate 'memory' within the Church.

Does the question of authorship make a great deal of difference here? At one level the answer is probably no. The interpretation of Mark's Gospel, say, is not necessarily dependent on one's decision about whether the author was the John Mark of Acts or an otherwise unknown Christian named Mark. The Gospel has its own individual characteristics which are independent of the question of the identity of its author.

At another level, it is often argued that the question of authorship is very important. This is the level of the historicity of the events described. If, for example, one believes that the author of Acts was a companion of Paul, then the we-passages in Acts may be regarded as the account of an eyewitness of the events described. As such, the whole story, especially the account of Paul's career, might be accepted as an historically trustworthy one. If one believes that Acts was not written by a companion of Paul, then this might affect one's assessment of the historicity of parts of the narrative.

We should again, however, be wary of confusing issues and of making things too black and white. Certainly the question of the historical reliability of a text should not be equated absolutely with the question of the eyewitness character of its author. Eyewitnesses can be very unreliable; non-eyewitness authors can have access to thoroughly reliable information. Thus the identity of the author does not necessarily settle the issue of how historically accurate his narrative is.

Further, a decision that a narrative is not written by an eyewitness can once again be liberating rather than negative. There are, for example, notorious difficulties involved in reconciling the picture of Paul which emerges from Acts and the picture of Paul which we get from his own letters.[7] If the author of Acts is to be identified as Luke the companion of Paul, and if Acts is also accepted as historically trustworthy, then one has to work quite hard to reconcile the Paul of Acts with the Paul of the letters. If, however, one believes that Luke was not a companion of Paul, and one accepts that Luke may have been at times 'inaccurate' in his account of some of Paul's activities, then one is free to accept the portrait of Paul in Acts on its own terms, perhaps to see how true it is to the real Paul, but also to see what Luke was trying to say to his readers by telling the story of Paul in the way he has. Yet we must be careful not to confuse the issues of authorship and reliability: Acts could have been written by a companion of Paul and yet present a somewhat distorted picture of Paul. A person's most ardent admirer is not always his ideal biographer!

In the case of the gospel tradition many complex issues are raised in assessing the historical reliability of various parts of the tradition. The whole problem will be discussed more fully in the chapter on form criticism. Here the issue will be limited to the question of how far decisions about historicity are affected by the question of the identity of the authors of the Gospels. One issue that arises is the question of how far the New Testament itself may provide a legitimate source of 'background' information. We have already looked at some aspects of this problem. Here we shall consider the problem as it relates to the question of authorship.

An example of the network of problems raised is Mark's account of the Sanhedrin trial of Jesus. It is well known that, according to Mark's narrative, the Jewish authorities appear to break almost all their own rules for the conduct of a capital trial.[8] What does this say about the author of the Gospel? One could argue that our evidence for Jewish rules about the conduct of capital trials comes from the Mishnah which was put together at a much later period (*c.* AD 200); hence we may not know for sure what rules were in force at the time of Jesus. Mark's account could therefore be taken as historically accurate, and as providing evidence for the way in which a Jewish trial could be conducted. In which case, Mark's Gospel could be the work of an eyewitness, or else based on eyewitness testimony (perhaps that of Peter).

On the other hand, one could argue that the evidence of the Mishnah should be accepted as valid for the time of Jesus. If Mark's account is historically accurate, then the Jewish leaders were guilty of gross illegality. Perhaps Mark deliberately intended to give this impression. Alternatively, one might argue that such gross illegality is historically implausible; Mark's account is unlikely to be historically accurate and so Mark cannot be based on eyewitness testimony here (or if he is, he has muddled his information very badly). Again though, one should not confuse the issues of authorship and reliability. Mark's account of Jesus' trial might be the work of a very confused eyewitness (though in that case, the fact that he was an eyewitness loses almost all of its evidential value).

At other levels, the question of the authorship of the Gospels may not be of over-riding importance. Indeed, decisions about the identity and situation of an evangelist may only emerge after a critical analysis of the Gospel. If we reject the traditional ascriptions of authorship of the Gospels, then we have no evidence external to the Gospels for determining who the authors were. We can still call them Matthew, Mark, Luke and John for convenience, but what we will be able to say about them will be more at the level of whether they were Jews or Gentiles, what kind of communities they were writing for, what sort of relationships they may have had with non-Christian Jewish neighbours, and so on. Most of these results will only emerge after the analysis of the Gospel.

In the case of the epistles it may be possible to make more of a logical separation between questions of 'introduction' and questions of 'theology'. One can (just) separate the problem of the nature and purpose of Romans, for example, from the problem of analysing the theological content of the letter in detail. In the case of the Gospels, any such separation is probably not possible: our only clues to the identity and situation of the evangelists may be via what they have to say to us theologically.

In the last two chapters we have seen how a genuinely historical understanding of a text is only possible if we are fully aware of the background of the text concerned. We have to try to discover something of the author's general background, linguistic, social, religious or whatever. We also have to try to discover something of the specific background of the particular text we are looking at: the identity of the author, the reason why the text was written, who the text was written for, and so on.

Very often we shall not be able to discover the answers to all such questions about a particular text. Nevertheless, if we are to arrive at an interpretation which is historically defensible, we must consider such questions. The problems associated with 'Introduction' are thus vitally important ones in the interpretation of the New Testament. Words and phrases in a text need a context before they can be fully understood. In these two chapters we have considered various historical contexts which affect the meaning of words and sentences. There is however another kind of context which it is vital to consider, and it is to this that we shall be turning in the next chapter.

Mark 3.1–6 and Parallels

The three accounts of this story in the Gospels raise a number of important 'introductory' problems. They can therefore serve as useful illustrations of some of the points made in the general discussion above.

In terms of the general background, it is clear that the story presupposes a background in Judaism. The incident recorded centres on the question of the legitimacy of Jesus to heal the man with the withered hand on the sabbath. Presupposed here is the command in the Jewish law, indeed in the decalogue, that one should do no work on the sabbath. The problem of Jesus' ability to perform the miracle is not raised: such ability is assumed by all concerned. Moreover, it appears to be assumed by all that Jesus' action in healing the man would constitute 'work'. Now it was recognized in Judaism that the commands of the law, including the sabbath law, were never to be applied rigidly or inflexibly. In some instances, two laws might appear to clash, and one would need guidance as to which law had precedence. In other instances, it was recognized that a particular law might be ignored if the circumstances warranted. Was the case of healing a man with a withered hand considered such an exceptional case as to warrant disregarding the law of the sabbath?

We know that such questions were discussed by Jews. At a later date, the Mishnah defined a number of specified actions as 'work' for the purposes of this law. Further, it was decided that in some circumstances it was legitimate to disregard the sabbath law if a human life was in danger, one could and should do 'work' on the sabbath to save that life; otherwise one should respect the law. (Cf. Yoma 8.6: 'Whenever there is doubt that life is in danger, this overrides the Sabbath.' Such a decision represents a very reasonable and humane compromise.)

As always when dealing with material from Jewish sources, there is the problem of knowing whether these principles were recognized at the time of Jesus. Our Jewish evidence comes from a later date, and it may be that the law was interpreted differently in the first century. Part of the problem in this Gospel story arises from the fact that Jesus' argument, at least in Mark, seems somewhat irrelevant.

In order to justify his action in healing the man, Jesus asks: 'Is it lawful on the sabbath to do good or to do harm, to save life or to kill?' (Mark 3.4). On the basis of the principles laid down in the Mishnah, these questions would be easy to answer: it is lawful to do good on the sabbath, but 'doing good' means doing no work since this is the divine commandment; also one should 'save life' on the sabbath, and if necessary 'work' to do so.

But in this case, there is no question of 'saving life'. A man with a withered hand is in no danger of dying. Thus 'doing good' in this instance should mean doing no work and perhaps waiting a day before healing the man. Against the background of the principles in the Mishnah, Jesus' questions would not in fact justify his proposed action of healing the man concerned. Thus one Jewish commentator says that Jesus here 'seems to evade the argument by a counter argument which, however ingenious, is not really to the point'.[9]

There are a number of ways of avoiding the difficulty. One is to say that in fact Jesus' action did not constitute 'work' and was technically not a breach of the sabbath law.[10] Another is to say that Jesus' question is not meant to be a legal defence of his action but more of a polemical assertion of his rights to disregard the sabbath law occasionally in the light of his own mission.[11] A third option would be to say that in the first century AD a wider class of activities than just saving life would have been regarded as legitimate breaches of the sabbath law. Thus Jesus' question in Mark

3.4 might have provided adequate justification for his action at the time. This is in effect using the New Testament story itself as evidence for the background situation. As far as I am aware, this option is not taken by scholars today in discussing the Marcan version of the story. Most in fact accept the evidence from the Mishnah as providing reliable information about the ways in which the sabbath law was interpreted in the first century.

There is much more debate about the interpretation of the Matthean version of the story, and this raises not only the question of the general background of first-century interpretations of the sabbath law, but also the specific 'introductory' problem of who 'Matthew', i.e. the author of the first Gospel, was.

As can be seen from a synopsis, Matthew's version of the story differs from Mark's in several ways. One difference arises from the fact that the issue of the legality of Jesus' action is not raised in the form of a blunt rhetorical question 'Is it lawful . . .?', as in Mark. Rather, in Matthew Jesus produces a reasoned argument based on a general case about rescuing a sheep which has fallen into a pit. As a result of this, Jesus in Matthew *concludes* the argument with the claim 'So it is lawful . . .' (Matt. 12.12). In this context the problems arise from the general example used here. For it seems to be assumed that if a sheep had fallen into a pit, then it would be regarded as legitimate to pull the animal out on the sabbath.

At this point the situation becomes rather complex. We know that the specific situation of an animal falling into a pit was discussed by the later rabbis as a possible instance where the sabbath law might be disregarded. The rabbis were in fact divided in their opinions. A strict school argued that only feeding and watering the animal should be allowed; a more lenient view allowed articles to be lowered into the pit to enable the animal to get out under its own steam if possible (Shabbath in the Babylonian Talmud 128b). But neither side argued that it was legitimate to drag the animal out oneself. This discussion comes to us from a period much later than the time of Jesus. There is also a statement in one of the Qumran texts, which comes from a date much nearer the time of Jesus; this specifically states that it is not legitimate to rescue an animal from a pit in the sabbath (Damascus Document from Qumran 11.13).[12]

There is thus some discrepancy between our Gospel text and the background information which we have. The later rabbinic rulings, and the explicit ruling from Qumran, appear to prohibit precisely what is presupposed as legitimate in Matthew's Gospel.

This then raises the question of how far Matthew himself was aware of the Jewish background, and hence whether Matthew himself was a Jew.

At this point there are a number of exegetical possibilities open. One is to argue that Jesus is here not appealing to an accepted legitimate breach of the law. Rather, he is appealing to common practice amongst his hearers: they would in fact break the law by rescuing a sheep on the sabbath, so why are they grumbling at him?[13] This would solve the problem at the historical level, though there is still the question of Matthew's own understanding of the situation. For Matthew himself appears to regard Jesus' argument here as providing a legal justification for the healing. He thus appears to assume that the rescue of a sheep was a legally acceptable breach of the sabbath law. If one accepts the Jewish evidence as it stands as providing the proper background for the story in the first century, then one must conclude that Matthew himself was working with presuppositions which were not those of Judaism, and therefore Matthew himself was probably not a Jew.[14]

There is however another way to read the evidence. This is to argue that our evidence of Jewish discussion about animals in pits on the sabbath may not furnish reliable information about the situation in the first century in the context of Jesus' ministry and/or Matthew's community. The rabbinic discussions we have all come from a much later period. Further, the Qumran evidence, although from approximately the right time, may also not be useful since we know that the Qumran sect interpreted the sabbath laws very much more strictly than other Jews at the time. One could also argue that Galilean Jews were in general somewhat lax in their application of the law.[15] Thus our background sources may be insufficient at this point to give us full knowledge of the situation presupposed by Jesus and/or Matthew.[16] One could then argue that the New Testament text itself should be taken as the evidence for the background situation. Possibly, the general thrust of Matthew's Gospel could be taken as a positive indication that Matthew was a Jew, and hence would have been well acquainted with Jewish interpretations of the law in the first century. Thus Matthew 12.11–12 itself shows that rescuing a sheep on the sabbath was a legitimate breach of the law.

Such a form of argument will be regarded as perfectly acceptable to some, and dangerously circular to others. Clearly a lot depends on how much weight is given to different factors in the discussion. Is Matthew's apparent Jewishness elsewhere determinative? Or should the evidence from outside the New Testament have priority over the New Testament itself in providing the necessary background information?

In fact, of course, such questions about this text in Matthew cannot be answered in isolation from the rest of Matthew or the rest of the New Testament. Other small details in Matthew's Gospel cast doubts on whether Matthew himself was a Jew.[17] Source-critical considerations may indicate that Matthew's version of the saying is secondary to the Lucan version (see p. 92 later). Hence the problem of the text is only one at the level of Matthew's redaction since the form of the saying does not go back to Matthew's source here, let alone to Jesus.

My own instinct in this case, for what it is worth, would be to respect the evidence from outside the New Testament, and to conclude that Matthew is not here reflecting Jewish presuppositions, and hence Matthew himself was probably not a Jew. However, enough has been said to show that this is not the only way to piece the evidence together. This discussion should also show that questions about 'background' and 'introduction' may not only have a complex interrelationship with each other, but may also have a significant bearing on the interpretation of the text itself.

Notes

1. cf. C. H. Dodd, 'The Mind of Paul', *BJRL* 18 (1934), pp. 3–34; reprinted in his *New Testament Studies* (Manchester 1953), pp. 83–128. Dodd clearly understood that any theory of development depended on an established relative chronology of the letters; he therefore devoted the first part of his article to establishing such a chronology.
2. See, for example, F. F. Bruce, *The Epistle of Paul to the Galatians* (Exeter 1982), pp. 43–5.
3. The problem is often known as 'The Romans Debate'. cf. K. P. Donfried (ed.), *The Romans Debate* (Minneapolis 1977).
4. cf. C. K. Barrett, *The First Epistle to the Corinthians* (London 1971), p. 154 and many other commentators.
5. ibid., pp. 157–8, though this is not the only interpretation of the passage.
6. It must be admitted that this paragraph adopts a very different attitude to authority from earlier studies of 'Introduction'. Such studies in the nineteenth century (and indeed in the present century) assumed that the authority of a work was determined by its apostolic authorship. A work written by someone other than an apostle did not have the same authority. The question of authorship thus assumed an importance out of all proportion to its inherent nature. For an alternative suggestion for how 'authority', or canonicity, might be thought of in the present, see ch. 1 above and the discussion there.

7. The *locus classicus* for such a view is the essay of P. Vielhauer, 'On the "Paulinism" of Acts', in L. E. Keck & J. L. Martyn (eds.), *Studies in Luke–Acts* (London 1966), pp. 35–50.
8. cf. D. E. Nineham, *Saint Mark* (Harmondsworth 1969), pp. 402–5.
9. C. G. Montefiore, *The Synoptic Gospels* vol. 1 (London 1927), pp. 81–2.
10. A. E. Harvey, *Jesus and the Constraints of History* (London 1982), p. 38; E. P. Sanders, *Jesus and Judaism* (London 1985), p. 266.
11. cf. (with varying nuances) Nineham, *Mark*, pp. 109–10; R. Banks, *Jesus and the Law in the Synoptic Tradition* (Cambridge 1975), pp. 124–5.
12. See Banks, *Jesus and the Law*, p. 126.
13. cf. T. W. Manson, *The Sayings of Jesus* (London 1949), pp. 188–9.
14. cf. G. Strecker, *Der Weg der Gerechtigkeit* (Göttingen 1961), p. 19.
15. cf. E. Lohse, 'Jesu Worte über den Sabbat', in W. Eltester (ed.), *Judentum Urchristentum Kirche* (FS for J. Jeremias. Berlin 1960), p. 88. However, there is no example of this in relation to the sabbath law.
16. cf. H. Hübner, *Das Gesetz in der synoptischen Tradition* (Witten 1973), p. 140.
17. cf. Strecker, *Der Weg der Gerechtigkeit*, pp. 15ff.

5

Genre

We have already seen that words can mean different things in different contexts. Most of us would not go quite as far as Humpty Dumpty and claim that any word can mean just what we want it to mean (especially if we pay it extra!). Nevertheless it is clear that language can be ambiguous. In the last two chapters we have seen how words can change their meanings if they are placed in different cultural or geographical contexts; and the same words can mean different things if said by different people. Now exactly the same is true if we look at different kinds of writing. For the proper interpretation of individual words or sentences depends, in part at least, on the type of text in which they occur.

When we started to look at textual criticism, I said that in order to interpret 'the text', one had to know what 'the text' was. At that stage, we were looking at the actual wording involved: in order to start to understand a text we have to establish precisely what the words are. But there is a deeper sense in which we have to know 'what a text is' before we can begin to make sense of it, even when we have established what the exact wording is. We need to have some idea of what sort of a text it is that we are dealing with, in order to know what the text is trying to say and what it is not trying to say. The technical word for this is the *genre* of a text. A few examples will hopefully clarify these rather general remarks.

Most of us make the kind of adjustment I am talking about quite unconsciously. We read words or sentences as parts of larger wholes, and we bring our awareness of what the wider context is to interpret the sentence in question. Suppose I am buying a house and I come across the sentence: 'There is a very small amount of rot in the window frames.' The context in which such a sentence might occur will determine my interpretation. If it is part of the report of my own independent surveyor, I might be inclined to sit back and breathe a sigh of relief that the trouble is not worse; if it is part of the details of the house given by the estate agent, I might be inclined to call the deal off immediately since an estate agent would only be likely to mention such a detail if the house is about to fall down in ruins.

Sometimes the genre of the whole text is absolutely vital for the proper interpretation of the text. Imagine that you are reading a newspaper and you come across the following sentence: 'Vicar gives directions to the Queen.' Interest might well be aroused. Where was the Queen? Perhaps at a garden party, and a kindly cleric showed her the way to the Ladies' tent? On the other hand, one might wonder why the Queen had to rely on a strange cleric in order to get directions: would she not have been surrounded by back-up staff who would tell her everything she needed to know?

Suppose we extend the extract slightly: 'Vicar gives directions to the Queen? Just the opposite.' Suspicions might now be aroused. The question mark suggests perhaps a shady vicar giving spurious directions to Her Majesty. Or perhaps they had a pleasant conversation, the vicar pointing in one direction and some people falsely assuming that he was telling her where to go.

Let us now extend the extract one stage further: '9. Vicar gives directions to the Queen? Just the opposite (7).' Hopefully by now the penny has dropped. This is no description of an historical event. It is a clue in a crossword puzzle. And those who enjoy such pastimes change gear completely in order to make proper 'sense' of the sentence. 'Vicar' does not conjure up a benign, smiling, dog-collared gentleman: it means 'REV' (short for 'reverend'); 'the Queen' is ER (Elizabeth Regina); 'directions' are points of the compass. And the answer to this not very clever cryptic clue is REV – ER – SE, the whole word meaning 'opposite'.

The point of this illustration is simply to show that our interpretation of the individual words of the text is determined in part by our understanding of what kind of a text the whole thing is, i.e. of its genre. As we saw just now, the sentence about the vicar and the Queen could have been a description of an event involving an ordained priest and the ruling Head of the country. In fact it was nothing of the kind. To read that sentence among the crossword clues and to ask about what historical encounter might lie behind it is just plain stupid. Rather, we make the mental adjustment which ensures that we interpret the sentences which appear as clues in the crossword puzzle quite differently from those which appear as headlines over news stories.

We make similar adjustments in other contexts. If we read books which tell stories, we distinguish between those which are fiction and those which are non-fiction. A good fictional novel may well be 'true to life' in the sense that we may be able to identify with some of the characters, and we may be able to recognize social situations as realistic. Yet if it is fiction, we recognize that the characters in the novel never had any historical existence. They may well be typical of real people, but they did not exist as such. To ask about the historical events described in a story is thus inappropriate if the story is fictional. Similarly, most of us make the necessary adjustment when we read a history textbook, a historical novel, a Shakespearean play, a detective story, or even a joke. Each type of writing, each genre, has its own character, its own limitations, its own aims. We realize that Shakespeare's *Julius Caesar* is not necessarily going to give us direct historical information about the events leading up to the murder of Caesar; and an Agatha Christie detective story about the activity of her famous Belgian detective Hercule Poirot cannot really be used to give insight into the ways in which Belgian detectives operate in real life. We read with certain expectations and we realize that some questions can be asked of some texts but not of others.

It must be admitted, however, that life is not always straightforward in this respect. All the examples we have looked at so far are instances where the genre of the text is already known: we know that a text is a crossword puzzle, or a fictional novel (by the disclaimer in the front), or a Shakespearean play, or a sonnet, or whatever. However, in dealing with ancient literature it is quite often the case that we do not know precisely what is the genre of the text in question. For example, are some of the later apocryphal stories about the apostles genuine historical accounts? Or are they fictional romances? Now in general terms we can only determine the genre of a text as a whole by looking at its individual parts: we can only know what the whole text says by considering each bit of it. Yet, the proper interpretation of each part of the text depends on having a proper appreciation of the whole. We are thus involved in a circular closed system, the technical phrase for this being the 'hermeneutical circle'.

Such a circularity in determining the genre of a text is to a certain extent inevitable. Indeed a certain amount of circularity is inherent in all literary study, and we have seen some examples of this already. There is no easy way out of this situation, though this does not mean that all study about genre is impossible. In practice, our understanding of the whole text (its genre) and our interpretation of the individual parts will interact with each other. Our understanding of the genre of the text should be constantly influenced, reinforced, or perhaps modified, by our understanding of the individual parts, and conversely, our developing understanding of the genre will continually influence our understanding of the individual parts of the text.

Many of these considerations about genre are extremely important when interpreting the texts of the New Testament. Most of us work quite unconsciously with some considerations like these. We accept, usually without thinking about it, that the parables of Jesus are fictional stories. We then make certain adjustments: we read certain things out of the parables, and we do not ask other questions about these stories which we might about other stories.

For example, the story of the rich young man who comes to Jesus (Mark 10.17–22) is presented in the Gospels as a true story. We could therefore legitimately ask whether the man in fact obeyed Jesus' instruction to sell everything that he had. Even if the Gospels give us no explicit answer, it is a legitimate question to raise. On the other hand, the parable of the Good Samaritan (Luke 10.29–37) is a fictional story. It is thus totally inappropriate to raise the question of precisely where on the road from Jerusalem to Jericho the man was robbed, of whether the Samaritan in fact came back to the innkeeper to pay the extra expenses incurred, of whether the wounded man ever thanked the Samaritan, and so on. The story is not describing a real event, and to raise other questions such as those just mentioned not only misinterprets the point of the story, it misinterprets the very nature of the story *qua* story.

Similar considerations apply in the metaphorical use of language. We often use language in a figurative sense, and it is the wider context that gives such language its meaning. When Jesus says in Mark 2.22 that 'no one puts new wine into old wineskins; if he does, the wine will burst the skins, and the wine is lost, and so are the skins; but new wine is for fresh skins', this is not a piece of advice about storing wine. A social historian might be interested in this verse as evidence for the methods of storing wine in first-century Palestine. But the primary interest of the text lies elsewhere. The language about new wine and old skins is being used to indicate the incompatibility of 'new' and 'old' in general, or rather the incompatibility of the ministry of Jesus (= the 'new') with the religion of Judaism (= the 'old'). What appears at first sight to be a statement about wine and its storing receptacles is in fact a statement about the relationship between Jesus and his Jewish contemporaries. Again most of us can quite easily make such adjustments in reading texts.

Sometimes the more precise determination of the genre of a text can make quite a difference to the interpretation of individual parts of it. Take, for example, the so-called 'letters' in the New Testament. Quite clearly these texts are not narratives, fictional or otherwise. They do not give direct descriptions of any historical events, even though they may allude to some events in passing. They are forms of communications from one party to another. Yet even in our own society it is clear that there are letters and letters. There are business letters; there are love letters; there are letters to newspapers which are primarily intended not as personal communications to the editor, but as mini-manifestos to be read publicly, and so on.

The same was true of the writing of 'letters' in the ancient world. A whole variety of different kinds of letter can be distinguished.[1] Some have tried to give some precision to this by distinguishing between a 'letter' and an 'epistle': a 'letter' is a genuine piece of communication integrally related to the situation of those to whom it is addressed, whereas an 'epistle' is a more general treatise which may have been written in the form of a letter but is not really specifically related to the addressees and is aimed at a wider audience.[2] The latter category would include, for example, the 'epistles' of Seneca which are really general treatises and not specifically related to the situation of the people to whom they are nominally addressed.

Most would agree that this distinction is probably too crude. How, for example, should Paul's correspondence be classified? Probably the answer must be somewhere in the middle between the two extremes of 'letter' and 'epistle'. Almost all of Paul's genuine letters are in one sense 'letters': they are written to specific congregations and try to deal with problems that have arisen there. The only possible exceptions to this are Romans and Ephesians (if indeed this is by Paul). Yet Paul himself expected his letters to be read in public (cf. 1 Thess. 5.27). Colossians 4.16 speaks of the letter to the Colossians being exchanged with a (now lost) letter to the Laodicean church and each letter being read to the other community. (Even if Colossians is not a genuine letter of Paul, this verse is still evidence of what was expected to happen to Paul's letters in Pauline communities.) Thus Paul evidently assumed that he was writing for a wider audience, and to this extent we could call his writings 'epistles'.

How though does one class the so-called 'Epistle to the Hebrews'? Is this a 'letter', a writing addressed to a specific situation? Or is it an 'epistle', a general theological treatise? Our answer to this question may determine our interpretation of the difficult passage in Hebrews, 6.4–6, which appears to state unequivocally that there is no possibility of hope for those who are guilty of apostasy. According to the writer, 'it is impossible to restore again to repentance those who have once been enlightened . . . if they then commit apostasy'. It was this harsh view which so angered Luther that he relegated Hebrews to the appendix of his Bible.

Now if Hebrews is an 'epistle', it is presumably justifiable to interpret the text as a considered theological statement: the author is claiming that it is impossible for those who commit grave sin after baptism to be restored and forgiven. If, however, Hebrews is a 'letter', the issue is not quite so clear cut. There are certainly parts of Hebrews that are exhortatory, interspersed amongst the more doctrinal parts. These paraenetic (encouraging, exhortatory) sections presuppose a situation where Christians are in danger of giving up their faith, perhaps by lapsing back into Judaism.

Now it is at least arguable that the whole of Hebrews is written with this very specific situation in mind and that the doctrinal parts of the letter are written to encourage Christians to remain steadfast in their faith. If this is the case, the warnings about the impossibility of second repentance after grave sin could be interpreted in a rather different way. They are not necessarily statements in the indicative of what inevitably and always is the case. They may be rather warnings of what *may* happen in the future *if* the readers lapse into apostasy; but they are made in full recognition that the readers have not yet fallen away from the faith and indeed are intended to function as exhortations for the readers not to do so.

It is true that the language is extreme, but then the writer thinks that the situation is extreme. However, the point is that the author is not necessarily giving a measured statement abut the effects of sin after baptism; rather, he is warning and exhorting his readers never to get into that situation. To take a very naive parallel, it may be not totally unlike a modern father saying, almost in desperation, to his small son: 'If you run across the road, I'll wallop you.' Father and probably son both know that no walloping will ever take place, but father wants to make it absolutely clear that if small children run across main roads, that is a desperate situation which must be avoided at all costs. So then, our understanding of the genre of the 'Letter/Epistle to the Hebrews' may have a considerable effect on our interpretation of the text itself.

Similar problems arise in the interpretation of the Book of Revelation. Revelation is an example of a type of writing known as 'apocalyptic'. There has been a great deal of debate about what precisely constitutes an apocalyptic writing.[3] This is not the place to enter into a detailed discussion of the issue. It is however perhaps worth raising the question of the relative time-scale of the events described in apocalyptic writings.

Apocalypses, including the Book of Revelation, are often regarded as predictions of events in the future: frequently the visions recorded in Revelation, at times very bizarre in form, are taken as detailed prophecies of events that are to come at the end of the world. However, it is by no means certain that these visions should be taken in this way. It has been cogently argued that the essence of apocalyptic is really not integrally related to the future: apocalyptic is the revealing of the heavenly mysteries in the present.[4] Whether this is true of all apocalyptic literature is at least debatable, but it should alert us to the possibility that apocalyptic writings are using language in a way that is rich and subtle and not always to be taken at face value. So, in terms of the time-scales involved, it may well be that some of the visions recorded in Revelation are insights into what is happening in the present rather than predictions of the future.[5]

The author of Revelation is faced with the situation of the Roman Empire threatening the Christian Church by demanding participation in the imperial cult:[6] Christians are expected to join other citizens of the empire in acknowledging the emperor as 'Lord and God'. Clearly many Christians would have regarded this as not too serious. If a pinch of incense offered to the emperor kept the peace, avoided violent persecution, and enabled the Christian Church to continue its activities of worship and mission, then why not? Does not God know the secrets of men's hearts? Does he not know that such an action would be done with no 'real', inner conviction?

'John's' answer to this is an uncompromising No. But in order to get his message across, he must show his readers the true reality of what is happening *in the present*. Thus part of his aim is to reveal the 'real' nature of the Roman Empire which on the surface seems to be so magnificent, so tolerant, and the provider of so much peace and security. In reality, the demands of the imperial cult are the demands of the great beast (Rev. 13); the city of Rome is in reality the great whore (Rev. 17) whose apparent magnificence will come to a disastrous end (Rev. 18).

The point is that John is writing primarily about the present and not about the future. Thus if we have a fixed idea that the genre of apocalyptic writing is one which deals exclusively with future events, we will mistake the force of what a text like Revelation is saying. Certainly if we look for events in world history many years after the first century as the 'fulfilments' of the 'prophecies' of Revelation, we will be totally misinterpreting the writer's message. Once again then an appreciation of the genre of the text is vital to its interpretation.

Genres are of course not fixed entities which cannot change for all eternity. Nor are they a set of rules, or boundary conditions, into which every writing of a particular genre must fit. There is debate amongst literary critics about the extent to which genres are prescriptive (i.e. they are rules within which one must work) or descriptive (i.e. they are simply generalizations of what a number of texts have in common). Perhaps most helpful is F. Kermode's description of genre as 'a context of expectation':[7] the genre provides the framework of reference necessary to interpret any text. This does not mean that every text within a single genre has to exhibit all the characteristics of that genre. Some texts make part of their point by departing from the standard expected form; but the existence of the expectation is itself what makes the departure a departure. Without the standard, the variant would not be recognizable as a deviation.[8]

One such example in the New Testament may be the opening of Galatians. Almost all the Pauline letters have a fixed form, starting with a formula 'A to B, greeting', followed by an extended thanksgiving. Galatians lacks the thanksgiving completely, presumably because Paul is so irate about what was happening to the Galatian communities. The significance of such an absence only becomes apparent when one realizes that it is an absence. Without the control of the 'genre' of the letters as a whole, the lack of a thanksgiving in Galatians would probably not be noticed.

Any discussion of the genre of New Testament texts cannot avoid at least mentioning one of the most difficult questions about genre in New Testament study, namely the problem of the genre of the Gospels. Is there a category, or genre, to which we can assign the four Gospels? Or should we assign some of the Gospels to one genre, some to another? (For example, Matthew's Gospel looks rather closer to the form of a 'biography' than Mark's Gospel does.)

Now it is not the aim of this book to provide answers to questions such as this. It is probably fair to say that majority opinion is still of the view that there is no close parallel to the genre of the Gospels amongst Hellenistic writings of the same period: the Gospels are *sui generis*.

It is true that recently there has been a revival of the view that the Gospels are quite close in kind to other writings known as 'biographies' in the ancient world.[9] On the other hand, others have argued that the alleged genre of 'biography' has to be stretched so far to include our Gospels that it really becomes of little value in helping us to interpret the actual Gospel texts.[10]

Certainly the Gospels do not provide us with the kind of information we would normally expect from a biography of Jesus. They tell us virtually nothing about Jesus' background, his upbringing, his mental or psychological development. Such features are entirely lacking from what was probably the earliest Gospel to be written, namely the Gospel of Mark. (It is true that Matthew and Luke provide some of this kind of information but this may simply illustrate that our Gospels are not necessarily all of the same genre.) For whatever reason, it appears that Christian writers produced a new type of writing to tell the story of the life of the central figure of their new faith.[11]

The importance of recognizing the proper genre of a text is acknowledged by literary critics. Most of us recognize genres unconsciously and adjust our interpretative spectacles accordingly. However, it is sometimes the case that genres cannot easily be determined (as in the case of the Gospels), or that the genre of a text is ambiguous (cf. the case of Hebrews which we looked at earlier). It is also perhaps worthwhile to think about some of the things we do subconsciously, and to realize some of the implications of what we do at the subconscious level. Hopefully enough has been said to show that a proper appreciation of the genre of a text is a vital part in understanding it. Perhaps then the lesson of this chapter is simply an extension of what we have said in the previous two chapters about the importance of the background and context of a biblical text. To understand individual sentences and words, we have to know not only something of the cultural, social and linguistic backgrounds, we also have to know something of the wider *literary* context in which the individual words and sentences have been set.

Notes

1. See the article on 'Letter' by N. A. Dahl in *The Interpreter's Dictionary of the Bible*, Supplementary Volume (Nashville 1976). Also W. G. Doty, *Letters in Primitive Christianity* (Philadelphia 1973), ch. 1.
2. This distinction between 'letters' and 'epistles' was made above all by Deissmann who argued that all Paul's correspondence should be seen as 'letters'. However, Deissmann had other things in mind as well: the distinction between 'epistle' and 'letter' was also that between a document deliberately written for artistic effect with general publication in mind (an 'epistle') and a genuine letter written without affectation in the heat of the moment (a 'letter'). Thus Paul's letters were to be seen as compositions of a natural and free religious impulse. For further discussion of Deissmann and his underlying presuppositions, see Doty, *Letters*, pp. 24–5, and his earlier article, 'The Classification of Epistolary Literature', *CBQ* 31 (1969), pp. 181–99.
3. cf. C. R. Rowland, *The Open Heaven* (London 1982); also P. D. Hanson (ed.), *Visionaries and their Apocalypses* (London 1983).
4. See especially Rowland, *Open Heaven*, pp. 70–2 and *passim*.

5. See the valuable series of short articles by G. B. Caird, 'On Deciphering the Book of Revelation', *Exp.T* 74 (1962–63), pp. 13–15, 51–3, 82–4, 103–5; also his commentary *The Revelation of St John the Divine* (London 1966).
6. cf. Rowland, *Open Heaven*, pp. 403–13.
7. F. Kermode, *The Genesis of Secrecy* (Cambridge, Mass., & London 1979), p. 162.
8. ibid., p. 53.
9. See C. H. Talbert, *What is a Gospel?* (Philadelphia 1977); P. Shuler, *A Genre for the Gospels* (Philadelphia 1982).
10. cf. R. Guelich, 'The Gospel Genre', in P. Stuhlmacher (ed.), *Das Evangelium und die Evangelien* (Tübingen 1983), pp. 183–219.
11. On the genre of the Gospels, there is a good brief discussion in R. P. Martin, *New Testament Foundations* vol. 1 (Grand Rapids 1975), pp. 15ff.; also H. C. Kee, *Jesus in History* (New York 1970), pp. 116ff.

6
Source Criticism

No author lives in a total vacuum. We have already seen that many of the New Testament authors write out of, and for, quite specific situations. Further, writers can take up and use words and ideas already spoken or written by somebody else. For example, Paul in 1 Corinthians regularly cites the views of his Corinthian readers (cf. p. 55 above). We have also seen that the recognition, or otherwise, of such elements in a text can have a significant bearing on its interpretation. It is thus important to be able to say how far an author is reproducing prior tradition, and how far he/she is writing freely. The branch of study which seeks to identify earlier traditions in a writer's text is usually known as source criticism.

In the study of the historical books of the New Testament there is one particular problem which has always aroused great interest, viz. the problem of the relationship between the three synoptic Gospels. These Gospels present three accounts of the life of Jesus which run so closely parallel to each other, both in the order of events and at the level of detailed wording in the Greek, that some form of literary relationship between them seems to be demanded: either one Gospel has been used as a source by the others, or the evangelists have used common sources which are now lost. The task of clarifying the mutual relationships between the three Gospels is usually known as the 'Synoptic problem'.

Although the Synoptic problem is often thought to be the source-critical problem *par excellence* in the New Testament, it is not the only such problem. There is a close literary relationship between Colossians and Ephesians, and between 2 Peter and Jude. Most would argue that again one writer has made use of the material in the other document. (The almost unanimous view today is that Ephesians is dependent on Colossians, and 2 Peter on Jude.)

There are also further source-critical problems in the New Testament texts. The examples considered so far are all cases where we have two or more texts which are probably in some literary relationship with each other. In other instances, the existence of sources has been suggested in cases where it is recognized that such sources are now lost. Thus many would argue that the writer of Acts has used sources for his story, even though these sources cannot be identified with any extant texts outside Acts. The only evidence for the source is the book where the alleged source is being used.

Similarly, many have argued that John 21 has a different origin from the rest of the Gospel. (Whether this is a 'source' in quite the same way as the other examples considered so far is perhaps debatable: one could call John 21 a 'secondary appendix', an expansion of an 'original' Gospel by a later writer; but methodologically the problem is similar to others considered here, and it seems reasonable to include the issue under 'source criticism'.)

So too many would agree that the Pauline letters sometimes use pre-formed hymnic units or credal summaries, and incorporate them into the argument. The so-called 'christological hymns' of Philippians 2.5–11 and Colossians 1.15–20 would come into this category. All these are possible instances where a writer has taken up traditions from elsewhere and used them in the final text as we now have it.

Source-critical problems are therefore of two kinds. We have instances where two existing texts are thought to be in some kind of literary relationship and the problem is to discover which way dependence lies; we can also have instances where the problem is to discover otherwise unknown sources in a single text. In view of the slightly different nature of these two kinds of problem, we shall look at each separately.

We start then with the problem of determining literary relationships between existing texts. Here the study of the Synoptic problem has always held an extremely important place within New Testament study, and so we shall spend a little time looking at some of the methodological problems raised.

Discussion of the literary relationships between the Gospels was at its most intensive in the nineteenth century, reaching its climax in the work of H. J. Holtzmann, *Die synoptischen Evangelien* (1861). Holtzmann's general solution to the problem was popularized for the English-speaking world by B. H. Streeter's *The Four Gospels* (1924). (It has not been a unique phenomenon for English scholarship to lag behind German scholarship by a generation or more!)

Many will be familiar with the solution which has found broad acceptance as a result of this work. This is the so-called 'two-source theory' or 'two-document hypothesis' (2DH). It consists of two claims: (i) Mark's Gospel was written first and was used by Matthew and Luke; (ii) Matthew and Luke also had access to another source known as Q which has now been lost. The agreements between the Gospels are thus due to dependence on two major sources, Mark and Q.[1] In broad terms, the 2DH is widely accepted today as providing the most satisfactory solution to the Synoptic problem.

It must also be said, however, that this theory has been under attack from a number of directions in recent discussions. The existence of Q has been questioned, with some maintaining that the evidence can be explained by the theory that Luke used Matthew in passages where Mark was not available.[2] There has also been a great revival of support for an older theory, the so-called Griesbach hypothesis (GH), which suggests that Mark's Gospel was written not first but last, making use of both Matthew and Luke as sources.[3] Now this is not the place to discuss the relative merits of each theory of synoptic interrelationships. I have discussed the matter more fully elsewhere, and, for what it is worth, have argued that the 2DH is preferable to some of its rivals.[4] Here all we shall do is look at the methods and forms of argument which we can use today.

Much of the more recent criticism of the 2DH has focused on the defence of the theory by Streeter.[5] Streeter put forward five arguments to sustain the claim that Mark's Gospel was written first. Probably none of these arguments offers any convincing *proof* of the priority of Mark. Others would go further and claim that none of the arguments offers any indication at all of the priority of Mark. We should however be wary of demanding the impossible when we look at arguments about literary dependence. We have already seen something similar in the case of claims about pseudonymity (cf. pp. 57f above), and the same is true here. We shall never be able to 'prove' that one solution to the Synoptic problem is right with the degree of finality which we could achieve in a mathematical proof. The nature of the evidence simply will not allow it.

In practice most source critics work with a rough criterion in mind which is very similar to that which we discussed when we were considering textual criticism. In textual criticism we are faced with two (or more) variant readings of the text; in the Synoptic problem we are faced with two (or more) different versions of a story with differences at various levels. We then have to ask, given two versions A and B, whether A is more likely to have been changed to B, or B to A. Or rather, can we give reasons why the change went one way and not the other. Very often we may well say that we can see how a change might have gone one way, but the reverse change is much harder to envisage. That is not to say that the reverse change is impossible. This means that all we shall have at the end of the day is a probability: a change from A to B is more likely than from B to A (or perhaps, we can only say that the reasons advanced so far for why B might have been changed to A seem unconvincing to us).

As an illustration of all this, let us take the first of Streeter's five famous arguments for the priority of Mark.[6] Streeter referred to the fact that almost all of the material in Mark appears in Matthew and/or Luke, and mostly in both. This fact is indisputable. Streeter then claimed that this could most easily be explained if Matthew and Luke had used Mark as a source, supplementing it with further material available to them from elsewhere. Now the facts can be explained in this way, but it would be quite wrong to pretend that there is no other explanation. The phenomenon could just as well be explained if Mark were writing last, pursuing a (general) policy of selecting from his two sources (Matthew and Luke) the material common to both. (This is the argument of advocates of the GH.)

In fact Streeter did supplement his argument about the content common to all three Gospels. In Streeter's day there had been a revival of the so-called 'Augustinian hypothesis', i.e. the theory that the Gospels were written in the order Matthew – Mark – Luke – John. Streeter ridiculed such a view, saying: 'only a lunatic would leave out Matthew's account of the Infancy, the Sermon on the Mount, and practically all the parables, in order to get room for purely verbal expansion of what was retained'.[7] Streeter can be accused of using rather strong language (cf. his use of the word 'lunatic'),[8] but the underlying form of the argument is clear and similar to what we have just discussed. A Mark–Matthew line of dependency seemed to Streeter to give a coherent picture of the development of the tradition: Matthew expanded Mark with extra material and cut out some of Mark's detail. The reverse line of dependency, Matthew–Mark, seemed to Streeter unintelligible: Mark must have made large-scale omissions of important material from Matthew, simply in order to expand the details of what he retained.

Now it is arguable that such a claim is not a convincing defence of the theory of Marcan priority. It does not, for example, meet the modern claims of the GH which asserts that Mark used both Matthew and Luke and deliberately decided to include only what was common to his sources (though to be fair to Streeter, the GH was not being advocated seriously in his day). Further, the fact that one modern critic can see no good reason why an ancient author behaved in one way does not mean that no such reason existed. The author may have acted in the way proposed for another, as yet unidentified, reason. All this simply illustrates the essential indeterminacy of many arguments in literary study, and we shall never be able totally to overcome this lack of finality in arguments of this kind.

Streeter's arguments tended to be somewhat wide-ranging, looking at patterns of agreement and disagreement in the whole synoptic tradition. Today, the debate is more often conducted at the level of individual stories, sayings and verses. To illustrate the kind of arguments which can be used, we shall look at three examples where a strong case can be made for the 2DH, though this is not to say that counter arguments cannot be brought.

(i) Consider the endings of the story of Jesus' rejection at Nazareth in Matthew and Mark:

Matt. 13.58	Mark 6.5–6
And he did not do many mighty works there,	And he could do no mighty work there, except that he laid his hands upon a few sick people and healed them. And he marvelled
because of their unbelief.	because of their unbelief.

In this case it seems relatively easy to explain how Mark's text could have been changed by Matthew. Mark's version suggests that Jesus was impotent: he was unable to do any mighty work/miracle. Matthew may have objected to such a suggestion about Jesus' lack of power. He thus cut out the central part of Mark's text; he also changed Mark's 'could do no' to 'did not do' and used the last phrase (the crowd's unbelief) to explain not Jesus' marvelling but Jesus' failure to perform many miracles. The lack of miracles is now blamed on the crowd's unbelief, not on Jesus' possible impotence. It seems quite easy to see why Matthew might have taken exception to Mark's text and altered it to produce his own version. The reverse line of dependency is much harder to explain, and so here the theory of Marcan priority gives a reasonably satisfactory explanation.

(ii) The three versions of Peter's confessions at Caesarea Philippi have different forms in the three Gospels:

Matt. 16.16	Mark 8.29	Luke 9.20
You are the Christ, the Son of the living God.	You are the Christ.	[You are] the Christ of God.

Again, the theory of Marcan priority can account for the texts fairly well: Matthew and Luke each expanded the very short Marcan version to give a fuller christological confession by Peter. The reverse line of dependency is very hard to explain. Especially if Mark knew Matthew, it is extremely difficult to explain why Mark dropped the reference to Jesus as 'Son of God' at a key point in his Gospel when 'Son of God' is such an important christological term for Mark (cf. p. 29 above). Again then, a Mark—Matthew line of dependence can be explained relatively easily; a Matthew—Mark (or even Matthew—Luke—Mark) line presents more problems.

(iii) The final example here comes from the so-called 'double tradition' (material common to both Matthew and Luke). The introductions to the final doom oracle at the end of the diatribe against the scribes and Pharisees in Matthew and Luke runs as follows:

Matt. 23.34	Luke 11.49
Therefore	Therefore also the Wisdom of God said,
I send you prophets . . .	'I will send them prophets . . .'

The prophecy, which in Matthew is a straight saying of Jesus, is in the form of a prediction by personified Wisdom in Luke. The theory that Luke used Matthew here is very hard to defend. If Luke is dependent on Matthew here, he must have substituted a Wisdom saying for Jesus' prophecy. Such a phenomenon would be unique in Luke–Acts. Nowhere else in the Lucan writings does Luke show any special interest in the figure of Wisdom, and there seems no good reason why he should have objected to the wording of the Matthean version. The reverse change is much easier to account for. Matthew shows a tendency elsewhere to see Jesus as comparable with the figure of Wisdom; it is therefore perfectly conceivable that Matthew changed a saying of Wisdom into a saying of Jesus. Since direct dependence of Matthew upon Luke is never seriously entertained, the only alternative is that Matthew and Luke depend on a common source here, which, in this instance, Luke has preserved more accurately than Matthew. The Q hypothesis here thus gives a reasonably satisfactory explanation of the texts concerned.

These are three examples where the case for the 2DH is a strong one. There may well be equally powerful arguments which could explain the texts on other source theories. There may well also be other instances in the synoptic tradition where the case for the GH, say, is a great deal stronger. Nevertheless, we have here some illustrations of how the argument might proceed.

In trying to determine how the tradition developed, we should however be wary of assuming that there are fixed and rigid 'laws of development', such as suggestions that a 'low' Christology was always changed to a 'higher' one, or a 'Jewish' form of the tradition always developed subsequently into a 'less Jewish' form.[9] Certainly studies of New Testament Christology have shown quite clearly that 'low' and 'high' Christologies cannot simply be equated with 'early' and 'late'. For example, Paul's Christology is probably far 'higher' than Luke's, and yet is considerably earlier. Thus in trying to work out which is the earlier and which the later of two forms of the same tradition, we may have to appeal to a wide variety of considerations. We shall also have to be aware that any 'results' we obtain will necessarily remain provisional and cannot be anything else.

We now turn to the slightly different problem of attempting to identify sources within existing texts in instances where those sources are now lost. Here the type of discussion tends to be rather different from the case of two extant texts, and the problems which are raised are also of a somewhat different nature.

Very often we suspect the existence of a source when we come across elements in the text which appear to be uncharacteristic of the author. This can be at the level of the vocabulary or style of the passage under consideration. For example, some of the vocabulary used in John 21 is rather different from that used elsewhere in the Gospel: the Greek word for 'to be able' used here is *ischuein* which is different from the word used elsewhere in John's Gospel, viz. *dunasthai*. The word for 'ask' (*exetazein*) in this chapter (v. 12) is not the same as that used elsewhere (*erotan*).[10] For these and other reasons, it can be argued that John 21 is not by the same author as the rest of the Gospel. Similarly, in Romans 3.25–26, Paul uses language and terminology that he does not use elsewhere: Christ's death is described as an 'expiation' (*hilasterion*); also God had 'passed over', or 'overlooked' (*paresis*) sins in the past. Both of these are unusual words for Paul. Thus many have argued that these verses may contain a little pre-Pauline summary which Paul has taken up and adapted for his purposes.[11]

Other cases where the existence of sources can be reasonably deduced are places where a writer seems to correct what he has just said. For example, John 4.1 implies in passing that Jesus and his disciples baptized people, but then the next verse, John 4.2, modifies this: 'although Jesus himself did not baptize, but only his disciples'. It looks very much as if the evangelist has inherited a tradition, or a source, which implied that Jesus did baptize, and for whatever reason, he wants to correct this impression. (In this case, however, it is very difficult to know the precise extent, or the wider context, of the prior tradition used by John.)

At other times, we may suspect that a source has been used because the contents of what is said are so tangential to the writer's evident purpose. Several of the notes about places visited by the Christian mission in Acts serve little purpose to the narrative as a whole. Acts 14.24–5, for example, says very baldly that Paul's mission visited Pisidia, Pamphylia, Perga and Attalia before reaching Antioch. No details at all are given. It seems quite reasonable to conclude that Luke has access to earlier tradition (a kind of 'travel diary' has been suggested) which gave some brief information about the names of places visited by the Christian missionaries.[12]

Attempts to isolate sources in these ways can however lead to certain methodological problems. Where we are appealing to differences in vocabulary, there is often enough evidence in the writer's text elsewhere for us to determine what his usual vocabulary is. However, it can be the case that we are not simply dealing with synonyms, for example whether the writer uses *dunasthai* or *ischuein* to express the idea 'to be able'. Part of the argument about the pre-Pauline nature of Romans 3.25–26 concerns the ideas, as well as the vocabulary, of the material in question. Some would say, for example, that the idea of God 'passing over', or 'overlooking', sins committed in the past is foreign to Paul's thought, since it appears to contradict what Paul says in Romans 1–2, where he argues that all sin is punished by God.

Now alleged differences in ideas are much harder to quantify than differences in the use of synonyms. This raises the question of whether we can determine what is fundamental in the thought of Paul, John, or whoever, so well that we can discriminate within a Pauline or Johannine text and say that something there is un-Pauline or un-Johannine. One could with some justification argue that we can only determine what is Pauline from Paul himself, and indeed it is almost a matter of self-definition that 'Pauline' means Paul himself. To put it crudely, can Paul ever be un-Pauline in any meaningful sense?

When the question is spelt out in this way, the answer is obviously no. If 'Pauline' means Paul, then Paul must by definition be Pauline. On the other hand, Paul may have incorporated ideas into his letters which do not cohere fully with his thought elsewhere. By bringing in other parts of the Pauline corpus we may be able to say that some elements in Paul's letters are not the work of Paul himself and hence attributable to a pre-Pauline tradition. For example, a strong case can be made for the pre-Pauline nature of passages like Romans 3.25–26, or Romans 1.3–4, or Philippians 2.5–11.

We should, however, be cautious about suggesting discontinuities within a single writer's text too readily, and we should make every effort to ensure that we have interpreted the relevant passages correctly. *Is* there a real tension between the ideas expressed in two contexts within the text of a single writer, so that one view is to be ascribed to the author and the other to his tradition?

To take another example, it is sometimes argued that the occurrences of the term 'Son of Man' in Mark's Gospel are rather uneven. The characteristic Marcan view is often claimed to be that Jesus *qua* Son of Man is the one who must suffer but who will be vindicated by God in the future. The evidence for this is the use of the term Son of Man in many texts expressing these twin ideas, suffering and future vindication, in the second half of the Gospel (Mark 8.31 onwards). There are, however, two Son of Man sayings earlier in the Gospel in Mark 2.10 and Mark 2.28, both of which seem to be concerned with a different theme, viz., the authority of Jesus *qua* Son of Man in the present. Should one argue that, since these references to Jesus as Son of Man apparently come too early in the Marcan scheme, before the point in Mark's Gospel where Jesus starts to teach about his suffering and vindication, they are un-Marcan and hence part of a pre-Marcan tradition?[13] Many have in fact argued in this way. Nevertheless, we could argue rather differently, and say that it is wrong methodologically to work out 'Mark's view about the Son of Man' excluding two Marcan Son of Man sayings from consideration, and then to say that these two sayings do not fit the pattern and hence are un-Marcan. Rather, we should perhaps try to incorporate all the Marcan Son of Man sayings into a single comprehensive pattern which may be different from that established on the basis of only some of the sayings about the Son of Man in Mark.[14]

Another similar example in terms of method occurs in the case of some of R. Bultmann's theories about the fourth Gospel. Bultmann argued that the final work of the evangelist was later expanded to form the Gospel as we have it today. A later ecclesiastical redactor added the apparent references to the Christian sacraments, i.e. the (baptismal?) references to being 'born *of water* and the Spirit' in John 3.5, and the section in John 6.51c–58 which seems clearly to reflect Christian eucharistic language. Thus, according to Bultmann, an un-sacramental, or even anti-sacramental, 'John' has been glossed by a later redactor who has added these later references.[15]

The difficulty is to know on what basis we can say that the sacramental language in John is 'un-Johannine'. At the level of style or vocabulary, there is nothing to distinguish these verses from the rest of the Gospel. The sole basis for the source-critical distinction is the alleged contradiction in ideas between these verses and other parts of the Gospel. For example, the eucharistic language of John 6.51c–58 is said to contradict the earlier parts of the Bread of Life discourse in John 6: in the earlier part of the discourse, eternal life is promised to those who simply believe in Jesus; vv. 51c–58 imply that eternal life is dependent on participation in the Christian sacrament.[16]

However, as in the case of the Son of Man sayings in Mark, we could argue in other ways. We could say that, since there is no other evidence for the un-Johannine nature of John 6.51c–58, these verses should be seen in the light of the rest of John 6 and interpreted non-eucharistically: the references to eating the flesh of the Son of Man and drinking his blood are to be seen as further *metaphors* of the basic idea, common to the whole of John 6, of coming to Jesus and believing in him.[17]

Alternatively, we could say that the eucharistic ideas are not to be interpreted too mechanically: sharing in the eucharistic meal is not to be seen as a piece of magic, but as the expression of full personal fellowship with the risen Jesus. On this view, the ideas expressed in the earlier part of the discourse, in terms of direct personal relationships with Jesus, and the eucharistic ideas of vv. 51c–58 are not mutually contradictory but rather complementary to each other.[18]

Bultmann's theories about the un-Johannine nature of these verses seem to be based in part on a polarization between the ideas of two parts of the same text and an apparent unwillingness to attempt to integrate them. Since the text itself, at least in its present form, has the two views side by side, we should initially try to interpret the text as it stands before splitting it up into sources and secondary accretions. Nevertheless, such work will always have to recognize that a total harmonization of the complete text may not be possible. Whether John 6.51c–58 falls into this category is at least debatable.

The question of whether Paul/John/Mark can be un-Pauline/un-Johannine/un-Marcan is an important one. Clearly it is not impossible that this might be the case. An author can take over and use traditions which do not always cohere perfectly with what he says elsewhere. If he never did so, then source-critical work would become almost impossible since we could never isolate features which were in part uncharacteristic of the author and were therefore indicative of a source being used.

We should, though, be aware of the problems raised by claiming that we can identify sources in this way. We should also remember that even if an author uses a tradition, this presumably implies some measure of agreement on the part of the author with what the tradition says. Thus we cannot drive too much of a wedge between an author and his tradition. (We shall return to this point later when we look at redaction criticism: see p. 121 below.)

Bultmann's source theories on John escape this difficulty, since he ascribes the sacramental references to a *post*-Johannine redactor: 'John' presumably would not have agreed with the inclusion of this tradition! Nevertheless, an argument which says that one part of a text is so uncharacteristic of the author as to contradict the rest of the text, must remain methodologically questionable.

So far we have looked at some of the methods used in source-critical study. Inevitably we must ask the question, What is the value of such study?

In the past, source criticism was often regarded as a discipline applicable primarily to the historical books of the New Testament, i.e. the Gospels and Acts. In the nineteenth century, an ability to establish the 'facts' of history, especially the facts about the life of Jesus, was regarded as being of tremendous theological importance. The Gospels were primarily regarded as sources for the history they were describing. Thus in order to discover information about the life of Jesus, one had to determine which was the earliest Gospel and which Gospels were secondary. If one accepts the theory of Marcan priority, Mark's Gospel is the earliest Gospel and provides a primary source of information; Matthew's and Luke's parallels to Mark are only secondary sources. Thus in considering material which is parallel in all three Gospels, the Marcan version is to be considered as the primary source for rediscovering information about Jesus.

Such a procedure is, of itself, admirable, provided it is not pressed too far. However, it is probably fair to say that in the past, scholars did press things too far. People tended to think that, since Mark's Gospel was earlier than Matthew and Luke, not only was Mark's Gospel more reliable than the other two but also it was reliable in absolute terms. One could therefore take Mark's Gospel as an exact transcript of the life and ministry of Jesus.

There is of course an important *non sequitur* here. The fact that Mark's Gospel may be more reliable than Matthew and Luke, does not necessarily mean that it is absolutely reliable. Exactly the same is true in relation to other sources which have been detected in the historical books of the New Testament. Many have argued for the existence of a Q source behind Matthew and Luke, for the existence of earlier traditions behind much of Luke's account of the trial of Jesus, for the existence of sources behind some of the accounts in Acts. Yet too often people have assumed that the isolation of an earlier source is almost *ipso facto* an indication of the historical reliability in absolute terms of the source in question.

It is now realized quite clearly that such 'optimism' in the use of the results of source criticism is misplaced. Ever since the turn of the century and the work of W. Wrede on the messianic secret in Mark, it has been acknowledged by many that Mark's Gospel is not necessarily an exact transcript of the life of Jesus: Mark's Gospel is just as theologically motivated as the other Gospels. Moreover, if we accept conventional datings for the Gospels, Mark's Gospel is to be dated in the 60s or early 70s AD, Matthew and Luke in the 80s or 90s. Source criticism thus enables the historian to get back from the 80s to the 60s/70s AD, but not necessarily any earlier. It is now becoming increasingly clear that the Q tradition in the Gospels also had its own distinctive theological slant, and hence we cannot simply make the jump from Q back to Jesus without a great deal of care. Similarly, the isolation of an 'L' tradition lying behind Luke's special material, e.g. in the passion narrative, may well indicate an earlier stage of the tradition; but this is no guarantee that the tradition is therefore historically any more reliable in absolute terms.

Source criticism can no longer provide the guarantee, looked for by many in the past, of the historical reliability of one part of the tradition. This is not to say that source criticism has nothing to contribute at this level: it is indeed the case that the results of source criticism have to be taken into account in deciding which is the earliest form of the tradition. Nevertheless, when this source-critical work has been done, there is still further work that is necessary in order to bridge the gap between the source material and the actual events themselves. Some aspects of this problem will be considered in the next chapter.

In terms of modern study of the New Testament it is probably the case that the value of source criticism lies primarily in the contribution it can make to redaction criticism, i.e. to the illumination of an author's own ideas. The whole topic of redaction criticism will be considered later. (To anticipate slightly, however, part of the way in which redaction criticism operates is to observe the ways in which a writer uses his sources, as this can tell us something about himself and his interests. Such a procedure presupposes that we can identify the sources in question, in order to be able to observe the way in which a writer alters and adapts those sources. Thus, for example, in Romans 3.25–26, most scholars who accept that Paul is using an earlier source here would also say that the reference to 'faith' in v. 25, and the note about God as the one 'who justifies [the person] who has faith in Jesus' in v. 26, are Paul's additions to the earlier formula, and they tell us something of Paul's own concerns in using his tradition here.)

Source-critical studies are thus indirectly of very great importance at a number of levels. In attempts to reach behind narrative accounts to historical events being described, we have to take full account of source criticism; and in any modern redaction-critical work, seeking to illuminate the thought of an individual writer, source-critical results can be brought to bear. Source criticism underlies a great deal of modern New Testament study, and so even though most of us have no desire to be specialist source critics, we all should be aware of some of the aims and methods, and also the limitations, of a source-critical approach to the New Testament.

Mark 3.1–6 and Parallels

The following remarks are simply intended to provide an illustration of how a modern source-critical study of a particular Gospel story might proceed. In order to keep the discussion within manageable limits, I shall have to restrict it to arguments which support a particular source theory. In this case, I believe that the texts can most adequately be explained by the 2DH, though that is not to say that other source theories may not be equally defensible here.

The three accounts of the story of the man with the withered hand run so closely parallel to each other that some literary relationship between them is demanded. In addition, Matthew has an appeal by Jesus to the example of a sheep falling into a pit on the sabbath (Matt. 12.11–12); and although this has no parallel in Matthew or Luke in their versions of this story, there is a parallel elsewhere in Luke (Luke 14.5).

Matthew's version of the story seems to be rather uneven. We have already seen something of the possible background to the story in Jewish regulations about the sabbath (see p. 63 above), and some of the difficulties which the story raises from a historical point of view. In particular, Mark's version of the story has Jesus asking polemically: 'Is it lawful on the sabbath to do good or to do harm, to save life or to kill?' This, as we have seen, cannot be a reasoned justification for healing the man with a withered hand, since the man's life is not in danger. Matthew appears to think differently. His version has Jesus appealing to the example of the sheep, and claiming that a man is of much greater value than a sheep (v. 12a). The logic seems to be that since a man is more than a sheep, what applies in the case of a sheep applies even more in the case of a man. Thus since a sheep can be rescued on the sabbath, so too can a man. Matthew's Jesus then continues: 'So it is lawful to do good on the sabbath' (v. 12b). The problem is that this conclusion, acting as the justification for Jesus' actually healing the man, in no ways follows from the preceding argument. The example of the sheep might justify saving a man's life, but it does not justify doing work in a less urgent situation. Matthew's conclusion, therefore, in v. 12b does not follow from the argument in vv. 11–12a. The statement 'it is lawful to do good on the sabbath', as a justification for doing work to help a man whose life is not in danger, can only be a polemical assertion. This suggests that there is a seam in Matthew's version between v. 12a and v. 12b, with the two parts perhaps coming from different strata of the tradition.

An analysis of Matthew's version alone thus suggests that Matthew is putting together two streams of tradition. A glance at the other two Gospels shows how well the 2DH can explain this. We saw that one of Matthew's sources probably contained a version of the story where the reference to 'doing good on the sabbath' was a polemical assertion. This is exactly the case in Mark. Mark's version coincides very closely with what we have reconstructed as one of Matthew's sources. Nothing in fact prevents us from actually identifying Mark as Matthew's source. Indeed all the other differences between Matthew and Mark can be adequately explained if Matthew is using Mark. For example, Matthew's omission of the note in Mark 3.5 about Jesus being angry could well be due to Matthew's reverence for the person of Jesus and a wish to avoid attributing anger to Jesus. Other small verbal differences can easily be explained by Matthew's known tendencies in his use of language.[19] A reverse line of dependence, i.e. Mark's being dependent on Matthew, would have to explain how Mark has neatly managed to reconstruct one of Matthew's sources.

The saying about the animal in the pit (Matt. 12.11–12) is the one item in Matthew which cannot be derived from Mark. There is however a parallel to the saying in Luke 14.5, which is close enough in substance to suggest a common origin. Either one

Gospel has used the other as a source (and here the only theory seriously entertained is that Luke used Matthew), or both depend on a common source. In this case, it is unlikely that Luke is dependent on Matthew, since Luke's version is probably more original. However, to defend such a claim involves a bit of textual criticism as well.

The text of Luke 14.5 is in some doubt. The question is who or what has fallen into the pit. In Matthew it is a sheep. In Luke there is variation in the manuscripts. Some have 'a son or an ox', some 'an ox or an ass', some 'an ox, an ass or a son', some 'a sheep or an ox' (with variation in the order as well). The last can almost certainly be rejected as assimilation to the text of Matthew. Distinguishing between the rest is more difficult. 'Ox and ass' is a well-known pair; 'son' seems rather incongruous in this context. We may get more help, and also solve the question of the most original form of the saying, if we look once again at the legal background implied.

We have already noted some of the problems involved here. As far as we know, it was not regarded as a legitimate breach of the sabbath law to rescue an animal which had fallen into a pit. However, it was apparently regarded as legitimate to rescue a man in such a situation. Now the appeal to unfortunate bodies in pits to justify working on the sabbath will only carry weight if it is accepted by all that the sabbath law can be breached in this case. This suggests that originally the saying referred to a human being who had fallen into a pit. Thus 'son' is probably an integral part of the earliest form of the saying (and we can use this to solve the text-critical problem as well). The 'ox' may have been added later because of some assonance between the Aramaic words for 'son', 'pit' and 'ox'. This means that Luke's version of the saying is probably closer to the original. Matthew's form, with a 'sheep', is thus secondary. This is also supported by the fact that Matthew is quite fond of using the sheep imagery. It occurs far more frequently in his Gospel than in the other Gospels and hence its presence here is probably redactional. Matthew and Luke therefore appear to be dependent on a common source for this saying, with Luke here preserving the more original form.

In this analysis of Matthew's account of the story, we have reached the conclusion that Matthew is dependent on two sources: one of these is the account in Mark; the other is a source which Matthew has in common with Luke. This is precisely the 2DH: Mark's Gospel is prior, and Matthew and Luke also use a common source, Q.

The argument given here is by no means complete. We have

not yet examined the relationship between Luke's account of the story of the man with the withered hand and the other two accounts, though it can be shown that the theory of Marcan priority can explain things just as well here.[20] Hopefully, however, enough has been said to show how the argument might proceed, what sorts of questions we are asking of the texts in source-critical study, what kinds of factors we are discussing, and what sort of results we can achieve at the end of the day.

Notes

1. The phrase 'two-document hypothesis' perhaps makes more assumptions about the nature of Q, viz. that Q was a single document. This would need further justification: Q might have been a single document; on the other hand, it might have been a more amorphous mass of traditions available to Matthew and Luke but never collected together beforehand in the tradition. However, this is a further problem which no one intends to prejudge by using the term 'two-document hypothesis'.
2. This is above all the theory of M. D. Goulder: see his *Midrash and Lection in Matthew* (London 1974), as well as other articles.
3. See especially W. R. Farmer, *The Synoptic Problem* (London & New York 1964).
4. See my *The Revival of the Griesbach Hypothesis* (Cambridge 1983), and 'On the Relationship between Matthew and Luke', *NTS* 30 (1984) pp. 130–42.
5. This may overrate the importance of Streeter: Streeter himself was only summarizing the views and arguments of others.
6. B. H. Streeter, *The Four Gospels* (London 1924), pp. 159ff.
7. ibid. p. 158.
8. The person who had revived the Augustinian hypothesis was H. G. Jameson. Farmer calls Streeter's treatment of Jameson 'the single most unparalleled act of academic bravado on record' (Farmer, *Synoptic Problem*, p. 152).
9. See especially E. P. Sanders, *The Tendencies of the Synoptic Tradition* (Cambridge 1969), who shows that many proposed 'laws of development' do not stand up to critical scrutiny.
10. cf. C. K. Barrett, *The Gospel according to St. John* (London 1955), p. 479.
11. cf. R. Bultmann, *Theology of the New Testament* vol. 1 (London 1951), p. 46; E. Käsemann, *Commentary on Romans* (London 1980), pp. 95ff.
12. cf. M. Dibelius, *Studies in the Acts of the Apostles* (London 1956), p. 197.
13. So H. E. Tödt, *The Son of Man in the Synoptic Tradition* (London 1965), p. 132.

14. I have tried to do this in my 'The Present Son of Man', *JSNT* 14 (1982) pp. 58–81.
15. See R. Bultmann, *The Gospel of John: A Commentary* (Oxford 1971), pp. 138, 218–19.
16. ibid., pp. 218–19.
17. So J. D. G. Dunn, 'John VI – A Eucharistic Discourse?', *NTS* 17 (1971) pp. 328–38.
18. cf. B. Lindars, *The Gospel of John* (London 1972), p. 251.
19. For more details, see my *Revival*, p. 101.
20. cf. *Revival*, pp. 101–2.

7
Form Criticism

The discipline of New Testament study known as form criticism (a piece of 'translationese' for the German word *Formgeschichte*) arose initially, for New Testament critics at least, as an aspect of study of the synoptic Gospels. As we have seen, synoptic studies in the nineteenth century were dominated by the work of source critics, as they endeavoured to clarify and identify the written sources which underlay the Gospels. However, the earliest Gospel to be written, probably Mark, is still to be dated no earlier than the 60s AD. Thus between the earliest written source and the events of the gospel story there is a gap of almost a generation. During this period the traditions about Jesus were probably handed down orally and used in various ways. Moreover, the process of putting all the various traditions into a connected whole was probably the work of the evangelists themselves. It was in the attempt to illuminate the way in which the traditions about Jesus were used in the period prior to the production of written sources that the work of New Testament form criticism was developed.

The main pieces of evidence considered by the form critic are the small units of tradition which now appear embedded within larger wholes; and one of the basic presuppositions in the work of form criticism is that these units originally existed separately. In the study of the synoptic Gospels, the 'units' concerned are the individual stories and/or sayings which can very often easily be isolated from their context. However, form criticism can also be applied, and indeed has been applied very fruitfully, to other writings of the New Testament. (On this, see p. 111 below.)

The fundamental axiom of form criticism is that there is a correlation between the way in which a unit of tradition is told, its form, and the type of situation where it is being used. (The technical term for the latter is the German phrase *Sitz im Leben*, loosely translated as 'setting in life'.) Many of us are no doubt familiar with such a correlation, and indeed presuppose it as providing certain conventions within which we can operate quite happily. We all know of the standard business letter which starts off 'Dear Sir' or 'Dear Madam', and ends 'Yours faithfully'. The start and finish of the letter are standard features where the words in themselves have almost no significance at all: 'Dear Sir' implies no note of endearment; 'yours faithfully' does not indicate that the sender of the letter will be 'faithful' to the person he/she is writing to in any meaningful sense of the word. The *Sitz im Leben* of the formal communication in a business transaction leads to a fairly well-defined form for that communication.

Similarly, many will be famliar with the type of letter which comes unexpectedly through the letter box informing the recipient that he/she has been specially chosen to take part in a fabulous lucky draw contest; the prize is a brand-new car which will make the reader the envy of the whole neighbourhood. Moreover, the reader is now in a uniquely privileged position to be able to buy a special book/atlas/encyclopaedia/greenhouse/subscription to a journal or whatever at a never-to-be repeated discount price, and this offer is backed up by the irresistible offer of a free trial of the product for fourteen days: 'If you are not absolutely satisfied with . . . you can send it back to us and owe nothing.' Furthermore, the format of the communication is often standard: a letter printed by a computer with the reader's name and/or address inserted in the letter (usually slightly out of line with the rest of the text), and all printed on colourful, high-quality paper. It is of course an advertising gimmick with the primary aim of selling a particular product. The form of the communication is highly stereotyped: again there is a close correlation between the *Sitz im Leben* (someone trying to sell a particular product to the general public) and the form used.

Most of us can recognize a 'form' and interpret what is said accordingly. We recognize immediately a business letter, an advertising circular, a short story, a poem, and adjust our interpretative spectacles to fit. We have already seen examples of this in looking at the question of genre. Indeed genre criticism and form criticism are in some respects two sides of the same coin, the main distinction between the two being that genre criticism looks at larger connected pieces of writing whereas form criticism considers the smaller units of tradition. In terms of the study of the Gospels, genre criticism looks at the question of what type of writing the finished Gospels are; form criticism looks at the individual stories within the Gospels.

Now in contemporary situations, we know the *Sitz im Leben* and can interpret the form appropriately. The study of form criticism in the New Testament seeks to go in the reverse direction: from a study of the form in which a tradition is being told, form criticism tries to identify the situation, or setting in life, which led to the tradition's being preserved in the way it has been. In terms of the classification of the units of the tradition, most work has been done on the synoptic tradition in the Gospels. The scholars most closely associated with this work have been M. Dibelius, R. Bultmann and V. Taylor,[1] and although they differ in some of their conclusions and also in some of the terminology they use, they also show an underlying agreement on a number of points, especially in their classification of the synoptic material.

One category of story in the synoptic tradition was called 'paradigm' by Dibelius, 'apophthegm' by Bultmann, 'pronouncement story' by Taylor. This is a brief account, told with a minimum of extraneous detail and designed to lead up to a single saying of Jesus, the 'pronouncement', which forms the climax of the story.

An example is the story of Jesus being asked about the ethics of paying taxes to the Roman Empire. Very few details are given beyond the barest minimum necessary for telling the story at all, and the narrative leads up to the 'punch line' from Jesus, 'Render to Caesar the things that are Caesar's, and to God the things that are God's' (Mark 12.13–17).

As far as the *Sitz im Leben* of such stories was concerned, Dibelius argued that the paradigms were used primarily in the context of preaching: they provided examples and illustrations for sermons. Bultmann tried to give rather more precision to the general category of what he called apophthegms, and he subdivided the class: there were controversy dialogues (of which the story of the man with the withered hand in Mark 3.1–6 is an example), arising from polemical situations between the early Church and its opponents; there were scholastic dialogues (e.g. the story about the greatest commandment in Mark 12.28–34) which are less polemical and more apologetic; and finally there were 'biographical apophthegms' (e.g. the story of the would-be disciples in Luke 9.57–62) which purport to give information about Jesus and which were used primarily as paradigms for sermons.

A second main category consists of some (though not all) of the miracle stories. Dibelius called these 'tales', Bultmann and Taylor called them 'miracle stories'. In contrast to the paradigms, these stories are much longer and contain far more detail. The 'form' of the story is basically a threefold one where the situation of the sufferer is described, an account of the miracle is given, and then there is a statement showing the success of the miracle.

A good example is the story of the Gerasene demoniac in Mark 5.1–20, where the simple fact that the story occupies twenty verses gives some idea that this story is being told in a rather different way from that of the more compact paradigms. Several features in the structure of these stories can be paralleled in other

Jewish and Hellenistic stories. Dibelius postulated a group of storytellers using these stories to show Jesus' superiority over other rival miracle-workers. Bultmann did not accept the existence of such a specific group of people, but agreed that the stories were preserved for propaganda and apologetic purposes.

Other categories are less easy to define. A third class of stories was called by both Dibelius and Bultmann 'legends'. This word in English has perhaps rather unfortunate overtones, suggesting that the story is fictitious; but Dibelius only meant 'religious narratives of a saintly man in whose work and fate interest is taken'.[2] An example is the story of Jesus in the temple in Luke 2.41–49. It is somewhat difficult to see either a common form in these stories or a common *Sitz im Leben*. A final category consists of the 'sayings' of Jesus. Dibelius took these as a single group, arguing that the *Sitz im Leben* for their preservation was catechetical instruction in the Church. As with the apophthegms, Bultmann endeavoured to give more precision to this teaching material. He distinguished proverbial sayings (e.g. Luke 10.7: 'the labourer deserves his wages'), prophetic and apocalyptic sayings where Jesus predicts the coming of the Kingdom of God etc. (e.g. Luke 10.23–24), legal sayings giving rules for the community (e.g. Mark 7.15), 'I sayings' where Jesus speaks of his own work and destiny (e.g. Matt. 5.17), and finally the parabolic teaching of Jesus where yet further subdivisions are made.

How valuable is the classification of the material in this way? In some instances, it may not be very useful. This is especially the case with Dibelius' categories which tend to be extremely broad. For example, if we are told that 'the labourer deserves his wages' is a 'saying of Jesus', we could be forgiven for thinking that this was crashingly obvious anyway. Bultmann's attempt to provide further precision within the broader categories is to be welcomed in this respect. So too the proposed *Sitze im Leben* are often very wide-ranging. Dibelius' proposed *Sitz im Leben* of 'preaching' for the paradigms, for example, seems to cover an enormous range of activity directed at a very wide cross section of society (e.g. preaching to Christians/non-Christians, preaching which is trying to convert, to defend, to encourage and so on). Once again Bultmann's attempt to give further precision here is welcome.

There is however a more important difference between the approaches of Dibelius and Bultmann, beyond the fact that the latter subdivides the broader categories. This concerns the method by which the two scholars try to determine the *Sitz im Leben* from the form of the tradition. Bultmann's approach in particular raises some important methodological issues and these deserve some discussion here.

Dibelius starts with preconceived ideas about what the activities of the members of the early Church were (e.g. preaching, worship), and he tries to correlate the forms of the tradition with these activities. Bultmann on the other hand starts with the texts themselves and deduces from them the activities and situations in the early Church which gave rise to the preservation (or even creation) of the texts. For example, the controversy stories about disputes between Jesus and the Jewish authorities are said to reflect very precisely the disputes in which the early Christian groups who preserved these stories were engaged with their contemporaries. Thus the stories in the Gospels where Jesus is in conflict with the Jewish authorities about the sabbath reflect conflicts in the early Church between Christians and their Jewish neighbours about the sabbath.

Now the precision with which Bultmann can make such a proposal is dependent on his whole approach, since there is often no evidence for the alleged situation in the Church apart from the Gospel texts themselves. The argument is of course circular (as Bultmann himself recognizes): the text implies the proposed situation, and the situation provides the background against which to interpret the text.

We have already seen a number of examples of inevitable circularity in arguments. However, in the case of some of Bultmann's alleged settings for the preservation of the controversy stories, we can perhaps raise a few critical questions about the circularity involved here.

Take again, for example, the controversies in the Gospels about the sabbath. We know of some of the controversies which arose in the early Church, both within the Christian community and in relationships between Christians and non-Christians. Circumcision was a big issue; so were the food laws. Sabbath observance, as far as we know, was not.[3] Are we then justified in saying that the sabbath controversies in the Gospels necessarily reflect precisely similar controversies in the later Church? A strong case for such a theory can be made for the story about food laws (Mark 7.1–23); similarly a strong case could be made if we had stories of Jesus' arguing about the value of circumcision (but we don't). Thus it may be that the sabbath stories in the Gospels were preserved for other reasons.

The attempt to see behind every controversy story of the Gospels an identical controversy in the early Church is therefore questionable. Nevertheless, one must say that Bultmann's attempt to give greater precision to the forms of the tradition and to their associated *Sitz im Leben*, is in general terms thoroughly justified.

Another criticism that is often made about the categorization of the material given by the form critics is that it really goes beyond its own terms of reference: it is a division based quite as much on content as on form. In some respects this may be true. Some of the categories are in any case extremely vague. The collection of 'legends', or 'stories about Jesus', is a rather amorphous mass of stories with no common characteristic beyond the fact that they are neither paradigms nor miracle stories/tales.[4] Other suggested divisions are indeed based as much on the content of the tradition as on its form. Thus B. S. Easton asked: 'What *formal* difference is there between the 'logion' – Whosoever exalteth himself shall be humbled – the 'apocalyptic word' – Whosoever shall be ashamed of me, the Son of Man shall be ashamed of him – and the 'church rule' – Whosoever putteth away his wife and marrieth another committeth adultery?'[5] At one level this is true: all three sayings have the same formal structure. Nevertheless, literary critics rightly warn us that we cannot make an absolute distinction between form and content.[6] In the case of the examples we started with, viz. the business letter and the advertising circular, both are in one sense 'letters'. (Both come through the letter box!) What distinguishes them, and what distinguishes their form, is the content of the letters. Thus whilst the form/content dichotomy may be apparently rather easier to make in some instances than in others, we can never make an absolute distinction.

A final comment about the categorization by form critics of the material can also be made. We can at least question what I have described as the fundamental axiom of form criticism, viz. the claim that there is a close correlation between form and *Sitz im Leben*. In the way in which this principle is put into practice, it is often assumed that there is a neat one-to-one correspondence between a form and a specific *Sitz im Leben*. Yet frequently this is not the case. One *Sitz im Leben* may give rise to a variety of forms of communication. For example, the context of cultic activity can lead to a wide variety of different 'formulae' (e.g. hymns, creeds, historical reminiscences). Conversely, the same form could be used in a variety of different situations. Cultic formulae used in worship can become the basis of paraenesis; similarly, the deutero-Pauline letters can appropriate the form of the genuine Pauline letters, whilst transposing it for use in a different situation.[7]

If form criticism had confined itself to analysing formal structures and correlating settings with forms, it would probably not have survived long, nor aroused much comment. In fact the discipline known as 'form criticism' in English has a much more ambitious aim as well. Form criticism is the rough English translation of the German word *Formgeschichte*. Now *Geschichte* does not mean 'criticism'; it is one of the German words for 'history'. The discipline of *Formgeschichte* is thus often conceived as not only looking at the forms of the tradition, but also at the history of the individual formal units and the whole development of the tradition, to see how the forms have been handed on as they have been used, and how they may have undergone adaptation in the course of their transmission.

Form criticism thus includes what is sometimes called 'tradition criticism'. Further, this extended idea of form criticism attempts to push the line of inquiry back as far as possible by investigating the origins of the individual traditions. Thus a *formgeschichtlich* analysis of an individual story seeks to analyse not only the present form of the story but also any developments in the tradition which may be discernible; and it will also try to say something about the origin of the story.

It is this last aspect of the work of form criticism that has given rise to the suspicion with which the discipline has been regarded by many people. For one of the leading form critics, Bultmann, was somewhat sceptical about the historicity of much of the tradition. However, it should be noted that such a historical scepticism is in no way necessarily implicit in form criticism as such. V. Taylor, for example, was a scholar who accepted many of the insights of form criticism and adopted many of the standard form-critical classifications of the tradition; yet Taylor himself was extremely 'conservative' when it came to assessing the historical reliability of the tradition.

In fact one should probably separate the various aspects of form criticism. For example, the question of where and how a particular tradition was preserved and used in the early Church is really logically independent of the question of its origin. Thus the classification of a story as a paradigm, or a miracle story, or even as a legend, does not necessarily in itself say anything about its origin. A miracle story may have been used by Dibelius' group of storytellers (if they ever existed): but that does not decide the issue of whether those storytellers made the story up *de novo*, or whether they were recounting an event which occurred in Jesus' lifetime. In order to make such a judgement we will have to analyse the development of the tradition, its form *and* content, in order to try to determine the origin of that tradition.

It is accepted by almost all scholars today that not every single part of every single story in every single Gospel can be traced back to an event in the life and teaching of Jesus. At times the early Christians adapted the traditions about the ministry of Jesus, and even occasionally 'invented' some details. We can see this quite clearly when we compare a story in Matthew's Gospel with its parallel in Mark's account. Assuming that Matthew used Mark as a source, then the points at which Matthew differs from Mark provide evidence of Matthew's editorial activity; they tell us nothing about Jesus himself.

Take, for example, the texts of Mark 9.1 and Matthew 16.28. Mark has Jesus say: 'there are some standing here who will not taste death before they see that the kingdom of God has come with power'; Matthew has: 'there are some standing here who will not taste death before they see the Son of man coming in his Kingdom.' Matthew's version is a secondary adaptation of Mark's, and hence it cannot be used to provide any evidence, for example, for Jesus' use of the term 'Son of Man'. In this case, a Son of Man saying has been 'invented' by a later Christian writer, Matthew.

In the case of the development of the tradition from the earliest Gospel to the later Gospels, this creative activity can clearly be seen and documented. But if such activity is clearly evidenced after the writing of the earliest Gospel, there is no reason to believe that such activity did not take place in the period before Mark as well. (Indeed *a priori* one would expect it to be more likely in that period. Whatever the result of writing the tradition down, one would expect it to make things less flexible than they were before.) Most would agree that such is the case.

A standard example (often cited in this context) is the small unit about fasting in Mark 2.18–20. Jesus is asked why his disciples do not fast. Jesus replies in v. 19: 'Can the wedding guests fast while the bridegroom is with them? As long as they have the bridegroom with them, they cannot fast.' This seems a straightforward, albeit indirect and metaphorical, reply to the question. Jesus is comparing the time of his ministry to a wedding: it is a time of joy and celebration and hence fasting is inappropriate.

But then in v. 20 a new note is introduced: 'The days will come, when the bridegroom is taken away from them, and then they will fast in that day.' The figure of the bridegroom himself seems suddenly to assume independent importance: the bridegroom will be 'taken away' and this will be the sign for the reintroduction of fasting. In terms of the context of the saying in Mark, it is clear that the 'bridegroom' is Jesus.

But the temporal distinction implied here seems quite foreign to the thrust of Jesus' reply in v. 19 which is primarily concerned with the joyful conditions of the present. Moreover, on form-critical grounds (in the strict sense of the word) v. 20 seems redundant. Vv. 18–19 form a good example of a paradigm/pronouncement story, leading up to the 'punch line' of Jesus in v. 19. Thus on grounds of both form and content we could argue that v. 20 is a secondary addition by the early Church to the more original story in vv. 18–19, and is not a genuine saying of Jesus.[8]

The precise extent of such creative activity by the early Church is much debated. The issue frequently arouses strong emotions, with some claiming that theories about the early Church 'creating' sayings of Jesus are tantamount to accusing the early Christians of forgery or dishonesty. In some respects the issue is similar to that of pseudonymous literature which we have looked at already.

In the case of the Gospels, any suggestion that the creation of sayings of Jesus is dishonest or disreputable is probably inappropriate. The Gospels were all written by Christians who believed that the man Jesus of Nazareth had been raised by God to God's right hand in glory and was now the living Lord of the Church. Jesus was thus believed to speak to the Church in the present, quite as much as from the past.

The distinction which we might wish to make between a pre-Easter 'earthly' Jesus and a post-Easter 'risen' Jesus might not have been very important for first-century Christians. For them, the really important fact was that Jesus was alive in the present and still spoke to the Church. The words of Jesus remembered in the tradition were presumably mostly (though not entirely) preserved because they were thought to be still relevant. As the risen Jesus also spoke to the present, words of the risen Jesus and words of the pre-Easter Jesus could be combined simply because it was the same Jesus who was believed to be speaking.

We have already seen that in some instances, the form of the saying of Jesus recorded is due to a Christian writer as much as to Jesus: Matthew 16.28 is due in part to Matthew's adaptation of his tradition. Further, at times Christian creative activity probably went beyond the stage of modifying an existing tradition and actually created a saying of Jesus. Mark 2.20 is probably a case in point, as we have seen. Most would also argue that the saying in Matthew 18.20 ('where two or three are gathered in my name, there am I in the midst of them') is not a saying of the pre-Easter Jesus, but represents a saying of the risen Jesus, perhaps given through the voice of a prophet speaking in Jesus' name.

That such creative activity occurred is undeniable. Its nature and extent are much more debated. How far, for instance, did the early Christians simply modify existing traditions about Jesus, and how far did they actually create whole stories and/or sayings of

Jesus *de novo*? In the case of the miracle stories, Bultmann regarded these as basically unhistorical on the grounds of their formal similarity to other Hellenistic miracle stories. This is probably an unjustifiable method of argument. The actual form in which the saying is now put does not necessarily imply that it originated in this form. Nevertheless, the general problem of the precise extent of the creative activity of the early Christians in the gospel tradition is a very complex one.

The fact that the study of form criticism in the Gospels is concerned with the origin of the traditions quite as much as with their present form means that the task of identifying how much of the tradition is 'genuine' to the pre-Easter Jesus is an integral part of form criticism. This so-called 'Quest for the historical Jesus' has led to discussion about the criteria which we can use to distinguish between material in the Gospels which can be traced back to the pre-Easter Jesus and material which is more probably due to the early Church. It is to this that we shall now turn.[9]

The most famous criterion is the so-called 'criterion of dissimilarity'. This says that if there is a tradition which shows Jesus as dissimilar to his Jewish environment and also dissimilar to the early Church, then we may be confident that this represents genuine material about the historical Jesus. The fact that the tradition is dissimilar to the early Church shows that it is unlikely to have been invented by early Christians; and the dissimilarity with Judaism shows that the tradition has not simply been copied from the background material.

As an example of the application of this criterion, one could refer again to Mark 2.18–20. Here Jesus is shown as advocating an end to the practice of fasting. This is dissimilar both to Judaism and to the early Church. (As far as we know, the early Christians did fast, as indeed Mark 2.20 suggests.) Hence it is likely that we are in touch here with the historical Jesus.

This criterion has engendered a lot of discussion. It has been pointed out by some that strong advocates of the criterion have not always been very consistent in its application.[10] Methodologically, however, this is immaterial. More to the point are the presuppositions and inevitable consequences which are involved here. The criterion is in theory admirable. The question is whether it can ever establish anything with any certainty.

One difficulty concerns the blanket terms 'Judaism' and 'the early Church'. It has been pointed out by many that we do not know enough about either of these categories to be able to say with any confidence what would be similar, and hence what would be dissimilar, to either Judaism or the early Church. We certainly know that both were extremely varied entities in the first century.

There is also a great deal which we do not know about within both Judaism and first-century Christianity. For example, we know that Christianity spread to Alexandria very early; how and when we do not know, and equally we know virtually nothing of the nature of early Alexandrian Christianity. Who is to say then that a tradition which at first sight appears to be dissimilar in outlook to the rest of the early Church is not in fact wholly continuous with the ideas of the primitive Alexandrian Christian community?

A second difficulty arises from the problem of determining what is to count as 'dissimilar'. At one level, it could be argued that the very fact that a tradition has been preserved by at least one part of the early Church shows that that part of the Christian community thought it worth preserving, presumably because of the similarity with its own beliefs. A strict application of the criterion would thus imply that nothing which has been preserved could be authentic: the very fact of its preservation means that it will fail to pass the test set by this criterion.[11]

A third difficulty arises from some presuppositions which lie behind the criterion. The criterion inevitably excludes material which shows Jesus in a line of continuity with either Judaism or the early Church. The result will inevitably be a Jesus who is cut off from his Jewish roots, and who is followed by a community which shows no continuity with him at all. The inevitable consequence of the application of this criterion is thus that there is an almost unbridgeable chasm created by the Easter event. Even if some of the problems created by the second difficulty mentioned above are avoided, so that at least some material gets through the net, the result is bound to be a Jesus who is quite unique.

Lurking here are some deep-seated presuppositions. It is often argued that advocates of the dissimilarity criterion are really threatening the basis of Christian faith by being so sceptical about the authenticity of so much of the Jesus tradition. In fact, paradoxically, it is probably precisely the opposite which is the case. For the strict application of the dissimilarity criterion will inevitably produce a unique Jesus, a Jesus who stands out against all his contemporaries, Jewish and Christian. The Jesus of this criterion is thus radically new in relation to Judaism; and he stands over and above his Church and cannot be absorbed into it. The criterion is thus almost bound to produce a suitable figure to act as a centre of religious faith. Far from threatening the basis of Christian faith, the dissimilarity criterion almost has the Christian faith built into it and is geared to supporting it.[12]

It is clear that the criterion of dissimilarity is on its own not entirely satisfactory. Others have thus advocated different criteria. One difficulty raised by the dissimilarity criterion is that it lets so little through the net; further, what is allowed as authentic by it may indeed be genuine material about Jesus but may not be wholly characteristic of him. By isolating a few authentic elements in the tradition, we may get a very distorted picture of Jesus.

One way of extending the material which is accepted as authentic is to apply the so-called 'criterion of coherence'. This argues that the body of authentic material can be extended if it can be shown that such material 'coheres with', or is consistent with, material already established as authentic.

Again, this criterion looks good in theory but also poses problems. There is, for example, the question of what constitutes 'consistency', or for that matter inconsistency. What appears inconsistency to some may not be so for others. Coherence and inconsistency are notoriously difficult to quantify. There is also the fact that what is coherent is not *ipso facto* authentic. A good novel is at one level 'coherent' and self-consistent, but totally fictitious. Further, if the early Church did in fact create traditions about Jesus, it would presumably have created material which, at one level at least, 'cohered' with the authentic material from the pre-Easter Jesus which it already had.

Another difficulty arises from the fact that when this criterion is used to supplement the material established as authentic by the dissimilarity criterion, the danger is enhanced that an original picture of Jesus, based on authentic but uncharacteristic material, will simply be magnified: the dangers of producing an uncharacteristic picture of Jesus are unaltered and we will simply have a bigger picture which is equally uncharacteristic.

A third criterion which is often proposed is that of 'multiple attestation'. This is based on the common-sense idea that a tradition which is supported by two independent witnesses is more trustworthy than one which is supported by only one. However, we must also take note of the results of synoptic source criticism and remember that the evangelists themselves are not independent of each other. If all three synoptic Gospels record the same saying of Jesus, this may not be because all three are independent witnesses: their mutual agreement may simply be due to the fact that one Gospel has provided the source for the other two. However, the case is rather different if we consider different synoptic sources. Thus, if a tradition appears independently in more than one strand of the synoptic tradition (Mark, Q, material peculiar to Matthew/Luke), then this is an indicator that it may go back to Jesus. One example is the parable of the mustard seed which appears in Mark (4.30–32) and also in Q (Luke 13.18–19; Matt. 13.31–32 conflates both versions).

In favour of this criterion is the fact that it is more free from subjectivity than those we have looked at already, although it is dependent on a particular solution to the synoptic problem. In practice, however, this criterion provides very little concrete help. It is true that general themes in the ministry and teaching of Jesus are multiply attested, e.g. Jesus' teaching about the Kingdom of God, or his friendship with tax-collectors and sinners. However, it is rare that a specific tradition is multiply attested. Thus Jesus' general openness to tax-collectors may be well documented across the different strands of the tradition; but this does not of itself guarantee the reliability of each story where Jesus meets a tax-collector, since each occurs in only one strand of the tradition. So too, very little of the teaching of Jesus is duplicated across the tradition. The parable of the mustard seed is the only parable to appear in more than one strand, and no one is going to suggest that this is the only authentic parable of Jesus! Further, the fact that a tradition is multiply attested shows that it is deeply embedded in the tradition; but this does not necessarily show that it is authentic. It could simply have been created very early in the development of the tradition.

A fourth criterion appeals to the Semitic character of a tradition. Our Gospels are written in Greek, but Jesus (probably) spoke Aramaic in a Semitic milieu. If, therefore, a tradition shows evidence of having come from a Semitic background, this may be an indication of its authenticity. For example, some of the Gospel sayings are couched in a form of Hebrew parallelism, saying the same thing twice either synonymously or antithetically (cf. Luke 12.8–9 for an example of the latter). Other Gospel sayings use the so-called 'divine passive': it is a typical feature of Semitic speech to use a passive verb to avoid mentioning the divine name when it is clear that God is the subject of the action of the verb (e.g. the beatitudes: 'Blessed are those who mourn, for they shall be comforted', Matt. 5.4, means 'God will comfort them'). These are examples where the Semitic nature of the text shines through.

Again, as with all the criteria considered so far, this one is not without its difficulties. Above all, there is the fact, obvious as soon as it is stated, that Jesus was not the only Aramaic speaker in the first century. Hence an Aramaic or Semitic idiom in a saying shows only that it originates in a Semitic milieu. This might mean that the tradition goes back to Jesus; but it might equally mean that it was created by the Aramaic-speaking Christian community. We know that Jewish Christianity continued to exist in Palestine at least as late as the second Jewish revolt of AD 135. Thus an Aramaic tradition is by no means *ipso facto* likely to be authentic, or even very early.

Further difficulties are raised if we extend the scope of the discussion to consider not only Aramaic idioms in speech, but also Palestinian customs and presuppositions. J. Jeremias is one scholar who has appealed to this sort of criterion very frequently, especially in his work on the parables: those features which fit the geographical, cultural and environmental features of Palestine are authentic.

There is no doubt that such a criterion can be extremely valuable in assessing the relative value of different versions of the same parable. For example, in the two versions of the small parable of the lamp lit in the house (Matt. 5.15; Luke 11.33), Matthew's version presupposes a small one-roomed house, typical of Palestine; Luke's version presupposes a larger house with a separate entrance passage. Matthew's version is the more Palestinian and thus more likely to be original.[13]

However, such a use of this criterion in interpreting the parables may at times be particularly misleading. Such a criterion has a built-in presupposition that Jesus' parables are all 'true to life' in the sense that they reflect the normal conditions of nature and human existence in Palestine. Indeed many accept this quite openly. Nevertheless, this cannot be assumed as axiomatic. It may well be that some of Jesus' parables use imagery which is quite unnatural and extraordinary, but that that is precisely their point.

Take, for example, the parable of the mustard seed. This exists in two versions, one in Mark (4.30–32) and one in Q (cf. Luke 13.18–19). In the Marcan version, the mustard seed is sown in the earth and becomes a shrub so that birds rest in its shade. In the Lucan version, the seed is sown in a garden and it becomes a tree so that the birds nest in its branches. Elementary Palestinian botany tells us that mustard seeds grow into shrubs, not trees; in fact they produce quick-growing shrubs which might provide shade for birds, but their branches are too weak and spindly to support actual nests. Further, it is pointed out in Jewish law that one should not sow mustard in gardens (to avoid your neighbour's garden being overshadowed).

Is then the Marcan version, which is truer to nature, more original? Not necessarily; the Q version gives a much more striking interpretation. Here the parable refers to the glorious future

Kingdom of God which was already present in germ in Jesus' ministry; but the continuity between the beginning and end of the process is not a matter of empirical observation and natural order. Rather, it is a divine miracle, that out of this, 'the smallest of all the seeds on earth' (Mark 4.31), i.e. from this insignificant start in one man's ministry in Galilee, God will produce his mighty Kingdom. Further, the seed is sown in the most unlikely of places, illegally in a garden: the start of the process lies outside the norms of respectable society. On this interpretation, the parable is making some striking claims; but the details are only striking by virtue of the fact that the botanical process described is contrary to nature and custom. Here the assumption that all Jesus' teaching fits its Palestinian environment may miss the point.

This survey of the criteria for assessing the authenticity of the sayings of Jesus shows that none of them is either perfect or foolproof. Nor indeed can they be. No one can prove that Jesus never said this or that he did say that. Provided that the criteria remain rough rules of thumb, then no harm will be done. It is only if they are taken too rigidly, or in isolation from one another, that disaster will probably ensue.

The work of the form critics has never attracted universal agreement in all its aspects. In part this may have been due to some of Bultmann's sceptical views about the historicity of parts of the tradition. We have seen that such scepticism is however not necessarily inherent in the method itself. Further, it has been pointed out that the term *Sitz im Leben* was used in a rather peculiar way by the classic form critics. In fact the term is a sociological one, describing a typical situation within any community.[14] It is not a description of a particular community. There is thus no necessary reason for driving a wedge between the pre-Easter community and the post-Easter community, as some form critics have tended to do, simply on the basis of a proposed *Sitz im Leben*.

A typical situation could be dated as either pre- or post-Easter and the situation itself does not necessarily determine the relative date. Thus one cannot talk of a '*Sitz im Leben Jesu*', contrasting it with a '*Sitz im Leben* of the early Church', without doing considerable violence to the term *Sitz im Leben* itself. H. Schürmann has argued this most strongly, and has appealed to sociological and confessional continuities between the pre-Easter community and the post-Easter community: at both stages the disciples were united by their commitment to Jesus' words and teaching.[15] Thus Schürmann postulates, as a *Sitz im Leben* for the preservation of Jesus' teaching, the disciples' remembering and handing on that tradition to others; further, this may have had its origin not only in the post-Easter community but also in the pre-Easter mission of the disciples. Schürmann is quite clearly using the insights and methods of form criticism, but his work shows that the discipline itself does not necessarily lead to historical agnosticism or scepticism about the historical Jesus, in fact just the opposite.

Other aspects of the work of the form critics have also been questioned over the years. Early form criticism tended to assume a model whereby the initial traditions about Jesus were handed down individually in oral form; these traditions then floated around freely in a way which we can deduce from the study of other oral traditions; finally the traditions were put into written form by the evangelists.

Many aspects of this model are now questionable. It is not clear precisely when the tradition first took written form, and indeed some have argued that, since in Judaism people sometimes took written notes from a teacher, the same might be true of the early Christians. Hence written traditions might go back very early, even to the time of Jesus.[16] Certainly it is not impossible that some collections of the individual traditions were made prior to the writing of the finished Gospels. Many have suspected that all, or part, of Mark 2.1–3.6 constituted a pre-Marcan collection of controversy stories prior to its inclusion by Mark in his finished Gospel. Indeed the whole question of the nature of collections of Jesus traditions is one which deserves more detailed consideration.

The question of how the traditions about Jesus were preserved in early Christianity is a complex one. Early form criticism tended to presuppose that the conditions were similar to those which preserved folk tales and similar traditions. Yet very often the time-scales involved were very different from those presupposed in early Christianity. New Testament form criticism grew out of Old Testament form criticism; but in the Old Testament we are dealing with traditions preserved over centuries, while in the New Testament we are dealing with a time-scale of at most one generation.

One particular theory which has aroused a lot of discussion has suggested a quite different model for the preservation of the Jesus tradition. This theory is associated with two Scandinavian scholars, Riesenfeld and Gerhardsson.[17] These scholars have suggested that we should take more seriously the Jewish milieu of the Jesus movement. Jesus was a Jew; so were his first disciples. Now rabbinic Judaism had various procedures for memorizing and passing on tradition. Thus these scholars have suggested that the early Christians may have handled their tradition in the same way, memorizing it and carefully preserving it, with the Twelve at Jerusalem acting as the guardians and guarantors of the tradition. Such a model might lead to a much more 'conservative' view of the activity of the early Church.[18]

This theory does however encounter some difficulties. Jesus was not a rabbi. His teaching, and the traditions about him, are quite unlike the traditions which are preserved in the rabbinic writings where the bulk of the material is dealing with legal rulings interpreting the law. Gerhardsson's appeal to later rabbinic traditions has been criticized as being anachronistic: one cannot easily read back the situation of later rabbinic Judaism into the pre-AD 70 era.[19] Further, the role of the Twelve in Jerusalem which Gerhardsson postulated is very difficult to substantiate.[20] Indeed the Gospels themselves show that the tradition was at times handled very freely. Matthew and Luke do not show the respect for the Jesus tradition in Mark which Gerhardsson's theory might lead us to expect. Nevertheless, although some of the details of the overall theory are questionable, Gerhardsson has underlined the importance of understanding more fully the Jewish milieu in which the early Church operated and which must therefore have influenced the way in which the Church preserved its tradition.

We have seen that the discipline of form criticism encompasses an enormous area. In the discussion in this chapter we have confined attention to the synoptic tradition, dealing with questions about the forms and tradition-history of the units which make up the synoptic Gospels. Form criticism can also be very fruitfully applied to material in the New Testament outside the Gospels. For example, the epistles contain several units which can be isolated and analysed from a form-critical point of view. We can sometimes isolate hymns (cf. Phil. 2.5–11), or elements which were probably used in Christian worship (cf. 1 Cor. 11.24–26). Several of the lists of codes of behaviour for various groups in the community, the so-called 'household codes' (e.g. Col. 3.18–4.1), show stereotyped forms. So too many have found evidence in various parts of the New Testament for a standard pattern of a catechetical teaching. All these can be examined very fruitfully from a form-critical point of view. There is not enough time or space to go into details here, but it should be noted that form criticism is not a discipline which is exclusive to synoptic studies.[21]

Form criticism has often had something of a bad press, perhaps because of the historical scepticism on the part of some leading form critics in the past. Yet form criticism has above all made us aware of the tremendous vitality of early Christianity. The first generations of Christians were very much alive and kicking. They worshipped, they taught, they believed in their risen Lord passionately. They had to struggle against opposition from non-Christians, they fought to spread their good news and to extend the boundaries of their communities. It is form criticism which has enabled us to see more of this very rich life of the earliest Christian churches. Form criticism has also made us aware of some of the ways in which early Christians used their historical traditions creatively to get their message across. It has therefore alerted us to the complex situation we face if we wish to get behind the text to try to recover something of the history being described. In all this, form criticism has brought nothing but gain to the study of the New Testament.

Mark 3.1–6 and Parallels

When we approach this story from the point of view of form criticism, our main concern is to look at the story as it circulated prior to its inclusion in our synoptic Gospels. We shall therefore not be so interested in the form the story took after it reached written form. Thus for these purposes the form of the story in Matthew and Luke will be ignored.

A full form-critical study of the whole tradition would be very interested in the tradition which underlies the saying about the sheep in the pit in Matthew 12.11–12. I shall leave that on one side here, simply in order to save space. (We shall in any case be looking at this briefly in the next chapter.) However, the modifications which Matthew and Luke introduce in their Marcan material are of less interest from a form-critical point of view. We shall therefore confine attention to the Marcan version of the story.

Most would agree that the Marcan version has undergone a certain amount of modification by Mark himself. The concluding verse, Mark 3.6, is probably due to Mark, providing a conclusion to the whole series of stories in Mark 2.1–3.6. Some of the details in the story may also be Mark's additions: for example, the phrase 'Again he entered the synagogue' in v.1a, and the note about Jesus looking round in v. 5.[22] These elements can therefore be discarded for the present purposes. The pre-Marcan tradition thus consists of a simple story where Jesus meets a man with a withered hand, the Pharisees watch closely, Jesus puts the rhetorical question in v. 4, and then heals the man.

Form critics are almost unanimous in classifying this story. Despite the fact that a miracle occurs in the story, and indeed is integral to it, the story is not a 'miracle story' in the form-critical sense. There is, for example, no acclamation from the crowds at the end, expressing astonishment and wonder at what has happened. The centre of attention is not the miracle as such. Nor is it Jesus' ability to heal the man. That is assumed as self-evident right from the start. Rather, the issue is whether it is right to perform such an action on the sabbath. A minimum of detail is given about the setting; the story leads up to a 'punch line' in v. 4 and ends with the healing itself. Thus all the major form critics agree in classifying this story as a paradigm or pronouncement story (or equivalent).[23]

Can we say anything about its *Sitz im Leben*? This is rather more difficult. A consistent form-critical approach, such as that of Bultmann, would see here a reflection of the Church's own situation, with Christians defending their own behaviour against opposition from non-Christian Jews.[24] However, precisely what kind of behaviour would be defended by this story is not clear. (Bultmann himself is rather vague at this point.) Is the community claiming total freedom from the sabbath law? Or is it trying to define its position more carefully whilst recognizing the basic validity of the sabbath law? The latter is the view of one modern form critic who claims that the story 'would have been composed in a community which continued to observe the sabbath, but which raised the question of the extent to which Pharisaic law was applicable'.[25] This is possible, though the implied criterion asserted in the story, that it is justifiable to 'do good' on the sabbath, seems so general that the sabbath laws are very radically questioned.

We have, however, already seen that such a form-critical approach, assuming that the story reflects directly the interests of the community, is at least questionable in the case of these sabbath stories. We do not have any evidence outside the Gospels that concern about the proper observance of the sabbath was ever a great issue in the early Church. It is thus possible that this story was preserved for reasons other than justifying the community's doing in real life what Jesus is portrayed as doing in the story.[26] For example, the story may have been preserved and valued as implying something about Jesus himself. It showed Jesus' unique authority in standing out against the Jewish leaders of his day and claiming to be able to dispense with the sabbath law. The main interest may thus have been as much christological as in any suggestion that the story gave direct justification for the behaviour of Christians themselves.

How much of the tradition in the story can be traced back to Jesus? Many would argue that the very difficulties created by a

Bultmannian approach serve to increase the likelihood that we have authentic material here. The very fact that disputes about the sabbath were not (as far as we know) a very live issue in the early Church suggests that this story is less likely to have been created by the early Church. Jesus here is in some ways 'dissimilar' to the early Church. Further, Jesus' attitude here in claiming almost sovereign freedom over one of the ten commandments sets him apart in a very radical way from his Jewish contemporaries. The Jesus of this story is thus seen to be 'dissimilar' to both Judaism and the early Church. Many would therefore claim that we are probably in touch with the pre-Easter Jesus at this point. Even Bultmann himself agreed that at Mark 3.4 we are hearing the authentic voice of Jesus himself.[27] This would therefore seem to be an instance where the criterion of dissimilarity can be applied positively to recover authentic Jesus material.

In summary we can say that, from a form-critical point of view, the story is a 'paradigm' (or some equivalent term) and not a 'miracle story' (in the form-critical sense); and if we ask about the whole tradition-history of the story, we have seen that a strong case can be made for the events narrated here having their origins in the ministry of the pre-Easter Jesus.

Notes

1. The classic works are M. Dibelius, *From Tradition to Gospel* (ET, London & New York 1934); R. Bultmann, *The History of the Synoptic Tradition* (ET, Oxford 1968). See also V. Taylor, *The Formation of the Gospel Tradition* (London 1933).
2. Dibelius, *Tradition to Gospel*, p. 104.
3. Gal. 4.10 (and perhaps Col. 2.16) may imply otherwise; but it is clear that in both cases, the real issue in the debates concerned was not primarily sabbath observance: in Galatians it is circumcision, in Colossians Christology, which forms the central issue.
4. cf. S. H. Travis, 'Form Criticism', in I. H. Marshall (ed.), *New Testament Interpretation* (Exeter 1977), p. 158.
5. B. S. Easton, *The Gospel before the Gospels* (New York 1928), p. 74, cited by Travis, 'Form Criticism', p. 157.
6. See R. Wellek & A. Warren, *Theory of Literature* (Harmondsworth [3]1963), esp. p. 140.
7. cf. W. G. Doty, 'The Discipline and Literature of New Testament Form Criticism', *ATR* 51 (1969), pp. 257–319, on p. 307; also G. N. Stanton, 'Form Criticism Revisited', in M. D. Hooker & C. J. A. Hickling (eds.) *What about the New Testament?* (London 1975), pp. 13–27, on p. 23.
8. See for example H. Anderson, *The Gospel of Mark* (London 1976), pp. 107–8 and many other commentators.

9. For a very useful discussion of the various criteria for authenticity, see W. O. Walker, 'The Quest for the Historical Jesus. A Discussion of Methodology', *ATR* 51 (1969), pp. 38–56; also R. H. Stein, 'The "Criteria" for Authenticity', in R. T. France & D. Wenham (eds.), *Gospel Perspectives I* (Sheffield 1980), pp. 225–63.
10. For this, and the following points, see the important article of M. D. Hooker, 'Christology and Methodology', *NTS* 17 (1971), pp. 480–7.
11. cf. D. R. Catchpole, 'Tradition History', in Marshall, *N T Interpretation*, p. 176.
12. cf. R. S. Barbour, *Traditio–Historical Criticism of the Gospels* (London 1972).
13. See J. Jeremias, *The Parables of Jesus* (ET, London 1963), p. 66.
14. As indeed Bultmann himself recognized: see his *History*, p. 4.
15. H. Schürmann, 'Die vorösterlichen Anfänge der Logientradition', *Traditionsgeschichtliche Untersuchungen zu den synoptischen Evangelien* (Düsseldorf 1968), pp. 39–65.
16. cf. E. E. Ellis, 'New Directions in Form Criticism', in G. Strecker (ed.), *Jesus Christus in Historie und Theologie* (FS for H. Conzelmann. Tübingen 1975), pp. 299–315; reprinted in E. E. Ellis, *Prophecy and Hermeneutic* (Tübingen 1978), pp. 237–53.
17. H. Riesenfeld, *The Gospel Tradition and Its Beginnings* (London 1957); B. Gerhardsson, *Memory and Manuscript* (Uppsala 1961), *The Origins of the Gospel Traditions* (London 1979).
18. Gerhardsson's views are often taken this way, though it is doubtful how far this would apply to Gerhardsson himself: see P. H. Davids, 'The Gospels and Jewish Tradition: Twenty Years after Gerhardsson', in France & Wenham, *Gospel Perspectives I*, pp. 75–99.
19. See M. Smith, 'A Comparison of Early Christian and Early Rabbinic Tradition', *JBL* 82 (1963), pp. 169–76.
20. W. D. Davies, *The Setting of the Sermon on the Mount* (Cambridge 1966), pp. 464–80.
21. For a useful survey, with further bibliography, see Doty, *Letters*, ch. 3.
22. For more details, see A. J. Hultgren, *Jesus and His Adversaries. The Form and Function of the Conflict Stories in the Synoptic Tradition* (Minneapolis 1979), p. 82.
23. cf. Bultmann, *History*, p. 12; Dibelius, *Tradition to Gospel*, p. 43; Taylor, *Formation*, p. 65.
24. Bultmann, *History*, p. 48.
25. Hultgren, *Jesus and His Adversaries*, p. 84.
26. See the valuable summary, with similar conclusions to those offered here, in J. Kiilunen, *Die Vollmacht im Widerstreit. Untersuchungen zum Werdegang von Mk 2, 1—3, 6* (Helsinki 1985), pp. 244–8.
27. Bultmann, *History*, p. 147; also Kiilunen, *Die Vollmacht im Widerstreit*, p. 246; Lohse, 'Jesu Worte über den Sabbat'.

8

Redaction Criticism

The last chapter has shown us that the New Testament can be interpreted at different levels. A story in the Gospels, for example, can tell us something about the events being described; it can also tell us something about the storyteller. In the previous chapter we considered typical situations which led to traditions being preserved in stereotyped forms. Now we are all probably aware that stories can also be told in highly individualistic ways. Moreover, the way in which a story is told can be very revealing about the individual who is telling it.

Take, for example, the following hypothetical reports of an imaginary incident during the miners' strike in Britain:

A. Four miners who tried to brave a picket line today failed to reach the colliery gates. A howling mob of angry pickets 'persuaded' the men to turn back with a volley of bricks, stones and other missiles. Police reinforcements trying to escort the men through were involved in violent scuffles with striking miners. Two policemen had to be treated in hospital later.

B. Four men who tried to break the strike today failed to reach the colliery gates. An official picket persuaded the men to turn back. Heavy-handed police reinforcements tried to prevent the picket from presenting its case to the men and in the resulting confusion several members of the picket were injured. Three miners had to be treated in hospital later.

It may be that a nearby hospital casualty department treated five men after the incident, and a TV camera crew recorded some scenes of violence. Yet it is clear that the same story can be presented in radically different ways. Writer A is clearly on the side of the strike-breakers and the police; writer B is clearly on the side of the strikers. Each writer picks and chooses what he will say (e.g. whose injuries are reported), and the choice of words (who, for instance, are the real 'miners'?) and punctuation (cf. the use of inverted commas) tells us quite a lot about the political views of the two writers concerned. Quite irrespective of the original 'facts' of the situation, the two accounts can tell us a lot about their authors.

It is now clear that similar considerations apply to the New Testament texts, especially to the Gospels. Form critics tended to have a rather low view of the activity of the evangelists themselves. The Gospel writers were simply 'scissors-and-paste' editors, or collectors, who assembled the individual stories of the tradition into a single document, but whose work was not seen as particularly significant theologically.

This view of the evangelists changed dramatically after the Second World War. As a result of a number of different studies on each of the synoptic Gospels, the three evangelists themselves came to be seen as far more than just 'editors' putting their material together in a rather mechanical way. Rather, it was realized that the evangelists had been far more creative and theologically active in what they had done. By putting the material together in the way they had, the evangelists had at times modified their traditions, and their adaptations were sometimes very revealing of an underlying theology in the work of the individual Gospel writers. This work of adapting the traditions that were available to an evangelist has come to be known as 'redaction' and the whole method of analysing the way in which the evangelists have creatively used their traditions is known as 'redaction criticism' (which, as in the case of 'form criticism', is a piece of translationese for the German word *Redaktionsgeschichte*).

The terminology is not altogether appropriate and it can at times be confusing. Strictly speaking, the German word *Redaktionsgeschichte* implies a history of redaction (cf. p. 101); it is thus not particularly appropriate for describing the study of one particular redaction, rather than a series of editings. Perhaps this is an instance where the standard English equivalent, redaction *criticism*, is an improvement on the German word!

The work of modern redaction criticism is frequently regarded as having started with the work of Marxsen on Mark, Bornkamm on Matthew and Conzelmann on Luke,[1] and has often been hailed as something decisively new in New Testament study.[2] In fact an awareness that each evangelist had his own individuality, and had to a certain extent imposed his own ideas on the tradition, is by no means new. During the last century F. C. Baur argued that all the Gospels were governed by an individual *Tendenz*, and in many respects the so-called *Tendenzkritik* of Baur and other members of the Tübingen school in the nineteenth century is very similar to modern redaction criticism. In the twentieth century, the work of R. H. Lightfoot on Mark's Gospel showed how Mark's theological concerns had creatively shaped the tradition, and Lightfoot effectively anticipated the era of redaction criticism by a generation.[3]

Nevertheless, however 'new' one decides that redaction criticism really is, it is the case that this method has, in various forms, dominated Gospel studies for over a generation. This is not to say that redaction criticism has not changed or developed. It has; and the purpose of this chapter is to provide a glance at some of these changes. However, it is also the case that despite the dominating position that redaction criticism has occupied within Gospel studies, there has been correspondingly little critical evaluation of the method itself.[4]

In the early days of the discipline, the redactional work of each evangelist was seen primarily as something active. In the initial redaction-critical studies, the 'redaction' was taken as the way in which a writer has actively altered his tradition. In the synoptic Gospels, this activity can often be seen quite readily with the aid of a synopsis. Thus if we assume that Mark is the source of Matthew and Luke, we can see the way in which Matthew and/or Luke have 'redacted' their Marcan source by the way in which they have altered that source. For example, Peter's confession at Caesarea Philippi takes the form in Mark 8.29 'You are the Christ'; in Matthew, this becomes 'You are the Christ, the Son of the living God' (Matt. 16.16). The extra words ('the Son of the living God') are thus due to Matthew's redaction and tell us something about Matthew's Christology.

Early redaction critics realized that the contribution of the evangelists could not necessarily be confined to the small differences in detailed wording within the individual pericopes. The evangelists imposed their own ideas quite as much by their arrangement of their material as by making small changes to their sources. For example, Luke gives a quite different perspective to the ministry of Jesus by bringing forward the account of the rejection of Jesus in Nazareth to make this story act as the programmatic summary of the whole narrative to come. The summary of Jesus' preaching is no longer 'the Kingdom of God is at hand' (Mark 1.15), but 'Today this scripture has been fulfilled' (Luke 4.21). Similarly, Matthew rearranges the teaching material of Jesus into five big 'blocks' of teaching. Whatever the precise significance of the arrangement (and it is debated), it seems to show at the very least Matthew's concern to present Jesus' teaching as something which is of vital importance for Matthew's own community (cf. also Matt. 28.19).

The term 'composition criticism' was at one stage proposed as an alternative to 'redaction criticism'.[5] In fact the change has not generally been made. The term 'redaction criticism' has stuck, though it is now usually used to cover the whole activity of the evangelists, not only in editing the detailed wording of their sources but also in arranging wider blocks of material to form their finished Gospels.

What are the criteria and methods used in redaction-critical studies of the Gospels? In one way they are self-evident. Redaction criticism seeks to identify the particular emphases of the evangelists by examining the ways in which they have altered their traditions and sources. Thus the method employed is to compare the evangelist's work with his source(s). In the case of Matthew and Luke, this is relatively straightforward since we can make a direct comparison (via a synopsis) between the work of each evangelist and his Marcan source. In the case of the Q material in Matthew and Luke, the same may also be possible though the task is more complicated since we do not have Q directly available to provide the reference point against which Matthew's and Luke's changes to their sources can be clearly identified.

It is however worth pointing out that a great deal of this work of redaction criticism is directly dependent on a particular solution to the Synoptic problem. If the sources of Matthew and Luke were different from those suggested by the 2DH, then the pattern of Matthew's/Luke's redactional activity would also be correspondingly different. Since a large number of theories about the nature of Matthew's/Luke's theology have been worked out on the basis of the 2DH, it can be seen that theories about the Synoptic problem may have a large number of 'knock-on' effects. One corollary of the reopening of the Synoptic problem in recent debates has thus been potentially to call into question the value of a large number of redaction-critical studies of the Gospels.

By the nature of the case, redaction-critical study of the earliest Gospel, Mark, is more problematical, since we do not have Mark's sources available to us to enable us to pinpoint Mark's redactional activity. Redaction criticism has also been extended to try to analyse the sayings source Q. Problems are even greater here since, not only do we not have Q's sources directly available to us, we do not even have Q itself immediately before us.

In the case of Mark (and also with Q where this is possible), critics have tried to identify the redactor's hand at work in the passages which link the various traditions together, in the conclusions which round sections off, in the generalizing summaries which come in the story (e.g. Mark 3.11–12), in the order and arrangement of the material, and so on.[6]

For example, Mark frequently refers to Jesus' activity of 'teaching' in many of the link passages in his Gospel, and this may well be a feature which Mark wishes to stress (though the fact that Mark gives relatively little of the actual content of Jesus' teaching suggests that Mark's interests do not lie in Jesus' teaching as such: possibly the fact that Jesus is a 'teacher' is a way of showing that Jesus has authority and that this brings him into conflict with the other authority figures of Judaism (cf. Mark 1.22, 27)).

Mark also has a well-known habit of fitting two stories together so that one is placed in the middle of another. For example, the story of the 'cleansing' of the temple is sandwiched between the two halves of the story of the cursing of the fig-tree (Mark 11.12–21). It looks very much as if Mark wants to let the two stories interpret each other: thus the incident in the temple is interpreted by the episode of the fig-tree (and vice versa). Hence, for Mark, Jesus' action in the temple is probably to be seen as the final cursing of the temple rather than its cleansing.[7] In ways such as these, Mark's own redactional activity can, with a reasonable amount of confidence, be identified.

It is clear that redaction criticism has brought tremendous gain to the study of the Gospels. It was probably the case that the early form critics overreacted in stressing the value of the pre-redactional, oral stage of the tradition at the expense of the redactional work of the evangelists themselves. However, it is at least arguable that the pendulum is in danger of swinging too far the other way. Certainly the tendency has been, amongst some scholars, to attribute all the compositional activity of combining the individual stories of the tradition into a connected narrative to the evangelists themselves. But if there were prior collections of traditions already before the work of the Gospel writers, then the creativity of the evangelists will have been correspondingly less. This has always been recognized in the case of the Q material in Matthew and Luke, where the arrangement in Matthew/Luke may be a reflection of Q's composition as much as of Matthew's/Luke's. But it is possible that this is only one example of a more wide-ranging phenomenon.[8]

A more serious problem is raised when we consider the question of the status of the results achieved by redaction criticism. As we have seen, early redaction critics looked at the alterations made by an author to his sources. If all such activity is considered and, hopefully, systematized, the result will be – what? Strictly, the result will be a total picture of the way in which an author altered his sources, *and nothing more.* However, very frequently redaction critics have assumed that there is considerably more: they have assumed that their results give a global picture of the theology of the individual author. There has been an implicit equation made between the theology of an evangelist and the ideas implied in the ways he has altered his sources.

For example, the English translation of H. Conzelmann's epoch-making redaction-critical study of the Lucan writings, which was initially published in German under the title *Die Mitte der Zeit* ('The Middle of Time'), appeared under the title *The Theology of St. Luke.* Conzelmann himself cannot be held directly responsible for the translator's freedom at this point, but the new title is only making explicit what is at least implicit (if not more) in Conzelmann's own work, viz. the claim that by analysing the changes Luke has made to his tradition we will arrive at an understanding of Luke's whole theology.

Now it would be quite clearly perverse to deny that Luke's theology has a great deal to do with the way he has altered his sources. The question is whether the two can simply be equated. As soon as one thinks about it, the answer must be No. For there may well be times when an author agrees with his tradition and is quite content to repeat it unaltered. Indeed, 'quite content' may be an understatement: an author may be passionately convinced of the value of his source material and he makes a thoroughly positive decision to include it without change. Indeed the decision of an author to include the material in the first place must presumably indicate some measure of agreement between the author and his tradition. However, the method of redaction criticism which looks only at the changes which a writer makes to his tradition will ignore such instances completely. Such a method may well end up with a thoroughly distorted picture of the evangelist's theology.

As an example of such a possible distortion, let us look once more at Conzelmann's work on Luke, especially his theories about Luke's eschatology. Conzelmann's famous theory was that Luke was concerned about the delay of the parousia; Luke then wrote his two-volume work as an attempt to 'apologize' for the delay of the parousia, and he altered his tradition at a number of points to replace the expectation in his sources of an imminent parousia event by a belief in salvation history (*Heilsgeschichte*) where the end had receded into the indefinite future.

This is not the place to enter into a full discussion of Conzelmann's theories. I only want to point to some methodological issues. Despite the many criticisms which Conzelmann's work has aroused, it is undeniable that Luke does appear to tone down some parts of his tradition which suggest that the end of the world and the parousia will take place soon. For example, at Mark 14.62, Jesus says in reply to the High Priest: 'you will see the Son of man seated at the right hand of Power, and coming with the clouds of heaven'; Luke's version has: 'from now on the Son of man shall be seated at the right hand of the power of God' (Luke 22.69). A prediction in Mark of a parousia-event which will be seen by the Jewish authorities themselves has become a claim in Luke of Jesus' heavenly position which will start immediately (or almost immediately: Luke is thinking of either Jesus' death or, more probably, his ascension, as the key moment). Any idea of Jesus' 'coming' has been eliminated by Luke.

This is not an isolated instance and Conzelmann pointed to other examples in the Lucan writings of the same phenomenon. However, there are other texts in Luke where the imminent expectation of the end is retained: for example, the preaching of John the Baptist (Luke 3.7–9) or the message of the disciples on mission: 'The kingdom of God has come near to you.' (Luke 10.9). Conzelmann's general answer was that these were simply vestiges from Luke's *tradition*: they were not evidence of his *redaction.*[9]

Now at one level this is true: these texts do not reveal Luke's redactional activity, provided the term 'redaction' is limited to referring to actual changes which Luke has introduced into his tradition. But can we go one stage further and say that these texts, as well as contributing nothing to Luke's redaction (narrowly understood), also contribute nothing to an understanding of Luke's overall theology? This seems very much more doubtful. In fact, if we are interested in discovering Luke's overall theology, we must be prepared to consider not only the changes Luke has made to his tradition, but also the places where Luke has preserved his tradition unaltered (as indeed more recent studies of Luke's eschatology have done).[10] For Luke's decision to adopt, and *not* adapt, a tradition may be just as revealing of his overall concerns as the changes he makes to his sources elsewhere. If redaction criticism imposes the restriction of looking only at the points where an author alters his tradition, then its results will be equally restricted.

In fact, redaction critics have always had in view the whole theology of the author of the text concerned. Hence, with the awareness of the limitations of the older type of redaction criticism, there has been a trend to look rather more at the works of the evangelists as wholes, as entities in themselves. We have therefore seen a move away from the older approach of what has been called 'emendation criticism' to what some have called 'rhetorical criticism' or even 'literary criticism', using that phrase in a sense closer to the way some secular critics use the term. This new approach would accept that an author has produced a final version of his text, and it is this whole text which is the main evidence for discovering something of the author and his concerns. A division of the text into 'tradition' and 'redaction' may tell us something, but the tradition should not necessarily be discarded when trying to discover the author's individual ideas. For this the whole text should be used, looking at the way individual parts of the text are related to other parts by the author, how the whole presents its message, and so on.

In such an approach there will be as much to be gained from the insights of secular literary criticism as there is from conventional source criticism with its analysis of a text into different layers of tradition. Thus this type of redaction criticism will seek help from the secular literary critic to learn how narratives function and how they gain their dramatic power.[11] So far in the area of the synoptic Gospels, such study has mostly been applied to the Gospel of Mark, though the work of J. D. Kingsbury on Matthew's theology is notable for taking a holistic approach to the text of Matthew and generally avoiding the method of making detailed comparisons between the text of Matthew and the text of Mark.[12]

This greater readiness to look at the whole text of an author has led to some important insights and also to some correctives of earlier theories in ways which other critical methods would find less easy to substantiate. Let us look at two examples, both of which occur in Mark's Gospel. The first concerns the phenomenon of the two feeding stories in Mark. Mark tells how Jesus fed vast numbers of people in a similar way on two occasions: 5,000 people are fed with five loaves and two fish (Mark 6.30–44), and a little later in the story, 4,000 people are fed with seven loaves and a few fish (Mark 8.1–10). What is the purpose of such duplication in the narrative? Many explanations have been given in the past. One of the most popular has been that the two stories are meant to symbolize the double mission of the Church to Jews and Gentiles.[13]

A more self-consciously literary reading of Mark might give a rather different picture.[14] On such a reading, the role of the disciples stands out very strongly. Mark's Gospel is well known for its bleak picture of the disciples: they fail to understand Jesus and in the end desert him completely. Now this theme can also be seen in Mark's narrative of the two feeding miracles, if one adopts a more literary approach. The two stories run very closely parallel with each other: the crowds are thronging round Jesus, the disciples ask Jesus what they should do, and Jesus then feeds all the people present.

In the first account, such a story line is quite natural. When Jesus tells the disciples to get the crowds some food, the disciples reply scornfully, 'Shall we go and buy two hundred denarii worth of bread?' (Mark. 6.37). Clearly they have no idea what is about to happen. But now exactly the same happens in the second story. The crowds are again thronging around, and again the disciples ask scornfully, 'How can one feed these men with bread here in the desert?' (Mark 8.4).

If one is operating at the level of source criticism, such a duplication gives rise to problems such as which question is more original, which one is a repetition of which, and so on. However, at the literary level, we can ask a quite different sort of question: what role does this repetition serve in the narrative as a whole? At this level, the second question of the disciples is clearly totally unjustified. Their first question is quite natural: 5,000 hungry people are around Jesus and the disciples have yet to see that Jesus' miraculous power can deal with such a situation. But in the second instance, they have no such excuse. An exactly similar situation with a hungry crowd has materialized, and they have just seen Jesus deal very easily with the problem. Yet they fail to realize that he can do so again, and they repeat their scornful question. Thus by being part of the later narrative as well as the earlier one, the disciples' question serves to highlight their ignorance and their almost total failure to respond positively to Jesus.

The point here is that such an analysis is only possible by looking at the text of the Gospel as a whole and seeing how individual features relate to each other within the whole narrative. Certainly such a result would be difficult to achieve using the older methods of analysing a text into its component parts of sources and redactional additions.

The second example also concerns the role of the disciples in Mark, this time in relation to the end of the Gospel. We have already seen that Mark's Gospel ends at Mark 16.8 (see p. 35 above). In its present form the Gospel ends with the angel's command to the women at the empty tomb to go and tell the disciples to go to Galilee where they will see Jesus; but the women run away from the tomb and say nothing to anyone 'for they were afraid' (Mark 16.8). What then happened to the angel's message? Did the disciples not receive it if the women really did say nothing to anyone?

One quite influential theory has been that this is indeed what Mark intended.[15] The ending of Mark is to be taken literally: the women said nothing to anyone and the angel's message did not get through to the disciples. This, it is argued, is part of a totally negative picture of the disciples which Mark portrays: the disciples failed Jesus in his ministry and in the end never received the angel's message and hence never saw the risen Jesus. Many have seen here a polemical situation within Mark's own community, whereby the disciples represent a group in Mark's day whom Mark is opposing. Mark writes his Gospel to discredit these people, who may have claimed to have experienced a special resurrection appearance. Thus Mark's way of telling the story is to show that any such claims by these people are bogus; if these people are represented by the disciples in the story, then Mark's account shows that the disciples never received the angel's message and so never saw the risen Jesus.

Such a theory can be very strongly criticized from a literary point of view.[16] Prior to Mark 16.8, the whole of the Gospel has been constructed with a view to showing that Mark himself is a 'reliable narrator', that Mark's 'point of view', his values and judgements and so on, are identical with those of Jesus as the main protagonist of the story, and hence that Jesus himself is to be regarded as 'reliable'.[17]

Sometimes in the Gospel Jesus predicts things that are going to happen in the future. Some of these are events that subsequently take place in the story. For example, Jesus predicts his passion in minute detail (Mark 8.31; 9.31; 10.33); within the passion itself he predicts Peter's denial even to the point about the cock crowing twice (Mark 14.30). All this happens just as Jesus has said (cf. Mark 14.72). Other predictions of Jesus are not fulfilled in the story itself. But the purpose of the fulfilled predictions is to show that Jesus can be relied upon, and hence the reader is given all the more assurance about the certainty of what, from the reader's standpoint, is still future.

What of the disciples and the risen Jesus? The angel's message in Mark 16.7 explicitly refers back to Jesus' own prediction in Mark 14.28 that he will 'go before you to Galilee' (cf. the end of Mark 16.7: 'as he told you'). Now if the disciples never received the angel's message, then this would indicate that this prediction of Jesus was not fulfilled. But then the reader would be thrown into total confusion: the whole narrative so far has been geared to showing that Jesus is reliable and that his predictions come true; the final ending would throw a gigantic question mark against this. It would in effect turn the values of the whole of the preceding narrative upside down. At the crucial point, Jesus would be seen to be unreliable. From a literary point of view this seems quite incredible. The only alernative is to reject the theory that Mark's ending is meant 'literally'. In order to preserve the literary integrity of Mark's narrative, it seems necessary to interpret the ending in some other way. Whatever it implies, it cannot mean that the disciples never saw the risen Jesus. The prediction of Mark 14.28 and the structure of the Gospel as a whole imply quite clearly that Mark believed that the angel's message did eventually get through.

Such a critique of the theory that Mark's ending is part of an anti-disciple polemic is possible using more traditional methods of interpretation; but the insights from literary criticism, together with some of the categories and arguments which we can bring into service from there, certainly serve to sharpen the critique and to concentrate the issues very forcefully.

The application of literary-critical techniques to the study of the New Testament, especially to the study of New Testament narratives, is still quite a recent development. One word of caution is perhaps necessary. When applied to the narrative books of the New Testament, a literary approach is something rather different from an older historical approach. A literary approach looks at the narrative in its present form and studies the narrative structure of the text as it now stands. It does not break the text up into different sources and strata. Nor does it ask questions about the historicity of the events being described. Thus in the case of the end of Mark's Gospel which we have just looked at, the literary approach is concerned with the literary question of what Mark implies in his narrative. We saw that Mark cannot have intended to suggest that the disciples never saw the risen Jesus. Whether in fact the disciples did see the risen Jesus or not is quite another matter. We cannot very easily solve historical problems by literary analyses such as these. So too literary analysis is rather different from a division of a text into tradition and redaction, and a literary analysis cannot solve problems of tradition and redaction very easily either. Analysing the present narrative will tell us how the present text is structured; but it cannot tell us where any one of the constituent parts of the narrative comes from.

So far, everything in this chapter has been related to the synoptic Gospels and it is often assumed that redaction criticism is primarily concerned with synoptic studies. In one sense this is true: when the discipline was developed it was directly related to study of the synoptic Gospels. Now such a restriction is by no means inherent in the method itself. Any text can be examined, both in relation to its sources and as a whole, with a view to determining the viewpoints of its author.

It is sometimes said that redaction-critical study of the fourth Gospel and of the epistles is still in its infancy.[18] This claim rather depends on precisely what is meant by 'redaction criticism'. If 'redaction' is taken to refer to the specific ways in which an author has modified his tradition, then such a claim is perhaps justified. Outside the synoptic Gospels we do not have the sources used by a New Testament author readily available to us. In the case of the epistles, such sources sometimes exist, but for the most part the writer is creating an entirely new text. However, when he does use a tradition, the modifications (if any) which he introduces can be very revealing.

We have already glanced briefly at Paul's modification of a prior tradition in Romans 3.25–26 (see p. 90 above). Another example may occur at the start of Romans in Romans 1.3–4. Many would agree that Paul here is using, and adapting, a mini-'creed'.[19] The tradition may have referred to Jesus as 'descended from David according to the flesh and designated Son of God according to the Spirit of holiness by his resurrection from the dead'. This could be interpreted in an 'adoptionist' way, suggesting that Jesus only became Son of God at the resurrection. Paul may then have adapted the tradition by prefacing it with the words 'concerning his Son' so that the whole creed is about Jesus *qua* Son; for the same reason Paul may have added 'in power' after the reference to Jesus as 'Son of God' (in v. 4): Jesus became 'Son of God in power' at the resurrection, which leaves open the possibility that he was also Son of God (? in weakness) prior to the resurrection. In cases like this, a redaction-critical approach can be very illuminating.

In the case of the fourth Gospel, the precise nature and wording of the sources or traditions available to the evangelist is uncertain, though attempts have been made to delineate their extent and even their exact wording at times.[20] However, if we extend the term 'redaction criticism' to cover the study of the whole thought of the author of the final text concerned (and indeed most synoptic redaction criticism claims to be interested primarily in this), then 'redaction criticism' of the fourth Gospel and of the epistles is as old as the hills. Certainly in the case of the epistles, interest has almost always been centred on the question of what the author meant. Introductory questions are often considered in great detail, as we have seen; but mostly the prime motivation behind the analysis of, say, the situation in the Roman church has been to come to a better understanding of what Paul himself meant in his letter to the Romans. In this looser sense of the term, all study of the epistles has been concerned with 'redaction criticism'.

The same has been true of the fourth Gospel for some considerable time. Certainly for the last 150 years of critical scholarship it has been recognized that, however much genuine historical information there may be embedded in the fourth Gospel, in its present form the Gospel is primarily a witness to the great Christian thinker who was its author. Thus most modern critical study of the fourth Gospel has been concerned with expounding the thought of John himself, rather than viewing the Gospel as a window through which we can see directly the historical events of the life and ministry of the pre-Easter Jesus. Thus 'redaction criticism', in the sense of study of the thought of the author of the text, is something which has been applied to the fourth Gospel for a very long time.

It must however be noted that the whole notion of 'the author of the text' is a problematic one when applied to the fourth Gospel. To put it more crudely, who is 'John'? Many have argued that the present text of John is the result of a number of stages of editing. We have already seen that John 21 was probably a later appendix added to the rest of the Gospel. In studying the thought of 'John', do we try to discover the thought of the person who took John 1–20 as his 'tradition' and redacted it by adding John 21? Most would argue not (though see ch. 11 below), and that 'the fourth evangelist' is the person who is primarily responsible for the bulk of the Gospel in 1–20. Even here, however, there are problems.

We have already noted Bultmann's theories about the origins of the fourth Gospel, whereby the work of the hero of the day, 'John', has been glossed by a later ecclesiastical redactor who has added the sacramental references (John 3.5; 6.51c–58). Bultmann also claims that the notes about a futurist eschatology (e.g. John 6.44b) are due to a later redactor. Added to this is a further theory of Bultmann's that the whole Gospel has been jumbled up so that the present text is out of order. Thus for Bultmann, the text of 'John' is the text of John 1–20, purged of the additions of the tiresome ecclesiastical redactor and also 'unscrambled'. Bultmann's 'John' is thus not 'the author of the final text'.[21]

However, Bultmann's theories are rather extreme in some respects. Many would argue, for example, that there is little justification for his theory of a muddling of the order of the text of John; and hence, despite the attractiveness of the allegedly 'unscrambled' text (and at times it is very logical), the present text of John should be analysed first of all to see if one can make sense of it as it stands before resorting to theories of reorderings. However, it should by now be clear that the whole question of the identity of 'John' is by no means a simple one, though most Johannine scholars do have in mind a single figure who was responsible for the text of the fourth Gospel in something like its present form.

So far we have looked briefly at the problems of applying redaction-critical methods to the Gospels and the epistles. One other book which we should perhaps consider here is the book of Acts. How far can we, or should we, apply redaction-critical techniques to Acts?

The dominant view in the past was that Acts was the work of a very accurate historian. Luke's reliability was confirmed by archaeological and other evidence which showed that he was remarkably accurate in some of his details (e.g. the titles given to various officials in the cities visited by the Christian mission). With the rise of redaction-critical studies of the Gospels, Luke has come to be seen as much more of a self-conscious theologian, using and shaping his traditions to get his message across.

The work of redaction criticism on Luke's Gospel has also had its effect on the study of Acts. The climax of such an approach to Acts (whether it is a high-point or a low-point depends on your point of view!) is probably the magisterial commentary on Acts by E. Haenchen.[22] Here Haenchen presents his interpretation of the message Luke was trying to get across to his readers. Thus, for Haenchen, interest is not primarily in the historical events which are described in Acts (and indeed at several points Haenchen argues that Luke is very inaccurate), but in Luke's own concerns in telling the story. Now this is certainly a perfectly legitimate way to use the text of Acts. An account such as Acts can be used to discover something about the events being described or something about the person telling the story.

The difficulty with Acts is to know just how we should proceed. Can we do some kind of 'emendation criticism', for example, or should we rely on a more 'literary' approach, using the text alone as it stands? Certainly the sort of 'emendation criticism' analogous to comparing Luke's Gospel with Mark's is very difficult in the case of Acts. We may suspect that Luke has used sources in his story, but we do not have any of those sources directly available to us. We may at times feel able to try to reconstruct pre-Lucan traditions, and to identify Lucan modifications of these, but this is not always easy or possible.

More delicate problems arise in those parts of Acts where we know from other sources something about what Luke is telling us, but we do not know what Luke's own sources of information were. This is particularly the case in Luke's account of Paul. A detailed comparison of Luke's account of Paul in Acts and Paul's own letters has shown a number of discrepancies. However accurate

Luke may be in giving titles to leading figures in cities in the Roman Empire (which he is), it is now clear that Luke is rather 'inaccurate' in his account of Paul.[23]

What is not so clear, however, is just how aware Luke is of this. Is he consciously changing his sources of information in presenting the story of Paul? Or has he simply got access to rather inaccurate information which he is reproducing to the best of his ability? A blanket, hard and fast answer to cover the whole of Luke's portrait of Paul in all its facets is clearly impossible. At times one suspects one thing is the case, at times another.

Take for example the vexed question of trying to reconcile Acts and Galatians with regard to the number of Paul's visits to Jerusalem (cf. p. 54 above). One suspects that the discrepancy between Acts and Galatians is simply due to the fact that Luke, writing perhaps forty years after the event, has got his information a bit muddled, and his sources were not quite clear about the precise chronology at this point.

On the other hand, the picture in Acts of Paul as a law-abiding Jew, which also presents difficulties in relation to Paul's own letters, seems to be rather more of a self-conscious matter. For whatever reason, Luke appears to want to underline the very close links between Christianity and Judaism and to show that Christians have always been loyal Jews: if there is now a split between Christians and Jews it is the fault of the Jews who have rejected the gospel, not of Christians who have hived off from Judaism.[24]

Given the fact that some of Paul's ideas and writings could be, and were, seen as much more threatening to the links between Christianity and Judaism (cf. some of Paul's statements about the law), it would seem likely that Luke's account is a more self-conscious attempt to 'correct' the picture of Paul. Yet whatever we decide in general terms we still cannot be certain of the precise extent to which Luke is actively changing his sources.

In fact most modern 'redaction-critical' study of Acts operates at the 'literary critical' level. Scholars look at the whole story which Luke presents, and then try to make sense of it on its own merits. (This is mostly Haenchen's approach.) We may well want to say something about the historicity of the story, the probability that events actually happened in the way Luke describes, the relation of Luke's narrative to other sources of information that we have, and so on. But this will only be possible after we have analysed the story on its own merits and on its own terms.

Redaction criticism has greatly enriched the study of the New Testament. In the case of the synoptic Gospels it has enabled us to see more clearly the contribution of the evangelists themselves to their texts and deepened our awareness of the influence which the early Christians had on their literary output. Certainly redaction criticism has shown us Christians struggling and wrestling with their traditions, seeking to make them relevant and applicable to their own situations. That for many will always be the fascination and interest which this aspect of New Testament study arouses.

Mark 3.1–6 and Parallels

When we considered this story from a form-critical point of view, we separated off the later accretions to the story added by Mark; we then ignored them in order to concentrate on the pre-Marcan version of the story. We also ignored the Matthean and Lucan versions of the story as telling us nothing about earlier stages in the tradition. When we turn to a redaction-critical study of the story, it is precisely those previously discarded parts which now become important. Whereas before we were looking at the form the story had in the oral stage of the tradition, we now concentrate on the meaning and significance which the evangelists themselves saw in the story, and here their editorial modifications to the tradition become highly significant.

We start by considering Mark's version of the story. We have already noted some small elements in his version which may be due to his hand, for example the reference to entering the synagogue in v. 1 and the note about Jesus looking round in v. 5 (cf. p. 112 above), but none of these is especially important theologically. More significant is the context which Mark has provided. Mark has this story as the last of a series of five controversy stories in Mark 2.1–3.6 which culminate in the note about the plot to kill Jesus (3.6). This final verse is almost certainly redactional.

There has been some debate about whether these five stories form a pre-Marcan collection. More and more, scholars are coming to the conclusion that, although some of the stories may have formed such a pre-Marcan collection, the present series of all five stories together is due to Mark's own composition.[25] Within the structure of the Gospel as a whole, their significance seems clear. All five stories show Jesus in conflict with the Jewish authorities, and it is a conflict which 3.6 clearly shows is one that leads to Jesus' death. Thus right at the start of the Gospel, the reader is shown that the course of Jesus' ministry is one which will lead to the cross.

The whole of the first part of the Gospel can in fact be shown to be very closely knit together with many themes crisscrossing with each other to point the reader forward to the passion narrative. Jesus teaches in the synagogue (Mark 1.21–28). Yet Mark is less interested in the content of Jesus' teaching than in the fact that it shows that Jesus has authority (Mark 1.22); moreover, this authority is different from that of the scribes (Mark 1.22). Then in Mark 2, the scribes are introduced again into the story (Mark 2.6), and they mutter the charge on which Jesus will finally be condemned to death: blasphemy (Mark 2.7; cf. 14.64).

The story of Mark 3.1–6 is thus the climax of a tightly-knit composition which shows Mark's interest in the passion narrative as the point to which his whole narrative is leading. Mark's Gospel is, in some sense, 'a passion narrative with an extended introduction',[26] and Mark 3.6 is Mark's way of foreshadowing what is to come. Mark's interests can thus be seen here partly by an 'emendation' type of redaction criticism, separating off Mark 3.6 as Mark's redaction, but also by a more literary approach, considering his narrative as a whole.

We have already seen that Matthew's account is rather different, and the logic of Jesus' argument in Matthew leaves something to be desired (see p. 91 above). Part of Matthew's lack of logic is due to his combining two traditions which do not quite fit perfectly. Why has he done this? Part of the answer seems to be that Matthew is concerned to show that Jesus' attitude to the law is not one of wanton disregard. This is part of a theme which recurs quite frequently in Matthew, almost as if the evangelist is trying to pull Jesus back within the fold of Judaism.

This can be seen happening here. Mark's Jesus is very free with regard to the law: the claim is made that any action of 'doing good' overrides the sabbath, and Mark has Jesus assert this bluntly via a rhetorical question. Matthew's Jesus is much more reasonable from a Jewish point of view. Matthew changes the structure of the story so that the bystanders are no longer simply watching to see if Jesus will heal the man so that they can accuse him (as in Mark 3.2). Rather Matthew forms a conversation between them and Jesus, so that they explicitly ask, 'Is it lawful to heal on the sabbath?' (Matt. 12.10). Jesus now appeals to the example of the sheep in the pit; he then says that men are worth more than sheep, and concludes 'So it is lawful to do good on the sabbath.' The blunt, provocative assertion of Mark 3.4 has been integrated into a reasoned conversation in Matthew. Mark's Jesus baldly asserts his authority; Matthew's Jesus argues his way to his conclusion in a typically rabbinic manner. (The difficulties only arise when one looks more closely at the details of Matthew's form of the argument, as we have seen: cf. p. 64 above.) Matthew's Jesus thus appears much more Jewish (on the surface at least), and Matthew's version appears to be the result of an attempt to soften the impact of the Jesus of Mark's Gospel in order to appease Jewish sensibilities. (Whether Matthew himself was a Jew is more problematic, as we have seen.)

It is perhaps worth noting that the source material which enables Matthew to do all this is Q. There is a certain amount of material in Q which is in a similar vein, showing Jesus as working firmly within the law. The clearest example is the saying in Matthew 5.18/Luke 16.17, which appears to assert that 'not an iota, not a dot, will pass from the law'. The precise wording of the Q version is uncertain, but it seems to show that the Q tradition represents a pocket of early Christianity which maintained very strongly that the Jewish law was still binding on Christians. So too in Matthew 12.11–12/Luke 14.5, we have a Q tradition which shows Jesus arguing his way to a legal justification for breaching the sabbath law in a particular instance. No Jew would object to working on the sabbath if you could provide a good enough reason (see p. 63 above). Q here has Jesus providing a good reason (and if the Q version had Jesus referring to a human being in the pit, as we argued on p. 92 above, the reason could be regarded as quite legitimate from a Jewish point of view.) We may have here an instance of a specific facet of a Q theology. Redaction criticism can be, and is increasingly being, applied to Q quite as much as to the Gospels themselves.

Luke's version does not differ greatly from Mark's, though Luke does not have the same tightly-knit structure as Mark has in this section of the Gospel. Luke has expanded his Marcan source with other material, and the series of five controversy stories in Luke do not have the same function as in Mark, where they foreshadow the passion to come. Luke thus rewrites the concluding verse and replaces the explicit death plot of Mark 3.6 with a more general note about the scribes and Pharisees being 'filled with fury' (Luke 6.11). Luke's other alterations to Mark are fairly small-scale. He tells us that it was the man's right hand which was withered (Luke 6.6), perhaps to heighten the unfortunate condition of the man. He also adds the note that Jesus 'knew their thoughts' (Luke 6.8), a motif which highlights Jesus' miraculous powers, and this is a theme of which Luke is especially fond.[27] There is not a lot of evidence to suggest that the sabbath law was of great concern to Luke and probably his main interest in this, as in all the sabbath healing stories, was the christological one of showing the power and authority of Jesus.[28]

It should now be clear that the same story can be used creatively by different authors to make a wide range of points. The account of the healing of the man with the withered hand can be used to show Jesus' authority clashing with Jewish authority and prefiguring the final point of that conflict, the cross (Mark); it can be used to show more simply Jesus' power and authority as a miracle-worker (Luke); it can be used to show Jesus' determination to stay within the law (Matthew; cf. also Q). Nor is this variation simply a matter of different authors stressing different parts of a common original. Mark's Jesus and Matthew's Jesus have very different attitudes to the law, and this is partly due to the evangelists reshaping their traditions, quite radically at times. The different forms of the story can thus tell us a great deal about the authors concerned quite irrespective of what we decide about the historical events being described.

Notes

1. See W. Marxsen, *Mark the Evangelist* (New York 1969); G. Bornkamm, G. Barth & H. J. Held, *Tradition and Interpretation in Matthew* (London 1963); H. Conzelmann, *The Theology of St. Luke* (London 1960). (The German originals of all these works first appeared in the mid 1950s or earlier.)
2. See especially the discussion, often in rather extravagant language, by N. Perrin, *What is Redaction Criticism?* (London 1970).
3. cf. R. H. Lightfoot, *History and Interpretation in the Gospels* (London 1935) and the discussion by Perrin, *Redaction*, pp. 21ff.
4. Though see J. Rohde, *Rediscovering the Teaching of the Evangelists* (London 1968); R. H. Stein, 'What is Redaktionsgeschichte?', *JBL* 88 (1969), pp. 45–56; M. D. Hooker, 'In His Own Image?', in Hooker & Hickling (eds.), *What about the New Testament?*, pp. 28–44.
5. See E. Haenchen, *Der Weg Jesu* (Berlin 1968), p. 24.
6. See R. H. Stein, 'The Proper Methodology for Ascertaining a Markan Redaction History', *NovT* 13 (1971), pp. 181–98.
7. cf. the commentaries on Mark here and see W. R. Telford, *The Barren Temple and the Withered Tree* (Sheffield 1980).
8. See C. J. A. Hickling, 'A Problem of Method in Gospel Research', *RelSt* 10 (1974), pp. 339–46.
9. Conzelmann, *Luke*, pp. 95ff.
10. See, for example, the treatment in S. G. Wilson, *The Gentiles and the Gentile Mission in Luke–Acts* (Cambridge 1973) ch. 3; also R. Maddox, *The Purpose of Luke–Acts* (Edinburgh 1982), ch. 5.
11. A useful survey is provided by N. R. Petersen, *Literary Criticism for New Testament Critics* (Philadelphia 1978), though some of his assertions about the bankruptcy of older methods, and the distinctiveness of 'literary' approaches, are probably too extreme. It should also be noted that the word 'literary' is being used in this

chapter rather differently from its use in ch. 11 below. Here I am using it to refer to a holistic approach to a text (i.e. not splitting the text up into tradition and redaction); in ch. 11, I shall be looking at suggestions that a text can be abstracted from its author and considered independently in its own right. The latter aim is not in mind here.

12. See J. D. Kingsbury, *Matthew: Structure, Christology, Kingdom* (London 1976), and his more overt use of literary-critical categories in 'The Figure of Jesus in Matthew's Story: A Literary-Critical Probe', *JSNT* 21 (1984), pp. 3–36, and his *Matthew as Story* (Philadelphia 1986).
13. cf. Nineham, *Mark*, p. 207.
14. For what follows, see R. M. Fowler, *Loaves and Fishes: The Function of the Feeding Stories in the Gospel of Mark* (Chico 1981).
15. See especially T. J. Weeden, *Mark – Traditions in Conflict* (Philadelphia 1971), esp. pp. 101ff.
16. See N. R. Petersen, 'When is the End not the End? Literary Reflections on the Ending of Mark's Narrative', *Interpretation* 34 (1980), pp. 151–66.
17. The terms in inverted commas here are slightly technical terms in modern literary study.
18. cf. Perrin, *Redaction*, p. 84 (in relation to John).
19. cf. C. K. Barrett, *The Epistle to the Romans* (London 1957), pp. 19–20.
20. The most ambitious is probably that of R. T. Fortna, *The Gospel of Signs* (Cambridge 1970), who tries to reconstruct very precisely the exact wording of the alleged 'Signs Source' used by John.
21. For details, see his commentary *The Gospel of John* (cf. n. 15 on p. 94 above).
22. E. Haenchen, *The Acts of the Apostles* (ET, Oxford 1971).
23. cf. Vielhauer, '"Paulinism" of Acts', (n. 7 on p. 67 above); see too Maddox, *Purpose*, ch. 3.
24. cf. Maddox, *Purpose*, p. 78; Haenchen, *Acts*, pp. 101–12.
25. cf. J. Dewey, *Markan Public Debate. Literary Technique, Concentric Structure and Theology in Mark 2:1–3:6* (Chico 1980), and Kiilunen, *Die Vollmacht im Widerstreit*, who both argue that at least the present structure of five controversy stories is due to Mark's redaction.
26. This famous description goes back to M. Kähler (though Kähler applied it to all the Gospels).
27. cf. P. J. Achtemeier, 'The Lucan Perspective on the Miracles of Jesus: A Preliminary Sketch', *JBL* 91 (1972), pp. 198–221.
28. cf. S. G. Wilson, *Luke and the Law* (Cambridge 1983), pp. 38–9.

9
The New Testament and Sociology

New Testament study has never been conducted in an academic vacuum. It has always been recognized that students of the New Testament can learn from and use the insights of many other disciplines. The use of ideas from philosophy, especially existentialist philosophy, by R. Bultmann is a classic example. So too we have seen how New Testament critics have learnt from some of the methods and insights of literary critics of secular literature in the interpretation of New Testament texts. Another academic discipline which has recently been regarded by many New Testament critics as being potentially extremely fruitful for New Testament study is that of sociology.

Sociological studies of the New Testament and the use of so-called 'sociological' methods to interpret New Testament texts are something of a 'new thing' in the world of New Testament scholarship. Moreover, it is clear that they have provided many challenging new insights and fresh avenues of approach for the New Testament critic. Sociological studies of the Old Testament do not seem to be quite such a new thing methodologically. The celebrated sociologist Max Weber published his studies on *Ancient Judaism* around the end of the First World War, and the work of scholars like A. Alt, M. Noth, G. von Rad and and N. Gottwald have continued this sort of approach to the study of the Old Testament documents. But in the area of New Testament scholarship, the use of sociological methods and insights is being hailed as something which is definitely new.[1]

Why has this approach been adopted so vigorously by some? The answer given by many scholars who have been attracted to the use of sociology is that they have become dissatisfied with the so-called 'idealism' of traditional New Testament scholarship, i.e. with its almost exclusive concentration on ideas, or theology. Thus R. Scroggs writes: 'To some it has seemed that too often the discipline of the theology of the New Testament (the history of *ideas*) operates out of a methodological docetism, as if believers had minds and spirits unconnected with their individual and corporate bodies.'[2] In similar vein, J. H. Elliott writes:

> . . . we have generally assumed . . . that history is basically or essentially the history of *ideas*. In our analysis of the literature

> and history of the early church we have conceived of the problems facing the early Christians almost exclusively in conceptual terms. Letters, gospels and other documents were composed, we have said, in order to combat wrongheaded ideas, false Christologies, and theological heresies, or to propagate ideas, say, of salvation as history. The significance or influence of specifically social needs, social conflicts, group interests and clashing ideologies has received little attention or mention.[3]

Hence, according to these scholars, New Testament scholarship has tended to ignore the *social* dimension of the New Testament documents, the social life in practical concrete terms of the primitive Christian communities, the social pressures which they experienced, and the possibility that social, rather than ideological, factors were determinative in some articulations of the early Christians' self-understanding. It is with this in mind that many scholars have turned to the discipline of sociology for help in considering the social aspects of early Christianity in much more depth.

As an example of the way in which such approaches have been used very fruitfully to illuminate the New Testament texts, we may look at the work of G. Theissen. Theissen has been a leading figure in the use of sociological insights for the study of the New Testament. Amongst his many writings he has published a number of important articles on the social situation of the Corinthian church addressed by Paul in 1 Corinthians.[4] Theissen here gives an extremely detailed and painstaking analysis of the social status of some members of the Corinthian community. Drawing on a wealth of background material from non-Christian sources, he shows how some, at least, of the Christians at Corinth were probably quite well-to-do and of a relatively high social standing. For example, he refers to the fact that some Christians at Corinth evidently had houses of their own; they were also very mobile and presumably therefore had the necessary money to be able to travel extensively. However it is also clear that other Christians were not well-off and were of a much lower social standing. Thus the Corinthian community may well have been made up of a very broad social cross section.

It is these social differences, Theissen argues, which may lie behind some of the troubles reflected in 1 Corinthians. For example, in 1 Corinthians 8, 10 Paul deals with the problem of whether a Christian should be allowed to eat food offered to idols. Evidently some Corinthian Christians argued that this was perfectly all right since 'all of us possess knowledge' (1 Cor. 8.1): Christians know that an idol does not exist (or rather that there is no divine being behind the lump of stone or whatever). Others evidently had great qualms about eating meat which had been offered to an idol. Paul refers to these two groups as the 'strong' and the 'weak', and, on theological grounds, accepts the arguments of the strong (at least in part).[5] However, he urges pastoral consideration so that the consciences of the weak are not offended. What lies behind the differences between the strong and the weak?

Traditionally New Testament critics have postulated that the strong may have been a quasi-gnostic group claiming to possess 'knowledge', while the weak may have been Jewish Christians having scruples about Jewish food laws. Theissen argues that the difference may have been more of a social one. In Corinth, well-off members of society would have eaten meat freely on various occasions. Lower social classes would have eaten meat only rarely because it would have been beyond their means. The main occasions when meat would have been available were public religious festivals. Thus the lower classes would have had difficulty in conceiving of eating meat in anything other than the context of a pagan festival. Theissen argues that the strong were the well-off Christians who were used to eating meat frequently; the weak were the less well-off whose scruples arose partly because of their social status. Theissen also suggests that exactly the same *social* division within the Corinthain community lies behind the troubles which evidently beset the celebration of the Eucharist at Corinth and which Paul deals with in 1 Corinthians 11.

Now this is not the place to go into a detailed examination of Theissen's individual suggestions. One suspects that there is more to the troubles at Corinth than *just* a social division within the community. After all, Paul deals with the problem at a rather different level![6] Nevertheless, Theissen's work has yielded many important new insights for the understanding of the social status of early Christians,[7] and his suggestions about the social stratification within the Corinthian community have shown how social factors may very well have aggravated tensions and differences within the community.

Now this book is intended to be primarily about the methods of studying the New Testament, rather than the individual results which emerge from the application of these methods. What then can we say about the method of sociological interpretation of the New Testament texts?

In any discipline it is a good thing to try to define one's terms first of all, at least as far as possible. This is especially the case in the present context, for it seems that a great diversity of work is being undertaken under the broad heading of 'sociology' and 'sociological'. At the very least we should perhaps make a distinction, admittedly a very crude one, between social *descriptions* of various aspects of first-century Christianity (e.g. the social standing of Christians, the social organization of the communities) and sociological *explanations.*[8] It may therefore be worthwhile to distinguish between sociological studies which use the methods, theories and explanations of modern sociology, and studies concerned in a broader way with the social nature of the early Christian communities. The same point is made more forcefully by Elliott:

> . . . The terms 'social' and 'sociological' have generally been used indiscriminately so that mere social description has been equated – erroneously – with sociological explanation. What has been lacking is a process for ascertaining not only *what* the sociohistorical circumstances of given traditions and compositions were but also *how* and *why* these circumstances gave rise to the productions under consideration.[9]

We shall therefore look at these two aspects, social description and sociological explanation, separately.

Social Description

There have been a number of studies in this area, investigating the social background in the first-century world and looking at the social organization of the Christian communities. Various works by M. Hengel, including his massive *Judaism and Hellenism* (ET, London 1974), and W. Meeks' study *The First Urban Christians* (New Haven & London 1983) could be mentioned here. A great deal of the work of Theissen also comes into this category: much of his writings, especially his studies of the Pauline letters, are taken up with minutely detailed analyses of the social background and social set-up of the first-century Christians.[10] Moreover, it is quite clear that works of this kind have contributed a tremendous amount to the New Testament student, bringing together and making available a massive amount of information about the social background of various Christian communities.

We may however raise the question here of just how new in terms of *method* all this is. For the importance of paying more than lip service to the background of the New Testament texts is what lies at the heart of the whole historical-critical method. Whether people have concentrated so much on the 'social' background is perhaps debatable.[11] As we have seen, 'the background' is a multifaceted entity and there will probably always be aspects of 'the' background which have received more, or less, attention than others. But the task of determining the background of the New Testament text is part of the whole area of New Testament 'Introduction' (at least as I have used that term in ch. 3 above). Thus a great deal of the work of 'social description' today falls within the broad category of 'New Testament Introduction'.[12] Indeed a great deal of older study in the general area of New Testament Introduction, part of which we have already looked at, can be seen as an application of the same basic method as is used in more recent social descriptions.

For example, F. C. Baur's epoch-making article 'Die Christuspartei in der korinthischen Gemeinde' of 1831 is often regarded as an important landmark at the start of the historical-critical approach. Baur's main point was that, in order to understand 1 Corinthians, one had to know about the background. Baur postulated here a great split between the Jewish and Gentile wings of the Church. Now whatever one makes of Baur's individual theories today (and they are indeed highly questionable), his method was precisely that of the modern New Testament social historian: one must be aware of the background in the Corinthian community – and for Baur it was in part the social background of the community as a divided one (according to Baur for ideological reasons)[13] – in order to make sense of Paul's letter.

Deissmann's work on the language of the New Testament we have already looked at briefly (see p. 44 above). Again, some of his detailed theories may well be questionable (e.g. about the degree to which New Testament Greek corresponds to that of the papyri, or about the precise social level of the early Christians),[14] but his underlying method is exactly that of the modern social historian. Deissmann's claim (and most would agree with him) was that the language of the New Testament could only be properly understood if full account was taken of the language of the surrounding culture.

There is too the whole approach of form criticism, especially as applied to the study of the gospel tradition. As we have seen, one of the basic assumptions of form criticism is that the individual pericopes of the gospel tradition were preserved for use in the community or society: hence the gospel tradition reflects the social realities of the communities which preserved the various parts of it.[15]

The historical-critical method has always recognized that a full knowledge of the background of the New Testament text, including the 'social' level, is essential for a proper understanding of the texts themselves. Thus despite some rather extravagant claims about the novelty of some sociological approaches to the New Testament,[16] it would seem to be the case that, in terms of method, such 'new' approaches are in fact very similar to, and closely related to, the disciplines of New Testament Introduction and form criticism.

Sociological Explanations

When we turn from the area of social description to the use of more specifically sociological methods, we are immediately confronted with a bewildering variety. Sociology itself is a multifaceted discipline and within its boundaries, various models and theories compete with each other. What is said here must therefore inevitably involve a somewhat restricted view, and any critiques given here will not necessarily apply to all possible uses of sociological theory by New Testament scholars. We shall limit attention to two areas: one is the use of insights from the so-called 'sociology of knowledge' by New Testament scholars, the other is the use of specific sociological categories as possibly applicable to New Testament data.

a) *Sociology of Knowledge*

Appeal has frequently been made by New Testament scholars to this aspect of sociological theory. Scroggs claims that it provides 'the single most important approach within the field of sociology' for New Testament studies.[17] Sociologists from this field would argue that the 'social world' in which we live, and which we create in order to provide structure, stability and meaning to the universe as we encounter it, is *socially* determined and constructed. This social world is determinative for the language of a society and, arguably, for its religious articulations as well. Thus W. Meeks writes: 'One's "world" in the sociology of knowledge is understood as the symbolic universe within which one functions, which has "objectivity" because it is constantly reinforced by the structures of the society to which it is specific.'[18] Or to cite Scroggs again:

> . . . the world we live in, the world we think, or assume, has ontological foundations, is really *socially constructed* and is created, communicated and sustained through language and symbol . . . language, *including theological language*, is never to be seen as independent of other social realities. *Thus theological language and the claims made therein can no longer be explained*

without taking into account socio-economic-cultural factors as essential ingredients in the production of that language.[19]

Now the way in which these insights have been applied by New Testament scholars has generally been to use them as justification for the claim that theological language is directly and positively revelatory of the community for which the language is written. One recent writer has referred to the work of W. Meeks on John, G. Theissen on the synoptics, and J. H. Elliott on 1 Peter, as good examples of this approach.[20]

For example, Meeks' article on the fourth Gospel starts by analysing the discourse between Jesus and Nicodemus in John 3. Meeks argues that the story there shows that Jesus remains totally incomprehensible to Nicodemus. Jesus does not bridge the gap between earth and heaven: he remains totally unintelligible and alien to the people of the earth. Meeks then appeals to the work of sociologists of knowledge to argue that this implies that John's *community* is alienated and isolated from the rest of its society. Thus what the text says about Jesus is taken as directly revelatory about the writer's social situation.

Similarly, Theissen considers the texts where Jesus calls the disciples to leave everything (e.g. Matt. 8.22), and he argues that these sayings must reflect the existence of a group of wandering charismatics in the early Palestinian churches who did leave everything. Thus once again a text about Jesus, or a saying of Jesus, is taken as directly indicative of the social situation of the later community.

Elliott considers in some depth the description of the readers of 1 Peter as *paroikoi* (cf. 1 Pet. 2.11). This is usually interpreted in terms of a religious metaphor: the readers are 'strangers' in the sense that their true homeland is in heaven. Elliott argues that the language should be taken much more literally, as an indication of their social status. The readers may well be social *paroikoi*, resident aliens who are being denied full citizenship rights here on earth.

A number of comments can be made about such an approach. First, we can again raise the question of just how new all this is. It is true that much of this scholarly literature is dressed up in new jargon (e.g. talk of 'life worlds' etc.). But fundamentally it scarcely differs from Bultmann's type of form criticism as applied to the Gospels. Bultmann too argued that the individual pericopes of the Gospels gave direct insight about the communities which preserved them: for example, stories about sabbath controversies between Jesus and the Jewish authorities in the Gospels reflect identical controversies between the Jews and the Christian communities who preserved these stories. Similarly, it has long been argued that, since there is a great stress in Mark's Gospel on the necessity of suffering, Mark's community was a suffering community. Thus once again, the allegedly 'new' insights brought by sociology are not very different in practice from insights which have been offered by form critics and others for some considerable time within New Testament scholarship.

Secondly, and perhaps more important, we should raise the question of how valid all this is. Scroggs warns: 'The difficult questions for the sociologist are, in concrete instances, *how* to move between language and social realities, and *which* social realities are to be related to *which* linguistic structures?'[21]

It is at least questionable whether literary texts are directly revelatory of the society for which they are written. Undoubtedly text and society are related, but the relationship is not always one of 100 per cent positive correlation. Thus A. Malherbe writes:

> It is at least possible that some documents were rescued from obscurity, not because they represented the viewpoints of communities, but precisely because they challenged them. It is too facile to view literature as the product of communities. The relationship could have been very complex.[22]

For example, it is arguable that people have gone too far too fast from the fact that Mark's Jesus has a lot to say about suffering to the conclusion that Mark's community is suffering. It may make much better sense of Mark if the Gospel were written against a community which was materially quite content and peaceful.[23] It may be as much a challenge to the community as a direct reflection of the life of the community. The same considerations can apply to the use of specific imagery. Certainly it cannot be assumed that an image is directly revelatory of the present state of the community. For example, Theissen refers to the use of the term 'body' as an image for the community: this may imply the great cohesion of Christian communities; but it is also used by Paul to establish such cohesion, so 'this image contains an unmistakable demand for the realization of its content'.[24]

The issue of how far we may deduce social and cultural settings from the imagery used by a writer or speaker is also one that needs a great deal of care. We can think too readily – if we are not careful – of Jesus as the great 'man of the earth', in touch with the world of nature and telling his parables which are all 'true to life', and contrast him with the urban Paul who knew so little about nature that he wrote the horticulturally impossible allegory of the olive tree in Romans 11. But Jesus' parables may not always be true to life. (Cf. our earlier discussion on pp. 108–9 above about the parable of the mustard seed.) We cannot always take language and imagery at face value as directly showing the social conditions of the speaker concerned. If we did, we might deduce from the parable of the Good Samaritan that Samaritans were socially very friendly with Jews; whereas the fact that Jews and Samaritans hated each other is precisely the 'social' background that gives the parable its force and 'punch' in a first-century context.

The interpretation of a writer's use of language and imagery thus needs a great deal of care. Yet sometimes it seems that much 'sociological' analysis of the New Testament fails to exercise such care. As an example I take part of H. C. Kee's argument that Mark's community was rural, not urban. He deduces this from an alleged 'anti-city' stance in Mark:

> . . . there is a clear antipathy towards the city in Mark. Not only are his images and metaphors drawn from the life of field and village, but he portrays Jesus in editorial sections as avoiding the cities, and many of the narratives are specifically located in open territory: on a hill, by the sea, in the 'desert', 'on the green grass'. Villages and fields are mentioned frequently. The city is the place from which Jesus withdraws . . . Jesus lives outside Jerusalem in a village, announces the city's destruction from a vantage point 'over against' it, gathers his disciples in a garden outside its walls, enters it again only under arrest as an insurrectionist, is condemned by its civil and religious authorities, and is led from it to be executed and buried.[25]

Now many of these features can be interpreted rather differently. For example, Jesus' standing 'outside', 'over against' the city and announcing its destruction, is probably nothing to do with Mark's being anti-city as such. Rather, Mark sees one city, Jerusalem, as symbolic and representative of the opposition to Jesus. Jerusalem for Mark, as has long been noted, is the focus for all the opposition to Jesus (cf. Mark 3.22; 7.1). To see the picture in the purely 'social' terms of an urban/rural distinction is probably to undermine the force of Mark's language and to miss much of the point of what he is saying.

These criticisms of some studies of New Testament texts from a sociological standpoint are not intended to undermine the whole enterprise of applying sociological insights to the New Testament text. Far from it. But there may be a danger of ignoring the varied way in which language can function. Language can reflect existing social structures; but it does not always do so. We need great care and delicacy in deciding which elements of language are socially determined and reflect existing social structures, which elements are directed *at* the existing structures seeking to alter them, and which elements are quite unrelated to the general social setting of the community for which they are written. All this is simply to say that insights from sociology cannot ignore insights from literary criticism, and vice versa!

Insights from the sociology of knowledge may well therefore have a lot to tell us; but it is questionable how far this approach really differs from that of form criticism (at least as practised by a Bultmann), and we have seen that such an approach has certain methodological problems built into its structure.

b) *The Use of Sociological Models*

In a survey article about the use of sociology in New Testament studies, J. Gager writes:

> What is revealed in the work of Elliott, Theissen, Meeks, and others is the potential fruitfulness of social scientific approaches to the study of the New Testament and early Christianity ... The value of these approaches is not just that they 'work', that sociological theories can be made to fit the data of early Christianity, but that they make a difference, they lead to new questions [etc.] ... such theories serve to 'set the historical imagination free from stereotypes'.[26]

This raises a number of questions. As far as the application of insights from the sociology of knowledge is concerned, the value of such an approach is in fact rather questionable. It may be that such an approach does enable a good 'fit' to be made between text and society; but the value of this is probably nil. For if we start with the presupposition that a text is revelatory of a society, that text and society correspond directly, then this inevitably leads to the result that text and society make a good fit. The result is predetermined by the method and the argument is circular, a fact which has frequently been pointed out in relation to Bultmann's method of form criticism.

Moreover, we may ask whether the results really help in the interpretation of the text. For example, Meeks' theories about the nature of the social situation of the Johannine community do not make much difference to the interpretation of the text itself.[27] The theory about the social situation has been derived from an interpretation of the text, and then it simply reinforces this interpretation which has already been achieved. In this area, therefore, the claim that sociological insights can be made to 'fit the data of early Christianity' may be true but is not ultimately very useful.

However, Gager probably has other things in mind as well, viz. the use of specific sociological theories or categories which may provide direct illumination of New Testament phenomena which other theories or categories fail to explain. Gager himself has argued that the strong missionary drive within primitive Christianity may be explicable along sociological lines by the theory of 'cognitive dissonance'. This theory suggests that when a group has very strongly held expectations which are clearly disconfirmed by events in the world, one reaction is to overcome the 'dissonance' by evangelistic zeal persuading other people that the system of belief is correct after all. Gager suggests that the death of Jesus acted as the clear disconfirmation of hopes that were entertained during his lifetime. The reaction of the early Christians immediately after the crucifixion of Jesus in strong missionary activity can thus be seen as an attempt to overcome the dissonance created by the crucifixion.[28] Others have suggested that the sociological categories of 'sect', or 'millenarian movement' or 'charismatic prophet' can be fruitfully applied to the early Christian communities and leading figures in it.[29]

Now it is certainly the case that the comparison of early Christian communities with other communities widely separated in space and time from the first-century Roman Empire may well be fruitful. Nevertheless, despite the claim that these comparative approaches 'set the historical imagination free from stereotypes', it may be that the New Testament evidence is pressed, by at least some New Testament sociologists, into *sociological* stereotypes in a way which represents an illegitimate use of these categories from the sociological point of view.

Take, for example, the claim that primitive Christianity can be regarded as a 'millenarian movement', or 'sect', with perhaps Jesus as a 'charismatic prophet'. All these terms are sociological stereotypes, and often New Testament critics have suggested that Christianity (or parts of Christianity) 'fit' these sociological descriptions extremely well.

However, some New Testament critics have argued in a slightly different way. They have pointed to a particular aspect of first-century Christianity as fitting most of the characteristics of the sociological model concerned, and have then claimed that we can assume that it fits the rest.[30] For example, Scroggs has argued that the earliest Christian communities fulfilled all the characteristics of what sociologists call a 'sect'.[31] He takes seven features said to define a sect (though this is only one amongst many possible definitions of a sect by sociologists). He then seeks to show that Christianity exhibits all these features; but in practice he is forced to argue that since Christianity exhibits most of the features concerned, the presence of the rest can be assumed.[32] Thus what starts as an empirical test about whether a sociological model fits the facts becomes a means whereby the model tells us what the facts must have been.

This probably represents a misuse of the sociological categories concerned. These categories should rather be seen as 'ideal types'; the models which sociologists use are not necessarily meant to be precise descriptions of empirical historical realities. Rather they are abstractions from realities, useful 'reference grids' by which we can measure different empirical realities and against which we can plot individual peculiarities. But we cannot necessarily assume that if one reality shows 90 per cent agreement with the ideal type, then we can assume agreement with the remaining 10 per cent. If these categories taken from the field of sociology become prescriptive rather than descriptive, if they are used not only to describe what is but also to infer what must have been, then we are in danger of abusing them.[33]

It is undeniable that 'sociology', if taken in a broad sense, has an enormous amount to contribute to the study of the New Testament. The work of the 'social historian' is absolutely indispensable in providing the New Testament student with the necessary knowledge of the social background against which the New Testament texts were written. The use of specific sociological theories and models perhaps needs more care, but it is certainly the case that many new and challenging insights have been produced by such approaches. It is still only relatively recently that this aspect of the use of sociology has begun to make an impact on New Testament studies, and we perhaps need more time to come to a full appreciation of the value of such an approach.

However in many respects we can, I think, say that at the level of *method*, many of these so-called 'new' approaches are not so new after all. The work of 'social description' (as I have called it here) is attempting to fill in part of the total background of the New Testament texts, though putting much more stress on the social background than perhaps has been the case in the past. These approaches therefore belong methodologically within the general area of New Testament 'Introduction', at least if we define that term as broadly as we have done here (cf. ch. 3 above). Further, some attempts at more strictly sociological explanations turn out to be extremely close methodologically to the well-established approaches associated with form criticism, as we have seen.

In terms of results obtained, much that is new and original has been achieved by approaches to the New Testament texts from a sociological point of view. In terms of basic method, however, it must be said that there is little here which differs fundamentally from the traditional approaches to the text associated with the historical-critical method. Sociological approaches have taught us to broaden our vision when interpreting the New Testament; but they do so by encouraging us to use many of the same basic methods as we have in the past.

Notes

1. cf J. G. Gager, *Kingdom and Community, The Social World of Early Christianity* (Engelwood Cliffs 1975), pp. xi–xii; J. H. Elliott, *A Home for the Homeless. A Sociological Exegesis of 1 Peter, its Situation and Strategy* (London 1982) calls his study 'an exercise in sociological exegesis – an attempt to articulate a fresh interdisciplinary approach' (p. 1).
2. R. Scroggs, 'The Sociological Interpretation of the New Testament. The Present State of Research', *NTS* 26 (1980), pp. 164–79, on pp. 165–6.
3. Elliott, *Home*, pp. 3–4; also W. A. Meeks, *The First Urban Christians* (New Haven & London 1983), p. 2, and many others.
4. These have now been translated and collected together in G. Theissen, *The Social Setting of Pauline Christianity* (Edinburgh 1982).
5. Though it is arguable that Paul does not in fact agree with them entirely: they may have been absolute monotheists, believing that no being existed at all behind the idol itself; Paul may have been more of a 'henotheist', believing that beings might exist but that Christians must under no circumstances give them recognition. This is what probably lies behind his argument in 1 Cor. 10. See the commentaries at this point.
6. cf. A. J. Malherbe, *Social Aspects of Early Christianity* (Philadelphia [2]1983), p. 84.
7. See Malherbe, *Social Aspects*, ch. 2, and Meeks, *Urban*, ch. 2, for further discussion of this important issue.
8. I am aware that such a distinction is rather naive: every 'description' may be making implicit assumptions about various 'explanations' of the relevant facts. cf. J. G. Gager, 'Shall We Marry Our Enemies? Sociology and the New Testament', *Interpretation* 36 (1982), pp. 256–65, on p. 259.
9. Elliott, *Home*, p. 3.
10. cf. J. H. Schütz's introduction in Theissen, *Social Setting*, p. 15: 'It would seem fair to characterize his [Theissen's] interests as more those of the social historian than those of the sociologist.'

11. In the modern discussion, especially in the work of those who are anxious to present the 'social' emphasis as something new in New Testament study, the word 'social' is implicitly often taken rather narrowly, and hence perhaps unhelpfully. cf. also n. 13 below.
12. cf. also the remarks made by G. Theissen at the start of his famous 'Wanderradikalismus' article, originally published in *ZThK* 70 (1973), pp. 245–71, and reprinted in his *Studien zur Soziologie des Urchristentums* (Tübingen 1979), pp. 79ff.
13. 'Social' and 'ideological' are not always easily separable. Ideological/religious differences probably had far greater social effects in the first century than they do today in a twentieth-century western pluralist society. Certainly the 'ideological'/religious division between Jew and non-Jew had very real *social* consequences.
14. cf. Meeks, *Urban Christians*, pp. 57–8.
15. In fact the continuity and firm links between modern sociological studies and older form criticism is fully recognized by some: see Schütz in Theissen, *Social Setting*, p. 7; also Theissen's own essay 'Zur forschungsgeschichtlichen Einordnung der soziologischen Fragestellung', in his *Studien* (n. 12 above), pp. 3ff.
16. cf., for example, the claims of H. C. Kee, *Miracle in the Early Christian World*, and the discussion on pp. 47–8 above.
17. Scroggs, 'Sociological Interpretation', p. 175. The sociological work to which reference is often made by New Testament scholars is P. Berger & T. Luckmann, *The Social Construction of Reality: A Treatise in the Sociology of Knowledge* (Harmondsworth 1967), though clearly their ideas have roots lying much further back within the field of academic sociology itself.
18. W. A. Meeks, 'The Man from Heaven in Johannine Sectarianism', *JBL* 91 (1972), pp. 44–72, on p. 70.
19. Scroggs, 'Sociological Interpretation', pp. 175–6. His italics.
20. See Gager, 'Shall We Marry Our Enemies?', referring to Meeks, 'Man from Heaven', G. Theissen, *The First Followers of Jesus* (London 1978), and Elliott, *Home*.
21. Scroggs, 'Sociological Interpretation', p. 176.
22. Malherbe, *Social Aspects*, p. 13.
23. cf. M. D. Hooker, *The Message of Mark* (London 1983), pp. 116–17.
24. Theissen, *Social Setting*, p. 187. Meeks, *Urban Christians*, ch. 6, is also much more cautious in his more recent book about deducing social conditions from the text than he may have been in his earlier article.
25. H. C. Kee, *Community of the New Age* (London 1977), p. 103. (I have omitted all the detailed references to Mark's text which Kee gives.)
26. Gager, 'Shall We Marry Our Enemies?', pp. 264–5. The last sentence is a quotation by Gager of P. Brown.
27. Unless it is that they question any absolute 'validity' of the text and relativize it: cf. Scroggs, 'Sociological Interpretation', p. 177.
28. Gager, *Kingdom*, pp. 37ff. For a powerful critique, see C. S. Rodd, 'On Applying a Sociological Theory to Biblical Studies', *JSOT* 19 (1981), pp. 95–106.

29. See D. Tidball, *An Introduction to the Sociology of the New Testament* (Exeter 1983), ch. 2 for a survey.
30. cf. Scroggs, 'Sociological Interpretation', p. 166.
31. R. Scroggs, 'The Earliest Christian Communities as Sectarian Movement', in J. Neusner (ed.), *Christianity, Judaism and Other Greco–Roman Cults* vol. ii (FS for M. Smith. Leiden 1975) pp. 1–23.
32. cf. Scroggs' statement, 'Earliest Christian Communities', p. 14: 'The pattern is, however, complex and not every part of the sequence is evidenced – *though it can be assumed*' (my italics).
33. This criticism does not apply to all New Testament critics who use sociological categories. See, for example, the recent studies on Paul by J. H. Schütz, *Paul and the Anatomy of Apostolic Authority* (Cambridge 1975) and B. Holmberg, *Paul and Power* (Philadelphia 1980); both authors refer to Weber's famous analysis of different kinds of authority (legal, rational, charismatic) to throw light on the nature of Paul's authority. Both are fully aware that Weber's categories are secondary abstractions and not descriptions of empirical realities, so that authority in any given situation may be a mixture of these categories.

10

The New Testament and Structuralism

So far, all the methods we have considered are, broadly speaking, part of the so-called historical-critical method. The New Testament texts have been taken as historical documents, stemming from a particular historical context; the various methods we have looked at have then been concerned to discover something about that context. Moreover, almost all these methods (with the possible exception of textual criticism) have implicitly assumed that there is something behind, or beyond, the actual text itself which the particular form of criticism aims to discover. This may be an historical event described, a feature of the life of the early Christian communities, the thought of the original author of the text, and so on. In all these cases the text itself is primarily regarded as of interest insofar as it acts as a window enabling us to see something or someone else beyond it.

Such an approach to the biblical texts has been challenged in recent years from a number of different directions, and the value of the historical-critical method (or methods) has been sharply questioned. Such attacks have not only come from the side of very 'conservative' Christian believers who would see all biblical criticism as subversive of the Christian faith. Rather, some of these questions have arisen from within the field of critical biblical scholarship itself; others have arisen on the basis of new movements in secular literary criticism. In the next two chapters we shall consider some of the ways in which the historical-critical approach can be questioned, and we start by looking at the method known as 'structuralism'.

Structuralist approaches to the New Testament tend to arouse strong reactions. Structuralism is not an easy method to understand, and structuralists can often be accused of presenting their work in a very confusing way, using a great deal of technical jargon as well as a plethora of diagrams and charts of ever-increasing complexity. We shall attempt in this chapter to look at the method of structuralism to see what it has to offer to the New Testament exegete, and what it is trying to do. In order to do this, we shall have to make a slight detour to discover something of what structuralism in general is all about, before we look at the question of how it can be related to study of the New Testament.

Structuralism is not in itself peculiar to the study of the Bible, or even to the study of literature. It is an approach, or a 'method', which is applicable to a wide range of disciplines including linguistics, anthropology, politics, mathematics and many other subjects as well. Indeed structuralism is applicable to any structured system and is basically concerned with the analysis of the structure of that system. However, such a vague and tentative definition of structuralism is probably meaningless until we fill this out in more concrete terms.

Fundamental to the whole approach of structuralism has been the work of F. de Saussure on linguistics, and this provides us with a useful starting point for seeing what structuralism is all about.[1] Saussure's theories are based on a number of claims about the nature of any language. First, he argued that language involves a series of 'signs' implying relationships between words and what the words refer to. Moreover, the relationship between a word and an object is *arbitrary*. There is nothing inherent in the ordered combination of the three letters d–o–g which necessarily determines that the word so formed must refer to a dog. Indeed in France it does not: the object referred to there is signified by a quite different collections of letters, c–h–i–e–n. The rule whereby the letters d–o–g in England refer to a certain kind of four-legged animal is thus a purely conventional one (though the convention is now firmly fixed).

A second basic insight of Saussure's, which follows from the first, is that meanings of words are determined by their relationships with other words in the set of conventions which forms the language. Words do not have any inherent meaning in themselves: they only acquire meaning in their relationships with other words. Moreover, these relationships can be of two kinds: a word can be related to other words *with* which it is used; it is also implicitly related to other words which are *not* used but which could have been used instead. (The technical terms for these relationships are syntagmatic and paradigmatic respectively.)

We have already seen some examples of meanings of words (especially of words which can have a variety of meanings) being determined by their syntagmatic relationships with other words in a phrase or sentence. (See pp. 42f above.) As examples of the second category, there are various words or phrases whose meaning would only be clear if we knew what the alternatives were which had *not* been used. For example, what do I mean if I say that 'I drove my wife round the bend'? Things might be rather clearer if I said what I did not do. Did I not stop the car before the bend (to save her having to walk an extra twenty yards), or did I not enable her to remain sane? Another stock example is the instruction: 'Only gym-shoes should be worn.' The instruction is plain, but to know its full meaning involves knowing what is excluded: is the instruction forbidding other kinds of footwear, or is it banning all other clothes?

Saussure's basic thesis is thus that meaning in language is not inherent in words themselves. Words are simply signs and their meaning depends on an underlying system of conventions and relationships. Saussure thus distinguished between what he called *langue* as the underlying system, and *parole* as the individual instances where the language is used in actual speech.

Further, given the fact that words only have meaning because of arbitrary conventions, much more stress should be laid on the study of words in their present usage to determine their meanings, rather than on their past history by studying their etymology. (The technical words of these different approaches to the study of language are synchronic and diachronic respectively.)

If the meaning of words is determined by relationships with other words, then the origin of words is largely irrelevant. Thus arguments based on the etymology of words are potentially misleading for determining the meanings of words in the present. (A standard example is the English word 'hussy' which derives etymologically from 'housewife'. Yet no official form today asks married ladies with no paid job to put down their occupation as 'hussy'!)[2]

A good parallel, which was used by Saussure himself to illustrate many of these points about the nature of language, is the game of chess. Chess has various rules which determine how individual pieces on the board may move: bishops may only move diagonally, only knights may jump over other pieces, and so on. These rules are really quite arbitrary. There is no inherent difference between queens and kings in real life which determines that queens are more mobile creatures than kings. The rule that a queen can move any number of squares at a time, whereas a king moves only one square at a time, is thus purely conventional. The whole set of rules of the game of chess corresponds to the *langue* of a language. Individual moves of specific pieces in a game correspond to the *parole*. Further, in the middle of a game of chess, all that matters is the current position of the pieces on the board. How that position has been reached, its 'etymology', is immaterial. All that matters is the situation at the present and the rules that govern the game.

Now in general terms the study of meaning in a language will involve study of the underlying *structure*, the *langue*, which determines the rules for 'playing the game' of using the language. It is this sense of the word 'structure' that is implied in the word 'structuralism'. Structuralist linguistics is thus a study of the underlying 'ground rules' of a language which enable individuals to use that language and to be understood by others. For example, it would involve a study of why the collection of words 'I walked to the shops' is an unambiguous sentence in English, 'I shot the lights' is ambiguous (did I fire a gun, or simply go past a red one?), and 'dogs shop walked the I' makes no sense at all.

Saussure's work was concerned with the study of language but his insights extend far beyond the field of linguistics alone. Language is a system of signs where all the signs are words. But signs can be other than verbal. Indeed a vast range of social activities and social phenomena are 'signs'. Moreover, the meaning of the vast majority of such signs has no inherent relationship to nature: rather they are purely arbitrary and determined by the social conventions of the culture.

Eating habits are an example of this. At one level one presumably eats three meals a day (if one does) to satisfy the pangs of hunger and to provide a diet which is conducive to health. But the actual content of each meal has become stereotyped. 'Toast and marmalade' has become standard fare as part of the English breakfast. There is no inherent reason why hunger has to be satisfied at the first meal of each day by eating these particular items of food. The connection between 'toast and marmalade' and 'breakfast' is thus a purely arbitrary one, being part of the conventions and patterns of eating habits in England.[3]

Clothing and fashion constitute another example of a set of somewhat arbitrary conventions in a society, though in this case, the conventions can change dramatically almost every year. The sign nature of a whole range of social phenomena means that these phenomena can readily be examined by a structuralist approach, looking at the underlying set of conventions, relationships and structures in the society which gives the various signs their meaning.

The extension of a structuralist approach to the field of social anthropology is associated above all with the work of C. Lévi-Strauss. Lévi-Strauss' work has been concentrated on the study of myth as well as other social phenomena. There is not enough time or space here to consider Lévi-Strauss' work on myth in any detail;[4] but one feature of his theories should be mentioned as it will crop up later in the discussion, and that is the notion of 'binary opposites'. Lévi-Strauss claims that many myths use pairs of elements which are opposite to each other: fire is opposed to water, human to divine, raw food to cooked food, and so on. The parallel in Saussure's theory of linguistics is the notion of a paradigmatic relationship: 'white' is opposite to 'black', so that the 'white knight' is in a paradigmatic relationship to the 'black knight'.

In practice such relationships are not always easily reducible to one element and just one opposite. At the level of language, the phenomenon of ambiguity means that one word or phrase may have more than one opposite. The opposite of 'white' is 'black' when discussing chess pieces, but 'red' when discussing wine. At the level of myth, the opposite of 'human' may be 'divine' in one context, 'inhuman' or 'animal' in another. Nevertheless, given a particular context, the notion of pairs of opposites can be a very useful one to bring to bear in the analysis.[5]

So far we have looked at structuralist approaches to the study of language and briefly in the field of social anthropology. It may now be a little clearer how and why the same process of analysing the underlying structure of a system might be applied to the study of literature. Insofar as literature functions as a form of communication using 'signs', it may then be based on sets of underlying conventions and rules which determine how individual pieces of literature may be produced. Thus a structuralist approach to literature is concerned with the study of the underlying 'structure', or 'code', which enables individual literary texts to be generated. (One should, however, distinguish between the 'structure' which is of concern to a structuralist, and the surface 'structure' of a piece of literature, its style and how the various parts fit together. The latter is of no concern to structuralism as defined here.)

One of the earliest works seeking to apply such insights to bodies of literature was that of V. Propp on Russian folk tales.[6] Propp analysed a large number of folk tales and showed that although the plots of individual stories varied amongst themselves, nevertheless the roles played by the individual characters of the story could be reduced to a finite number of fixed roles or functions. (Propp suggested thirty-one such roles.) Although not every function would take place in every folk tale, nevertheless the functions which were used would always be identifiable as coming from the basic list. The 'structure' of the folk tale could thus be isolated: the thirty-one basic roles provided the 'rules' or the 'code' which then generated individual folk tales.

Propp's work was developed further by A. J. Greimas who also introduced some notions of binary opposition into the system.[7] Greimas reduced Propp's basic functions to twenty in number. He also proposed an alternative model for analysing the structure of stories. He argued that each story can be conceived of as a 'plot' whereby a 'sender' wishes to communicate some 'object' to a 'receiver'. (Hence 'sender' and 'receiver' constitute a binary pair.) The sender initiates action in order to achieve this aim. The 'plot' of getting the object to the receiver is sustained by the action of the 'subject' who may be assisted or hindered by various 'helpers' or 'opponents' respectively. Diagrammatically this is represented as:

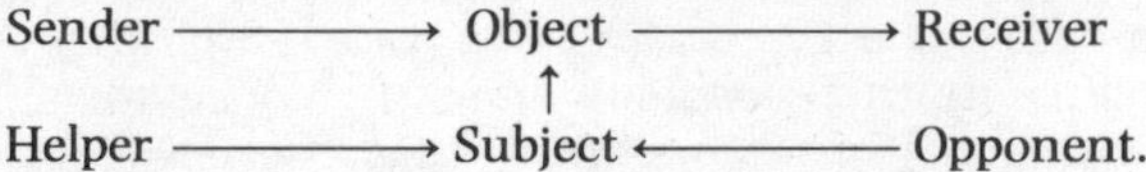

This is what has been called an 'actantial model', where each of the six poles on the grid represents an 'actant' of the story. (An 'actant' is not necessarily the same as an 'actor' – actants may well be inanimate objects. Further, the actual characters of the story might fulfil none, or more than one, of these roles. However, the purpose of the grid is not to analyse an individual story but to consider the underlying structure of the story form.) As an example, the parable of the Good Samaritan (Luke 10.30–35) could be analysed via this grid as follows:[8]

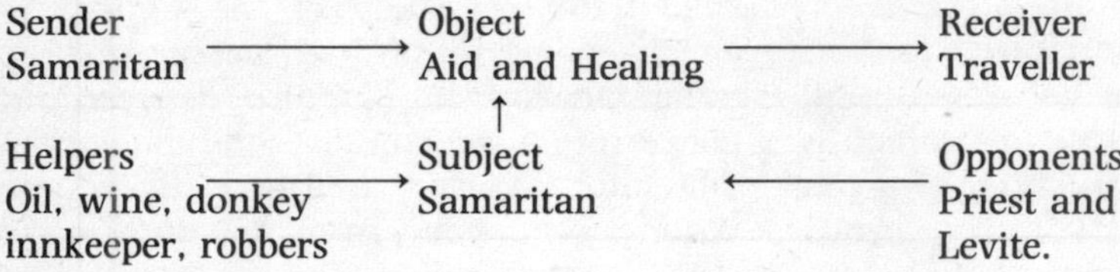

It must be emphasized that such analyses are not *per se* aimed at providing 'the meaning' of the individual story. Structuralist analysis is much more concerned with analysing how individual stories have meanings, rather than with identifying a particular meaning in an individual story. It is concerned with 'showing *how* texts "make sense", that is, what are the "mechanisms" through which a text is meaningful'.[9] The situation is thus analogous to that in linguistics, where structuralist approaches aim not to determine what individual words mean, but to show what users of the language know innately about the rules governing the use of the language.

An example frequently cited in this context is part of the analysis of the story of Jacob wrestling with the angel (Gen. 32.22–32) by the famous structuralist literary critic R. Barthes.[10] Barthes uses Greimas' actantial model to show that in this particular story, the 'sender' or 'originator' of the task in hand (Jacob's crossing the river) turns out to be the same as the 'opponent': thus in the story

God fills both roles. It is this unexpected duality in roles, whereby God appears to frustrate his own ends, which gives the story its power and strangeness as a story.

In general terms it should be noted that structuralism claims to be basically unconcerned with the problems which are usually of interest in the more traditional historical-critical approach. The identity of the author of a text is regarded as irrelevant: what is important is the *text* and what is to be analysed is the text itself rather than any hypothetical ideas of an original author. (In this, therefore, structuralists join forces with the so-called 'New Criticism' movement in literary criticism;[11] we shall look at possible implications of the latter for biblical criticism briefly in the next chapter.)

Further, structuralism is basically atemporal in its approach. Just as Saussure stressed the importance of a synchronic, as opposed to a diachronic, approach to the study of language, so literary structuralists would argue that they are not interested in the history of the tradition which culminated in the present text. The text is taken as an entity in its own right, independent of its history, and is worthy of analysis as it stands.

Before proceeding further, it may be worth distinguishing between structuralism as a full-blown ideology and a more limited use of structuralist methods to analyse individual texts.[12] The former approach would argue that the meaning of individual texts is really wholly determined by the rules and conventions of the underlying system.[13] Meaning is thus a product of the structured system, and the identity of the original author is quite irrelevant. The other approach would be less dogmatic. It would appeal to the methods and tools which structuralism uses to analyse a text or a structure; but it would be prepared to allow these to supplement other, more traditional, ways of looking at the text.

How are we to evaluate structuralist approaches to the New Testament? For many, the use of structuralist methods to interpret biblical texts appears strange, bizarre and of little value. Others have welcomed these methods as liberating New Testament studies from the straitjacket laid on the discipline by the historical-critical method. Since it is probably fair to declare one's hand, I must confess to being one who has a number of doubts about what I have called full-blown structuralist ideology applied to the study of literature; but a moderate use of a structuralist-type analysis may well enable us to enter more deeply into a text. Others will no doubt disagree, but the following methodological observations are offered here for what they are worth.

Structuralist approaches to literature are quite explicitly based on structuralist approaches to language, as we have seen. Just as the meaning of language is allegedly determined by the relationships within the system, so it is claimed, the meaning of literature is determinable by the structure of an underlying system. Now it would be foolish to deny *a priori* that this is the case, and in fairly general terms there may be a lot to be gained by considering literature on the basis of the analogy with language. However, there is a real question here of how exact this analogy can possibly be.

A favourite term within structuralism is 'competence'. A person who has 'linguistic competence' is one who knows the rules and system of a language, knows how to form real sentences, knows (intuitively perhaps) that some collocations of words are nonsense, and so on. Can one speak of literary competence in precisely the same way? Certainly we can in general terms. We can think of a general kind of competence which enables us to make sense of the collection of sentences which make up a whole text being considered. We can also conceive of a competence which enables us to understand Shakespeare, or poetry, at a level deeper than simply understanding the grammar of each individual sentence. Indeed we have already looked at this (although I did not use the word 'competence' itself) when considering the questions of genre and form: a knowledge of the genre gives us the 'competence' to be able to interpret a wisdom-type saying like 'Consider the lilies of the field' in the New Testament as something other than a call at the start of a botany field day.

Difficulties arise when we try to press the analogy between language and literature further than this. For example, a structuralist approach to language will claim (with some justification) that there is an innate competence which can say that the sequence of words 'dogs shop walked the I' is a meaningless sentence in English. It is difficult to conceive of a parallel situation in literature in general. What would count as disobeying the 'rules' of 'literature'?

One possible answer is given by J. Barton in his discussion of Propp's analysis of the folk tale:

> . . . no one would have the slightest hesitation in denying the name 'folk-tale' to a version of *Red Riding Hood* in which the woodcutter freed the wolf, shot the grandmother and married Red Riding Hood. It will come as no surprise that Propp's rules declare such a plot to be impossible – indeed, it will come as a relief.[14]

At one level this is true. But in what sense could such a story be 'impossible'? It is of course a highly unusual form of a folk tale – indeed it would be unique (if Propp's analysis is correct). It would thus have difficulty claiming a place within the specific genre 'folk tale'. But it is still a tale, or story, and nothing in Propp's analysis can possibly deny that.

Thus it may well be that a great deal of structuralist analysis is in fact not very different from genre analysis or form criticism.[15] For the 'competence' which excludes the variation of the Red Riding Hood story as 'impossible' is not a competence in 'literature' in general, but a competence in one particular genre/form within the body of all literature. The 'impossibility' of this version of Red Riding Hood lies in the fact that the version cannot belong to a particular genre, rather than its having an impossible plot in the same way as 'dogs shop walked the I' is an impossible English sentence.

Such an overlap between a structuralist and a form-critical approach should not however surprise us. We have already seen that structuralism is not in itself a method by which we can determine the meaning of a text. Rather, it is a way of showing *how* stories have meanings. At the level of language, we know what sentences mean, and structuralism tries to explain why that meaning is what it is. So too with literature, we may know intuitively what the meaning of a text is, and whether a story belongs to a particular form or genre. Structuralism than tries to analyse more precisely how we have arrived at these intuitive results. We shall see another instance of this overlap between structuralism and form criticism when we look at the story of the healing of the man with the withered hand.

Another important issue raised by structuralism is how far we can determine the meaning of a text solely on the basis of its form and structure. Some structuralists, especially those who would espouse what I have called a full-blown structuralist ideology, appear to claim that the meaning of a text can be determined in this way. It is however doubtful if such a claim can be sustained.

One example which tells against such a theory is that of irony. As E. D. Hirsch says:

> Possible irony is not a special case, only a particularly telling one (like possible allegory) that exemplifies the potential plurisignificance of all word-sequences. Irony is particularly convenient because its presence or absence changes nothing in the text except its fundamental meaning.[16]

Thus although the form and structure of a text can remain constant, the meaning can change drastically depending on whether the text is meant ironically or not. Hirsch cites the case of D. Defoe's work *The Shortest Way with Dissenters?*, which appeared to argue with all seriousness that all dissenters should be hanged. Defoe himself was a dissenter and it is quite clear that the text was not meant 'literally' (though it was taken so by some at the time!). It is thus extremely dubious to claim with 'full-blooded' structuralism that all texts can be interpreted on the basis of their underlying structure.

This raises the further question of how far we can ignore all questions of history and authorship in the interpretation of a text. As we have seen, structuralism tends to bracket off the question of authorship in order to concentrate on the text alone. This whole problem of the importance of authorship is an enormous one, and it cannot be adequately discussed in a few paragraphs here. We shall return to this question again in the next chapter too, but some attempt must be made here to say something about the topic.

It would seem (at least to one non-structuralist!) that we cannot bracket off the question of authorship totally in seeking to interpret a text. To take an illustration at a very naive level, we must know the language in which a text is written: if we come across the collection of letters p–a–i–n, we must know whether this is intended to be French or English, whether the word is referring to something to eat or to an unpleasant sensation of some kind.

We have also seen that the same words may have very different meanings when used by different people (see p. 43 above).[17] Moreover, everything that Saussure said about the importance of synchronic study of language is perfectly valid: the meaning of a word derives from its use in the present, not from its past history. But it is still the case that languages change with time. We have already seen this by implication: for example, 'hussy' and 'housewife' were at one time the same word but now have very different overtones. It then may be a matter of some importance to know something about the state of the language at the time when a text was written, and so we must know something about the historical situation of the author. At the very least, if a writer says that 'Elizabeth is a hussy', we shall need to know something of the author's historical situation to know if he is giving a neutral description of Elizabeth's occupation as a housewife or making a pejorative slur on her character! Thus not all historical considerations can be banished from the scene in interpreting a text.[18] Not even the strongest opponents of the 'intentionalist fallacy'[19] would deny that words can have identifiable meanings and that these meanings may be dependent in some respects on the identity of the author.

In fact it would appear that the importance of knowing something of the author is implicitly accepted by most structuralist critics. Consider, for example, the question of what text can appropriately be analysed by the methods of structural analysis. In theory any text could be analysed in this way. Any collection of sentences constitutes a text which is then worthy of analysis in its own right. It must be admitted that some structuralist critics accept this; they will take any text as the object of analysis, or they may even argue that the analysis itself determines the contours of the text. Beauchamp's analysis of the creation story in Genesis 1, for example, finds a deep structure in Genesis 1.1–2.1, which is not a passage that many would usually regard as a well-defined 'text'. (Most Old Testament scholars would see the creation account of Genesis 1 continuing until at least 2.4a.) But the deep structure found in this passage may be part of the justification for taking this set of verses as a unity, rather than, say, Genesis 1.1–2.4.[20]

Nevertheless, in practice most structuralists assume that a text which can properly be analysed structurally should be a unified text in some sense or other. For example, the Gospel of Matthew could be analysed structurally; so could the parable of the Good Samaritan. But a text consisting of Matthew's twenty-eight chapters followed by the first chapter of Mark's Gospel would not, I think, generally be regarded as a 'text' worthy of analysis by a structuralist critic. Nor would the first thirteen lines of a sonnet. Most would accept that a text which is capable of being analysed structurally should be a unity, and that some consideration of authorial intent is an important factor in determining whether there is such a unity or not. Thus if an author wrote a fourteen-line sonnet, we should respect his intentions and not cut out the last line before analysing the resultant 'text'.

These somewhat negative remarks made so far apply to what I called a 'full-blown' structuralist ideology applied to literature. This is not to say, however, that other 'structuralist' approaches (in a looser sense of the word) have nothing to contribute to New Testament studies. By its very nature structuralism aims to bring to the surface and clarify what is intuitively perceived anyway, and this can sometimes be very helpful. At other times the use of a structuralist approach can highlight more clearly the distinctive nature of a particular text.

Take for example the work of J. D. Crossan, who is one of the ablest proponents of these new methods and who has contributed an enormous amount to the study of the parables of Jesus. Crossan is no full-blooded structuralist in the sense of being uninterested in the author of the texts he is considering: he is very concerned to rediscover the parables *of Jesus.*

In his study *Finding is the First Act*[21] Crossan takes the parable of the treasure in Matthew 13.44, and compares it with an enormous number of similar folk tales which have to do with finding treasure. His method of reducing to order the apparent chaos of a vast number of tales from a wide variety of times and cultures is that of a 'structuralist' approach, in a loose sense. He separates the various motifs in the stories into a series of binary opposites: hiding treasure/not hiding treasure; seeking/not seeking; finding/not finding.

By reducing the various stories to these component parts, Crossan is able to show precisely where Jesus' parable breaks new ground: the man who finds a treasure in someone else's field, and buys the field without telling the original owner that the treasure is there, is generally regarded as reprehensible. Jesus' parable, which presents such an action in positive terms, is thus strikingly original in its application of the stock themes used so prominently in folk tales about finding treasure.

Here the analysis into binary opposites, whereby a vast range of related stories can be easily compared, is extremely useful and can be highly suggestive for the interpretation of the story. Nevertheless, it must also be said that such an analysis is only making a relatively limited use of structuralist methods. It is still, for example, maintaining a firm interest in the intention of the original 'author' of the parable, as Crossan goes on to appeal to other parables of Jesus to support his interpretation of this particular parable.

A full-blown structuralist approach has a more limited aim, but is not thereby valueless. It helps us to see more precisely why we give certain interpretations and meanings to texts. It can clarify certain issues for us, but it will not usually generate new meanings of the text. Its abiding value for any student of literature is that it focuses attention on the text. It reminds us, at times forcibly, that study of literature involves study of a text, even if we may often wish to move beyond or behind the text to something else.

Provided then that we bear in mind the methods, aims and limitations of structuralism, and provided too that we can develop a healthy scepticism about the value of complex charts and a battery of neologisms, we can learn from this discipline and accept its value for us. Its scope will however be a limited one. We should not expect new meanings of a text to emerge from structuralist analyses. Indeed if we learn nothing new, that will be some confirmation of the appropriateness of the analysis. Structuralism should be explaining what we 'know' already and clarifying how and why we do so. A structuralist approach which suggests meanings in a text which nobody has ever seen before might be rather suspect.[22]

Mark 3.1–6 and Parallels

We shall now try to give a structuralist analysis of the story of the healing of the man with the withered hand, which has functioned as a test passage throughout this book. We have already seen that the story has a different slant in each of the three Gospels, so that structuralist analyses of each version might be different. In order not to take up too much space here we shall confine our attention to Mark's version of the story. A discussion of this story along structuralist lines has already been given by P. Geoltrain, and what follows is in large measure a summary of his analysis.[23]

An actantial analysis of the story might well start with the theory that the plot of the story is centred on the action of Jesus or God wishing to heal the man's withered hand. The means by which this is achieved is Jesus and his power to heal, although this is opposed by the Pharisees and others, who question the legality of Jesus' doing such an action on the sabbath. The actantial diagram would thus be as follows:

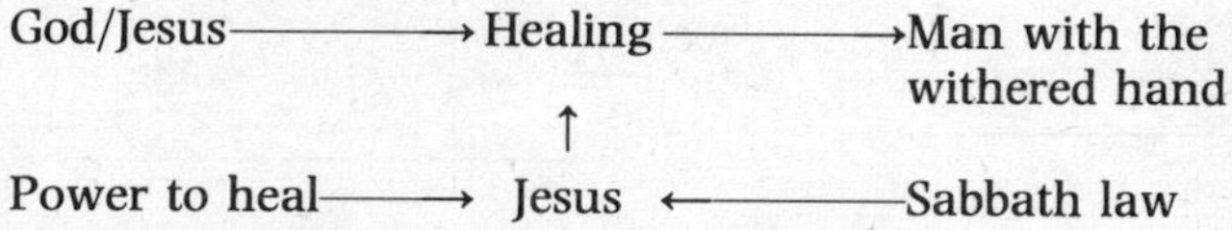

God/Jesus	⟶	Healing	⟶	Man with the withered hand
		↑		
Power to heal	⟶	Jesus	⟵	Sabbath law

Geoltrain points out that this does not really fit the text of Mark very well. The story as it now stands exhibits a number of elements which are in opposition to each other: Jesus is opposed by the Pharisees; Jesus goes into the synagogue (v. 1)/the Pharisees leave the synagogue (v. 6) (perhaps the 'synagogue' here symbolizes the place of the law); healing is opposed to keeping the sabbath; Jesus speaks to the Pharisees/they do not speak to him; the Pharisees watch Jesus (v. 2)/Jesus looks round at them (v. 5). All these (binary) oppositions suggest that the true 'plot' of the story is not primarily to bring healing to the man, but to establish something about the law. The oppositions are to do with Jesus and the Pharisees and their respective interpretations of, or attitudes to, the law. The man himself is almost a dumb actor. This suggests a different actantial model:[24]

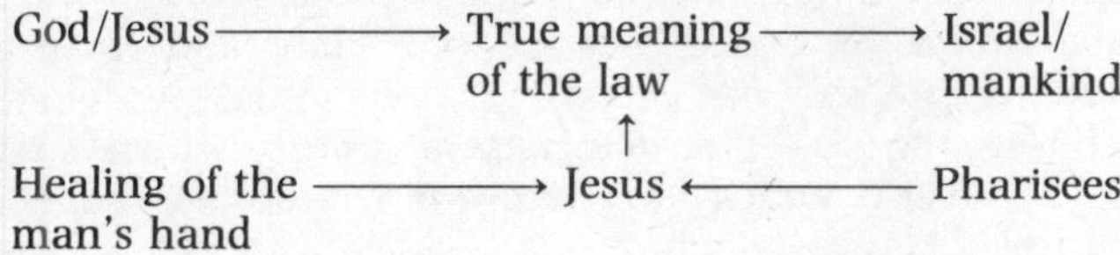

Now one could be forgiven for complaining that this is not very startling, and indeed not very new. The result of this analysis is virtually the same as what we claimed when considering the story from the point of view of form criticism, viz. that this story in the Gospels is not a 'miracle story' in terms of its form-critical category, but rather a pronouncement story or controversy story. The main point in Mark's account is not the miracle itself, but the dispute between Jesus and the Jewish authorities over the question of the law. The first actantial model we looked at would fit a 'miracle story', where the centre of attention is the miracle itself; the second model is that of a controversy story, where the central point of the story is a controversy about the law.

Such a duplication and repetition in our analysis should not however surprise us in the light of our general discussion earlier in this chapter. We saw there that structuralism is not really a method by which we achieve results in the interpretation of a text. Rather, it is a way of analysing the means by which a story has a particular meaning. (Cf. p. 156 above.) Moreover, we also saw that structuralism and form/genre criticism are very closely related. It is therefore not unexpected that the application of structuralist techniques to a particular story such as Mark 3.1–6 produces 'results' at the end of the day which overlap considerably with those of form criticism.

Where perhaps structuralism has something more to offer is in the fact that it tries to give more detailed justification for results which we would simply assume as self-evident in other contexts. As we have seen, the analogy in linguistics is that structuralist linguistics aims to explain how words and sentences can have the meanings which any user of the language in question knows intuitively. The situation is very similar here. When discussing Mark 3.1–6 from the point of view of form criticism, I simply stated that the story was not a (form-critical) 'miracle story' but a controversy story, and hoped that this was obvious. The structuralist approach seeks to analyse precisely why this 'obvious' fact is the case (if indeed it is!). By considering the binary oppositions in the text, it shows how the text is structured and enables us to see precisely why and how the plot of the story is centred on the law and not on the healing.

The fact that this approach does not offer anything new is not only something of a relief but also a justification for the application of the method. Structuralist approaches should not generally be imposing new meanings on a text, but simply explaining how and why a text has the meaning which readers with some literary 'competence' have already discerned intuitively.

Notes

1. F. de Saussure, *A Course in General Linguistics* (ET, London 1959).
2. For further discussion of this issue in relation to older word-studies of key biblical words, see J. Barr, *The Semantics of Biblical Language* (Oxford 1961).
3. cf. K. Leach, 'Structuralism in Social Anthropology', in D. Robey (ed.), *Structuralism: An Introduction* (Oxford 1973), pp. 37–8.
4. Useful discussions can be found in K. Leach, *Lévi-Strauss* (London 1970); also J. Rogerson, *Myth in Old Testament Interpretation* (Berlin 1974), pp. 101–27.
5. Though it must be said that some of Lévi-Strauss' actual pairs are at times fanciful: cf. Rogerson, *Myth*, pp. 106–7.
6. V. Propp, *Morphology of the Folk-Tale* (ET, Austin 1968).
7. A. J. Greimas, *Sémantique structurale* (Paris 1966).
8. cf. D. Via, 'Parable and Example Story: A Literary–Structuralist Approach', *Semeia* 1 (1974), pp. 105–33, esp. p. 112.
9. D. & A. Patte, *Structural Analysis. From Theory to Practice* (Philadelphia 1978), p. 10.
10. R. Barthes, 'La Lutte avec l'ange: analyse textuelle de Genèse 32.23–33', in R. Barthes & F. Bovon (eds.), *Analyse structurale et exégèse biblique* (Neuchatel 1971), pp. 27–40. ET in A. M. Johnson (ed.), *Structural Analysis and Biblical Exegesis* (Pittsburgh 1974), pp. 21–33. See the discussion by J. Barton, *Reading the Old Testament* (London 1984), pp. 116ff. I am greatly indebted to Barton's discussion of structuralism throughout this chapter. For a fuller discussion of Barthes' treatment of the Genesis story, see D. C. Greenwood, *Structuralism and the Biblical Text* (New York & Amsterdam 1985), ch. 3.
11. cf. Barton, *Reading the OT*, pp. 181ff., who points out some of the similarities, as well as the differences, between structuralism and the New Criticism.
12. cf. A. C. Thiselton, 'Structuralism and Biblical Studies: Method or Ideology?', *ExpT* 89 (1978), p. 329–35, appealing to Ricoeur; also Barton, *Reading the OT*, pp. 133ff., who distinguished 'structuralist dogma' and 'structuralist style'.

13. cf. also Lévi-Strauss' theories in the field of social anthropology about the universal meaning of myths.
14. Barton, *Reading the OT*, p. 116.
15. The links between the 'new' structuralism and older form criticism are well brought out by N. R. Petersen, 'On the Notion of Genre in Via's "Parable and Example Story: A Literary–Structuralist Approach"', *Semeia* 1 (1974), pp. 134–81: e.g. p. 154: 'Even though the word "structuralism" was only coined by the Prague school in 1934, the thing to which the word referred had been around for some time' (i.e. in the work of the form critics). Cf. also Barton, *Reading the OT*, p. 116.
16. E. D. Hirsch, *The Aims of Interpretation* (Chicago & London 1976), p. 23.
17. cf. also Barton, *Reading the OT*, p. 173, who, referring to a story of J. L. Borges, cites the example of what can happen when words of an ancient text (Cervantes' *Don Quixote*) are repeated verbatim 300 years later as the words of someone in the twentieth century. The result is an enormous change in meaning.
18. So also Thiselton, 'Structuralism and Biblical Studies', p. 334, referring to Wittgenstein.
19. The 'intentional fallacy' is the (allegedly mistaken) belief that the meaning of a text can be identified with the author's intended meaning. See the classic essay of W. K. Wimsatt & M. C. Beardsley, 'The Intentional Fallacy', *The Sewanee Review* 54 (1946), reprinted in W. K. Wimsatt, *The Verbal Icon: Studies in the Meaning of Poetry* (Lexington 1954), pp. 3–17. For a robust reply, see E. D. Hirsch, *Validity in Interpretation* (New Haven & London 1967), ch. 1. We shall look again at the whole question of authorial intention in the next chapter.
20. See P. Beauchamp, *Création et Séparation* (Paris 1969), discussed by Barton, *Reading the OT*, pp. 122ff.
21. J. D. Crossan, *Finding is the First Act* (Philadelphia & Missoula 1979).
22. cf. also J. Culler, *Structuralist Poetics* (London 1975), esp. pp. 68, 74. Culler's book is a very valuable discussion of structuralist approaches to literature in general.
23. P. Geoltrain, 'La violation du Sabbat: Une lecture de Marc 3, 1–6', *Foi et Vie* 69 (1970), pp. 70–90.
24. A very similar model is also suggested by D. Via, *Kerygma and Comedy in the New Testament* (Philadelphia 1975), p. 132.

11
Other Approaches

In the last chapter we considered one alternative, structuralism, to the more traditional, historical-critical approach to interpreting the New Testament. In this chapter we shall look at other ways in which the historical-critical method has been questioned in recent study. In particular we shall look at approaches which have questioned the value of being concerned primarily with the author's original meaning in interpreting a text.

In the more traditional, historical approaches to New Testament study, it has generally been assumed, almost without question, that the meaning of a text is the original author's intended meaning. It is true that there has always been ambiguity in interpreting a text like a Gospel. A saying of Jesus recorded by Mark, say, could be interpreted in terms of Jesus' intended meaning, or Mark's; but in either case, the 'meaning' implied is that intended by a historical figure of the past. In the case of texts like the Pauline letters, there is no such ambiguity. The meaning of Paul's letter to the Romans is assumed to be Paul's intended meaning.

Such an approach to the New Testament texts is however not the only possible one. Many of us are aware, intuitively perhaps, that the original meaning of a text may not be the only possible 'meaning' which a text can have. The very word 'meaning' itself has a variety of nuances. For example, we may be able to recognize that the 'meaning' of the lists of genealogies in 1 Chronicles 1–8 is quite clear at one level. The text 'means' that A was the father of B, C, D and so on. However, at another level, we may say that the text 'means' nothing to us. It is no longer meaningful in the sense of having any contemporary relevance. It has become a 'dead letter'.

Other ancient texts often 'come alive' as they are seen to have new 'meaning' and relevance for contemporary situations. We may think, for example, of Augustine's reading of Paul's words in Romans 13 ('not in revelling and drunkenness, not in debauchery or licentiousness, not in quarelling and jealousy, but put on the Lord Jesus Christ and make no provision for the flesh'), words which sparked off his conversion to Christianity (*Confessions* VIII.29).

Further, the meaning seen by a later reader may at times be tangential to the author's original meaning. Paul's words in Romans 13, for example, were not originally a plea to non-Christians to be converted. Such transference of meaning is of the essence of much Christian preaching. Very often in sermons, the preacher will take a biblical text and try to show that this text has meaning for the audience in the present. Moreover, preaching is not just exegesis. A sermon which simply expounded the thought of the original writer without relating it to contemporary concerns might well be regarded as a poor sermon. Many therefore wish to make a move from 'what a text meant' to 'what it means', and are aware that the two 'meanings' are not necessarily identical with each other.[1]

How important then is the concern, so characteristic of the historical-critical method, for discovering something about the original context of the biblical texts? Should the search for the author's intended meaning be the one that occupies all our attention? In this chapter we shall look at two ways in which such an approach can be questioned, firstly from the side of 'canonical criticism', and secondly from the side of what I have called here 'literary criticism'.[2]

Canonical Criticism

In the first chapter we looked at some of the more theological issues raised by the claim that the New Testament texts constitute a canon of Scripture for the Christian Church. We also saw that, in some contexts, the limits of the canon are ignored entirely (see p. 10 above). What though of those who respect those limits in some way or other? Does the canonical status of the New Testament make any difference to its interpretation? Can a Christian who accepts the New Testament as canonical Scripture come to an understanding of the meaning of the biblical text which differs from that of the person who is not a Christian? The assumption of most traditional historical interpretation of the New Testament has been that this is not the case. The meaning of the letter to the Romans, say, is Paul's intended meaning, and we should be able to discover this whether we ourselves are Christians, Buddhists or atheists.

There has, however, recently been a movement within biblical studies which would question such a traditional approach. This trend has come to be called 'canonical criticism' and, in the sense in which I shall use the term, is associated with the work of B. S. Childs and his supporters.[3] The Christian, it is claimed, accepts the

Bible as a canon of Scripture and this should affect the interpretation of the text itself. In particular, the Christian should not necessarily be tied to any 'original' meaning as established by the historical-critical method. Very often theories about the 'original context' of a biblical text are extremely uncertain and dependent on modern scholarly whims and fancies. The same also applies to modern theories of complex tradition-histories lying behind our present texts. However, the canon of the Christian Church does not consist of these modern theories. It consists of the texts themselves. Thus those who take the canon seriously should recognize its status by interpreting the biblical texts in their present form. They should also recognize that the canon provides not only a text but also a con-text within which the individual texts should be interpreted. This context is not necessarily that of the original author, and hence a rather different interpretation may arise; but this context of the canon should be taken seriously by all those who take the canon seriously.

As an example of the way in which canonical criticism operates, we may look at one of Childs' best-known examples, his interpretation of the ideas expressed about man in Psalm 8:[4]

> what is man that thou art mindful of him, and the son of man that thou dost care for him?
> Yet thou hast made him little less than God, and dost crown him with glory and honour.
> Thou hast given him dominion over the works of thy hands; thou hast put all things under his feet.

As they stand, these verses from the psalm are statements about the exalted position of man. The psalmist may have the creation story of Genesis 1 in mind, and he marvels at the uniquely privileged position which man occupies in relation to the rest of the world. However, a canonical perspective can note that the same words are adopted by the writer of Hebrews and applied to Jesus. The words 'son of man', which were used by the psalmist to mean 'man in general', now become a reference to one particular man, Jesus. Jesus is the one who is now crowned with glory and honour because of his obedience and suffering. Thus the wider context of the canon allows new depths of meaning to be read into the psalm. For the canonical critic, Jesus provides the key to interpreting just how man can be elevated to a position of glory: 'the way by which man attains his position of honor is through suffering and death'.[5] No one is suggesting that this is what the psalmist had in mind originally; but this view of man can be read into (or out of) the text when the canon provides the wider context of interpretation.

Childs' work has provoked a number of detailed discussions, and at times quite trenchant criticisms, from Old Testament scholars.[6] In the light of these fuller treatments, no comprehensive discussion of canonical criticism will be attempted here. Instead we shall offer just a few observations about this new approach, especially in the form it appears in in Childs' own work on the New Testament. Further, in order to keep the discussion within manageable limits, we shall concentrate on the work of canonical criticism as applied to the Pauline letters. This body of material provides a useful basis whereby we can look at the new approach critically (though different considerations might apply when looking at, say, the Gospels).

Firstly, it must be said that, however much is claimed for the value of the new approach, the results are often rather meagre. It is not always very clear how much difference, or at what level, Childs' approach makes to the actual interpretation of the detailed wording of the text. To illustrate this, let us look at the problem of pseudonymity in the Pauline corpus. Many commentators on Childs' work have pointed out that, however much similarity there may appear to be between canonical criticism and a highly 'conservative', or 'fundamentalist', approach, the two are very different. For example, Childs argues quite explicitly that several of the New Testament documents are pseudonymous. He claims that Ephesians and the Pastorals are probably not by Paul, since there are fundamental theological discrepancies between these letters and the genuine letters of Paul. Thus for Childs, the 'canonical Paul' is not the same as the 'historical Paul'. The latter is the Paul of history, about whom the pseudonymous letters provide no direct evidence at all. The 'canonical Paul' is the Paul of the canon, the 'Paul' who is the subject of the letters to the Romans and to the Ephesians. This Paul evidently had no historical existence, but, according to Childs, it is this Paul who is the norm and basis for a Christian faith which takes the canon seriously.

What is still not clear in Childs' work, however, is how one reconciles all the differences between the various letters, differences which have led many to argue that some letters are pseudonymous. If the difference in content between two letters is too great to attribute to the historical Paul, what sense or meaning is gained by attributing them to a 'canonical Paul'? At times Childs argues that these differences can be resolved. Thus in dealing with Ephesians (which he accepts as pseudonymous), he argues that the suggestion that ecclesiology has replaced Christology at the centre of the stage is quite wrong.[7] By this means the gap between the ideas of Ephesians and the ideas of the historical Paul is sharply reduced. However, such a claim has nothing to do with canonical criticism as such. All the arguments here are based on the 'original' meaning of the text of Ephesians itself. The case for Christology being just as dominant in Ephesians as elsewhere in Paul is being conducted precisely on the basis of the historical-critical approach.

What though of other differences between Ephesians and Paul? Many have argued that the eschatology of Ephesians is quite unlike Paul's (cf. p. 58 above). What then is the truly 'canonical' view of Paul's eschatology? Is the Christian who takes the canon seriously to believe that 'the night is far gone, the day is at hand' (Rom. 13.12), or that glory is to be given to God 'in the church . . . to all generations, for ever and ever' (Eph. 3.21), without apparently the embarrassing interruption of a parousia?

Elsewhere Childs does discuss the question of the eschatology of the 'canonical Paul' in his section on 2 Thessalonians. Childs argues that 2 Thessalonians is also pseudonymous, again because of its incompatibility with the thought of the real Paul. On the specific question of eschatology, Childs claims that a canonical view would regard the eschatology of 2 Thessalonians (with its detailed apocalyptic timetable) as 'holding in tension' the eschatology of 1 Thessalonians (with its expectation of an imminent parousia).[8]

No attempt is made to reconcile the two letters and they are rightly seen to be in some tension. But the tension is not resolved. Nor does a canonical approach tell us which view is to regarded as the dominant one and which is secondary to it. Is the truly canonical view that the end will come very soon (1 Thess.) or not for some time (2 Thess.)? This example of eschatology in the Pauline corpus is only one example of a more general phenomenon in relation to canonical criticism. The canonical approach does not tell us which parts of the canon are central and which provide the primary context against which the rest should be interpreted.[9]

The fact that no attempt is made to explain away the differences in the meaning of the individual texts suggests that, at one level at least, canonical criticism is still operating with the historical-critical method. Certainly the meaning of the individual words of the text are still determined by the historical-critical approach.[10] The Greek words of the Greek New Testament are still understood as words of first-century writers, using first-century language and presupposing first-century backgrounds. Childs' approach does not seem to be geared to providing a new meaning for the individual words of the text. Even in his example from Psalm 8, where the words 'son of man' are interpreted by the author of Hebrews as a reference to Jesus *qua* Son of Man, Childs does not suggest that the 'original' meaning of the psalm should be altered in this way. The psalmist used the phrase 'son of man' to mean 'man in general'. The use of the psalm in Hebrews 2 is then taken to provide a further meaning about the nature of man in general, not about a particular man.

Childs' approach seems to be attempting to provide a secondary synthesis of the New Testament (and Old Testament) texts via a rather broader sweep of the material concerned. The synthesis is attempted with the prior assumption that it will be possible to produce a coherent and reasonably self-consistent pattern from the various materials. In the case of the Pauline corpus, for example, the aim seems to be to produce a global 'theology' of all the letters attributed to Paul which is not self-contradictory and which is also in harmony with the rest of the New Testament. But the actual meaning of the individual words and smaller phrases is unaltered in this approach. Whether the whole enterprise is successful is another matter, but the starting point remains the basic historical-critical approach which is still used to determine what the individual words and sentences in the texts mean. It is thus difficult to see how the historical-critical approach can ever be fully given up in the work of canonical criticism.

One theme running through the work of canonical critics is that the canon is a 'good thing' and this method is appropriate above all for the Christian who accepts the status of the canon. This may be so, but it is also the case that in fact canonical criticism as such is religiously neutral. You do not have to be a Christian to be a canonical critic. The fact that the New Testament (or the Old Testament) is a canon can simply be taken as a given datum. Any text needs a context for interpretation, and canonical criticism decrees that that context shall be the canon of Christian (or Jewish) Scripture. We can then take this context, provided it is sufficiently well-defined,[11] and proceed to interpret the texts accordingly, quite irrespective of whether we think that this context has any religious value at all.[12] There is thus nothing inherently Christian about the work of canonical criticism.

However, it is still the case that most canonical critics are themselves believers who accept the canon in question as normative for their own beliefs. But even within the context of Christian faith, many will find the approach of canonical criticism rather unsatisfactory for a more theological reason. This unease arises from the nature of the authority of the canon which is implied here. Canonical criticism has an inherent tendency to resolve differences within the biblical tradition. All parts of the canon are to be seen as potentially harmonious and mutually supportive of each other. Moreover, this unified theology is presumed to be the work of those who produced the canon, or as it is sometimes stated more abstractly, the canonizing process. The canonizers, those who placed four Gospels next to each other, those who placed the Pastorals alongside Romans, those who supplemented Paul with James, are given a unique position of authority in this approach.

Such a model can be questioned at a number of levels. At the level of simple historical fact, it is hard to believe that the decision to place 2 Thessalonians or the Pastorals in the canon was a self-conscious act by which someone decided that the historical Paul was now to be replaced by a canonical Paul whose features were rather different. One suspects that life was rather more mundane: the Pastorals may have got into the canon partly because they were useful in some sectors of the Church (in combating 'heresy'), partly because it was simply assumed that they were by Paul. Ephesians was almost certainly accepted because it was thought to be Paul's own work; it was not canonized in order to provide a redefinition of 'Paul'. As we saw when we glanced at the history of the canon, the precise boundaries of the canon may have been more accidental than consciously thought out.

There is however a more fundamental problem about where authority is being located by the approach of canonical criticism. The authority now seems to be less the biblical text and more the canonizers working later in the Church's tradition (or if such people never existed, we should have to say the activity of an impersonal, albeit perhaps divinely inspired, canonizing process).

Many will find such a view of authority rather unsettling. The authority of Paul's letter to the Romans would not then be the authority of the text itself (despite the claim of canonical criticism to be interested primarily in the text alone); nor would it be the authority of Paul himself. The authority would be that of the later canonizers who placed Romans in the canon and provided it with a wider context of other Pauline letters (some of which Paul himself might have disowned), so that we can have as our norm a 'canonical Paul' who may be rather tamer than the turbulent individual of the first century. Moreover, this canonical Paul's thought is sufficiently incoherent for traditional historical critics to have suggested that he must have been so schizoid that he probably never existed (since the inconsistencies between the letters are too much to attribute to a single author)! Such a view of authority is not one that many will find easy to accept.

There is too the problem of how the New Testament can or should function as a norm. Most would argue that if the New

Testament is to be normative, it must be capable of being a critical norm.[13] The Bible should be capable of providing the basis by which later tradition in the Christian Church can be critically assessed. Such a view of the normative nature of Scripture would, I think, be shared by Catholic and Protestant alike. But this would seem to demand some use of the historical-critical method so that the meaning of Scripture can be determined independently of the Church's later use of Scripture.[14] The work of canonical criticism seems to turn the relationship between Scripture and tradition on its head. Far from Scripture being the sole arbiter of tradition (the traditional Protestant view), or Scripture and tradition being equal forces (the traditional Catholic view), Scripture here seems to be made subservient to a part of later ecclesiastical tradition.[15]

Even with the relatively lowly model for the role of Scripture which I suggested in the initial chapter, some sense of historical criticism is still required. I argued that Scripture is to be seen as the primary source of subsequent tradition, so that all later tradition is effectively an interpretation of the scriptural witness. But if this is to be used in any critical way, we shall need some means of testing whether later interpretations are valid or acceptable, and this will only be possible if we can determine the meaning of Scripture independently of tradition itself. We shall thus be driven back to the historical-critical method.

It is doubtful if canonical criticism can replace the traditional historical-critical approach.[16] Indeed, I have suggested that it incorporates this approach anyway. In making suggestions about how the various biblical witnesses can supplement each other in relation to broad themes (such as the place of man in God's creation), canonical criticism has a lot to offer. But this approach will always need the historical approach to determine the meanings of actual words and sentences before it attempts the larger synthesis. Canonical criticism can be extremely fruitful as a complement to traditional historical criticism. It is doubtful if it can ever replace totally the traditional approach, even for those who approach the biblical text from a standpoint of Christian commitment and who accept the Bible as in some sense a canon of Scripture.

'Literary' Criticism

The question of the importance of the author's original intention in the interpretation of a text is also raised by other approaches besides canonical criticism. In particular, the views of some literary critics of secular literature may be relevant here. Many such critics would argue that a literary text can have multiple meanings, and that concentration on the author's original meaning is an unjustified limitation to the critical task of understanding the *text*. A poem, for example, is an entity in its own right which can take on new depths of meaning quite independently of the poet's original intentions and thoughts at the time of writing the poem. Could the same considerations apply to the biblical texts?

As a possible example, let us take the well-known parable of the sheep and the goats (Matt. 25.31–46). Many historical critics argue that the parable 'originally' (or at least in Matthew's view) had nothing to do with charitable giving to the poor and needy as such. For Matthew, the recipients of the charitable actions concerned, 'these my brothers' (v. 40), were probably Christian missionaries; the parable is about responses to Christian missionaries, not about responses to basic human needs.[17] Nevertheless, the parable has fired Christian imagination, and many would regard it as incorporating the demand on the Christian today to act on behalf of the hungry and homeless, irrespective of the latter's colour, class or creed. *If* we decide that the original meaning of the parable was to do with giving support to Christian missionaries, what can we say of a claim that its meaning today concerns giving aid to the starving? Is such a meaning justifiable? Would a sermon which used this parable as a basis for a plea to give money to Christian Aid represent a legitimate or an illegitimate use of the parable?

Before we tackle this question, we should perhaps clarify the issues raised by the views of secular literary critics referred to just now. We have already considered aspects of this problem very briefly in our discussion of structuralism. I argued then that the author's intention was an important factor, at least at some levels, in interpreting a text. We generally respect the author's intended limits of his text, in that we accept that the text to be analysed is the whole text which the author produced. We also usually have regard for the author's historical circumstances, in that we respect that the words used in a text should be understood as words from the author's own situation. Words in the text of a nineteenth-century English author are usually interpreted as words of nineteenth-century English language. (See p. 160 above.)

There is however a further level at which the author's intention may become relevant, and this raises the question of how far insights from the study of secular literature can apply to the Bible. The basic problem is determining just what constitutes 'literature' in this context. Now this is an enormous topic, and no neat answers can be given. What is clear, however, is that when secular critics talk about 'literature' and the value or otherwise of determining the author's original intention, they are not talking about any text which has been set down in writing. 'Literature', in this context, is a much smaller body of material than the sum of all written texts. Quite how it should be defined is not certain, but we are all probably intuitively aware of the distinction which is involved here. T. S. Eliot's *Four Quartets* and Shakespeare's *King Lear* are one thing; a policeman's report of the position of the cars after a motorway crash, or the instructions of the Highway Code, are another. To say that a text can have different meanings, independent of the author's original intentions, may make sense for Eliot's work; it would be absurd, and indeed positively dangerous, to take an instruction from the Highway Code that all cars must stop at red traffic lights and regard it as a text where we can read our own meaning into an alleged use of vivid colour imagery!

There is clearly a difference here, though it is not always easy to specify precisely what it is. Take, for example, two modern discussions of the problem. Wellek and Warren argue that language in 'literature' is to be distinguished from scientific language and also from everyday language. 'Literature' narrowly conceived is not necessarily describing something apart from itself, as scientific language does; rather, it aims to evoke the senses and the imagination. Moreover, 'literature' is different from everyday language in that it deliberately and systematically sets out to exploit the imaginative use of language. They would also see it as crucial that 'literature' is primarily fictional. The reference in a work of 'literature' is not necessarily to any real object outside the written test itself.[18] E. D. Hirsch too would agree on the existence of a valid distinction between 'literature' narrowly conceived and other texts. He suggests as a definition: 'Literature comprises any linguistic work, written or oral, which has significant aesthetic qualities *when described in aesthetic categories*.'[19] This overlaps in part with Wellek and Warren's suggestions, but not entirely.

The fact that the definitions have inevitably to be rather imprecise means that it is not always clear whether a text should or should not be regarded as 'literature'. Indeed Hirsch's suggestion would imply that such a decision is not really an innate property of the text as such, but rather a decision of the interpreter. One can choose to interpret a text as literature by inquiring about its aesthetic qualities even though others may choose not to do so. Nevertheless, there is still a question whether such an approach is an appropriate one for the text concerned. It may be here that the author's intention becomes relevant once again. We may feel free to see ever-increasing depths of meaning in a poem because it is a poem; and we usually assume that it is a poem because the author intended to write a poem. We usually take sentences like 'Cars must stop at red traffic lights', or 'Smoking damages your health', quite differently. We do not let our imagination run free with symbolism and metaphor associated with redness or smoke. The reason is primarily that the original 'author's' intention in producing these sentences makes such an approach inappropriate or even farcical! We do then have respect for the author's intentions in many contexts.[20]

How do the New Testament texts fit into this understanding of 'literature'? It will be clear that hardly any parts of the New Testament can really be classed as 'literature' narrowly defined, according to at least one definition of the term. The New Testament texts are (mostly) not claiming to be fictional, for example. They include reports of what are claimed to be real events of history; they include statements about the activity of God which is regarded by the writers themselves as quite clearly non-fictional. These texts are then descriptive and referential in a way that 'literature' is perhaps not. We may then choose to regard the New Testament as if it were 'literature'. We can analyse the aesthetic qualities of the texts.[21] However, we shall have to be aware of what we are doing if we bracket off completely the question of what the text is referring to in the world outside itself. For we shall be ignoring the author's intention completely, at least at the level of the kind of writing he has produced.

There may however be one important class of texts in the New Testament which constitutes a special category in this connection. This is Jesus' teaching in parables. Quite clearly these are fictional stories which are intended to be evocative and to provoke the imagination to further reflection. C. H. Dodd's famous description of a parable was 'a metaphor or simile drawn from nature or common life, arresting the reader by its vividness or strangeness, and leaving the mind in sufficient doubt about its precise application to tease it into active thought'.[22] This is very similar to Wellek and Warren's description of 'literature'. It is thus at least possible that the parables could fruitfully be regarded as 'literature' narrowly defined.[23] Further, it is clear that the parables are capable of taking on multiple meanings. Certainly as a matter of history, they have given rise to a wide variety of interpretations.

This issue has recently been carefully analysed by M. A. Tolbert.[24] She shows that the parables function in a way very similar to metaphors, by setting up a comparison between a story and a reality. The full meaning of the parable emerges when this whole comparative scheme is made clear. However, the story on its own provides only one part of the scheme. The interpreter has to provide the other part. Thus different parables can have different meanings simply because they are placed in different contexts.

Thus to return to the parable of the sheep and the goats, the story may mean one thing in Matthew's Gospel where prime concern is for the persecuted Christian missionaries; in a contemporary situation of a sermon during Christian Aid week, the parable might signify something rather different. How can we assess whether new interpretations are legitimate? Tolbert suggests that one such criterion could be the legitimacy of the context itself. A parable read in the context of support for Nazi ideology could be regarded as illegitimate because the ideology itself is unacceptable.[25] In this sense then, the Christian Aid interpretation of the parable of the sheep and the goats could be regarded as acceptable on the grounds that giving aid to the starving is a worthwhile endeavour.

However, it would be dangerous to let such an approach to the study of the parables carry all before it. We saw that one factor in the decision to treat a text as 'literature' may be the author's intention. We generally respect the author's end product for what it is generically (poem, history, romance, rule-book or whatever). The parables do not in fact fall neatly into the category of 'literature'. Whether they go back to Jesus or the early Church, they were presumably created for a fairly well-defined purpose. They were not like poems, made up by the poet and left to literary critics to make whatever they like out of them. The parables *of Jesus* were part of his total preaching, other parts of which were quite clearly not in the form of imaginative literature. 'Come, follow me!', 'love your enemies', and 'turn the other cheek' are quite concrete ethical demands. They are not simply evocative phrases left floating in the air for the interpreter to make of them what he/she wills. It would thus seem dangerous to abstract the parables *of Jesus* from their original setting and to make them say almost what one wants them to say. If they are to be interpreted as the parables *of Jesus*, then some account must be taken of their original context to justify any alleged new interpretation, or new application, of them.

In all this, however, we must be aware of our own context as interpreters, of what we are doing with the text, and hence of what we can claim for the text. Quite clearly we can interpret a parable as we would a modern poem, even though Jesus never intended to produce a poem. If we do interpret a parable in this way we will achieve an interpretation of it. Where life becomes more problematic is over the question of what authority such an interpretation will have. In what sense can we say that such a reading of the parable is legitimate or appropriate? It is clearly legitimate within its own terms of reference, but can we say more?

The use of a biblical text in the context of Christian preaching is an example where a certain 'more' is implicitly being claimed. A sermon based on Matthew 25.31–46 to promote Christian Aid week may be claiming that a fairly 'literary' approach to the parable is appropriate not only within a guild of literary critics but also in producing a contemporary Christian ethic. The validity of this depends on whose, or what, authority is being claimed. By using the parable at all, the preacher may be claiming the authority of Jesus: 'Jesus said "do this", so we must do this' (to put it at its crudest). If this is indeed the authority structure implied, then a 'literary' approach is probably inappropriate, and we would have to stick to the 'original' meaning of the parable (insofar as we could discover this).

On the other hand, it could be argued that the authority structure is not necessarily quite like this. The New Testament texts provide a basic source and resource for the Christian Church. The words of the parables are deeply embedded in the Church's tradition and can be drawn on in a wide variety of contexts. Within the Church's tradition there is also a strong belief in certain values. We may thus be able to link values and parables via a more 'literary' approach to support a plea for the values concerned. Thus there is a firm belief today that giving aid to the starving is a fundamental Christian obligation. This could be based on a whole variety of reasons, some of which would include appeals to Jesus' teaching and his example, others would include appeal to direct Christian insight today (though that insight has also been formed and moulded from within the Christian tradition).

In this way an appeal to the parable of the sheep and the goats to support Christian Aid week could be seen as legitimate, even though it is recognized that this interpretation may not be the original meaning of the parable. In this way one could be arguing implicitly that such a message is congruent with the overall message of Jesus. One is then appealing to the parable as part of the tradition, and the authority is essentially that of the present Jesus, not the Jesus of the past. Put crudely, the claim might be 'Jesus says (present tense) "do this!"'

Some may feel uneasy with this approach. It is admittedly an attempt to steer a rather wobbly middle course between two extremes. One extreme view would argue that the only acceptable meaning of a parable is its 'original' meaning; the other would argue that a parable is a piece of 'literature' whose meaning is potentially completely open-ended. But the first view ignores the plain fact that people have found different meanings in the parables, some of which it would be hard to categorize as 'wrong'. The second view gives *carte blanche* to the interpreter and ignores the author's intention of the parables, and we have seen that authorial intention may be an important factor in determining what is 'literature'.

However, even if we are prepared to accept that a more 'literary' approach to the parables may be justified in some contexts, we shall still need the historical-critical approach to act as a check and a control on our suggestions. Above all, if we use such approaches in contexts where the text (and interpretation) are being given some authority (for example, in the context of preaching), if we appeal to the example of 'Jesus' to back up our interpretation, we shall have to respect the original preaching and meaning of Jesus' parables if the name Jesus is not to become a meaningless cipher. The parables *of Jesus* cannot be made to mean anything at all. If they are to have a meaning which is acceptably Christian, then they must show some positive links with the teaching of the pre-Easter Jesus (cf. p. 14 above). We can thus never rid ourselves of the necessity of applying historical methods to the study of the parables.

The upshot of this discussion is that the historical-critical method is and remains vitally important in interpreting the New Testament. For most of the New Testament, it is of fundamental importance in determining the meaning of the texts themselves. What texts like Romans, Hebrews, 1 Peter and the rest mean is what their respective authors meant, and in order to determine this we shall need the whole battery of support which the historical-critical method provides. In the case of narrative texts like the Gospels, there is more scope for variety in meaning since there are at least two historical contexts involved: there is the context of the author of the text, and there is the context of the events being described. But whichever level we choose to look at, most would usually respect the historical nature of the contexts concerned. In the case of the parables, there may be more of a case to be made for the historical approach being not the only way to look at the text. But even here, the historical nature of the text will still have to be respected if my argument above has any value.

We have looked at two possible ways in which the historical approach to the New Testament has been questioned. In both cases, I would argue, the historical-critical approach cannot be jettisoned completely. It remains an integral part of New Testament study, whether such study is undertaken from a purely historical point of view or from a more religious standpoint which accepts the texts studied as in some sense foundational for religious faith.

Notes

1. For a classic statement distinguishing these two 'meanings', see the article of K. Stendahl, 'Biblical Theology', *Interpreter's Dictionary of the Bible* vol. 1 (Nashville 1962). However, this use of language, in particular the common use of the verb 'to mean' in two contexts, may be confusing. Hirsch, for example, argues that we should distinguish between 'meaning' and 'significance': what a text meant originally is its 'meaning'; what it means for us today is its 'significance'. See his *Validity*, p. 8, and in more detail pp. 209–44. This has some merit, though it runs the danger of arbitrarily abolishing the problem by defining the terms differently. The problem would seem to re-emerge in slightly different guise: can a text have a multiple significance? And how does 'significance' relate to 'meaning'? I have tried to follow Hirsch's suggestion in part here, though the demands of producing reasonably unconvoluted English prevent this being done consistently.

   Stendahl's article expressed what many New Testament critics probably believe: that the job of the New Testament critic is to find out what a text 'meant', and that it is then the subsequent task of the systematic theologian to work out what it might 'mean'. For a powerful critique of such a model, see N. Lash, 'What might Martyrdom Mean?', in W. Horbury & B. McNeil (eds.), *Suffering and Martyrdom in the New Testament* (Cambridge 1981), pp. 183–98, reprinted in Lash, *Theology on the Way to Emmaus* (London 1986), pp. 75–92, who argues that perhaps we can only really determine what a text meant if we already have some idea of what it might 'mean'.
2. Though, one should note that the 'literary' approaches considered in this chapter are rather different from the 'literary' approaches considered in ch. 8 above. See n. 11 of that chapter.
3. It is perhaps unfortunate that the term 'canonical criticism' has become associated with two rather different approaches to the biblical texts. The term is used by many to describe the approach of Childs, even though Childs himself is rather unhappy about it as a description of this work. (See B. S. Childs, *Introduction to the Old Testament as Scripture* (London 1979), p. 82.) Childs is primarily an Old Testament scholar and much of his work in canonical criticism has concerned the Old Testament. But he has recently extended his discussion with a very full 'Introduction' to the New Testament: see *The New Testament as Canon: An Introduction* (London 1984). A rather different approach, which does welcome the name 'canonical criticism', is that of J. A. Sanders. See his *Torah and Canon* (Philadelphia 1972) and a number of articles, including his 'Text and Canon: Concepts and

Methods', *JBL* 98 (1979), pp. 5–29. Also his recent *Canon and Community*. (Philadephia 1984). For a valuable study of the two approaches, see F. W. Spina, 'Canonical Criticism: Childs versus Sanders', in W. McCown & J. E. Massey (eds.), *Interpreting God's Word for Today: An Inquiry into Hermeneutics from a Biblical Theological Perspective* (Anderson, Ind. 1982), pp. 165–94. As opposed to Childs' interest in the end-product of the completed canon, Sanders' interest is in the process by which later writers (some within the present canon) used earlier authoritative traditions creatively. In terms of method, it seems doubtful if Sanders' approach can be classified as very different from traditional form and redaction criticism. He is above all concerned with the meaning of the texts of historical authors, though concentrating on particular aspects of texts, viz., a later author's creative use of earlier traditions.

4. See B. S. Childs, *Biblical Theology in Crisis* (Philadelphia 1970), pp. 151–63.
5. ibid., p. 162.
6. See the series of articles in *JSOT* 16 (1980) and *HorBibTheol* 2 (1980); also J. Barr, *Holy Scripture*, and J. Barton, *Reading the OT*, who both devote large sections to discussing canonical criticism (by which they mean the work of Childs rather than Sanders).
7. Childs, *NT as Canon*, p. 327.
8. ibid., p. 368.
9. cf. Barr, *Holy Scripture*, p. 67: 'Canons are not particularly hermeneutical in their character'; also pp. 90ff.
10. cf. Barr, ibid., pp. 85ff.
11. Part of the problems faced by canonical criticism applied to the Old Testament texts is to know which canon one should adopt. Should it be the Hebrew Old Testament? Or the books of the LXX (which contain the apocrypha as well)? Or should it be the Christian Bible of the Old Testament and New Testament? 'Canonical' views of death and the after-life may well be radically different depending on which canon is adopted. See Barton, *Reading the OT*, pp. 91–2.
12. cf. Barton, ibid., pp. 93f.; Barr, *Holy Scripture*, p. 111.
13. Barr, ibid., *passim*. cf. also C. K. Barrett, 'What is New Testament Theology? Some Reflections', *HorBibTheol* 3 (1981), pp. 1–22, on p. 18: 'New Testament theology is always critical theology'.
14. cf. Barton, *Reading the OT*, pp. 94–5.
15. Why should this particular part of the Church's tradition be normative? Or, if one is to think of a divinely inspired impersonal process, why should God's inspirational activity be so apparently limited? Childs appears to assume that this is self-evident for the Christian.
16. However, it must be said that Childs does not set out to 'replace' the more traditional methods. Nevertheless, it does seem to be the case that Childs' own approach does use the older historical approach in a rather deeper way than he seems prepared to admit.
17. See for example, J. Friedrich, *Gott im Bruder?* (Stuttgart 1977); also E. Schweizer, 'Matthew's Church', in G. N. Stanton (ed), *The Inter-*

pretation of Matthew (London 1983), p. 138, with further references. This is not to say that the parable might have been taken by Matthew to mean one thing, but might have meant something rather different earlier in the tradition. See D. R. Catchpole, 'The Poor on Earth and the Son of Man in Heaven. A Re-appraisal of Matthew XXV.31–46', *BJRL* 61 (1979), pp. 355–97, who argues that it is Matthew who has limited the recipients of the charitable action to members of the Christian community.

18. See Wellek & Warren, *Theory of Literature*, p. 25.
19. Hirsch, *Aims*, p. 134. His italics.
20. cf. also Barton, *Reading the OT*, pp. 166–7.
21. cf. Hirsch, *Aims*, pp. 133–4.
22. C. H. Dodd, *The Parables of the Kingdom* (London 1935), p. 16.
23. Indeed it is no surprise that a great deal of the work based on secular literary study has been focused on the parables in the New Testament.

24 M. A. Tolbert, *Perspectives on the Parables* (Philadelphia 1979).

25. ibid., p. 71.

Conclusion

We have tried to look critically at the various methods scholars use to interpret the New Testament texts. We have in fact spent most of the time considering scholarship as conducted within institutions devoted to the study of theology or religion; and even within this context we have seen that the New Testament texts can be used in many different ways. We have also seen, sometimes in passing, that the New Testament can also be used in contexts other than that of academic theology. The New Testament can be used in liturgy, in preaching, in academic study of literature (rather than religion), in private devotion, and so on.

It should be clear by now that different approaches will get different things out of the same text. The test passage which we have used in this book, the story of the healing of the man with the withered hand, can tell us various things depending on how we approach the text. It can possibly tell us something about Jesus' own ministry; it can tell us something of the evangelists' concerns in their own day; it may tell us something of various intervening stages between these two poles. There is thus no single result which we can say constitutes 'the' interpretation of the story.

At this very naive level we might then agree, somewhat tongue in cheek, with the views of some critics of secular literature in saying that a text can have multiple meanings. This is of course a travesty of what such critics really mean. Indeed the discussion in ch. 11 above was intended to preclude such possibilities in all but a few instances.

The conclusion reached several times in this book has been that the historical-critical method remains of fundamental importance in the interpretation of the New Testament. All the traditional approaches of source, form and redaction criticism are essentially historically oriented, recognizing that the New Testament texts are historical texts stemming from a particular point in history. The variety of interpretation is simply a reflection of the fact that the context in question is a highly complex one, and we can concentrate on different aspects of it.

In the case of a narrative text, part of the complexity is due to the fact that there are at least two historical contexts; the context of the author and the context of the history he is narrating. However, almost all traditional approaches have accepted that these contexts, however complex and interrelated, are essentially historical ones.

Even if we adopt a highly 'literary' approach to a text such as Mark's Gospel, most would still accept that the 'narrative world' created by Mark's text is one created by a first-century Christian Greek writer using first-century language. Hence in order to understand the language we have to read it in its historical context of first-century Greek-speaking Christianity. We may not be able to discover as much as we would like about its context. However, to take an extreme example, we shall try to understand what Mark might have meant in referring to Jesus as 'Son of God' by looking at a first-century background in Judaism and the Hellenistic world; we shall reject completely the ideas implied in the Chalcedonian definition of the fifth century AD as a possible background for interpreting Mark's language.

Such dependence on the historical approach has been questioned by some. I have tried to argue, especially in the last two chapters, that the historical approach remains deeply embedded even in methods which appear to reject it. Some of these approaches claim to have no interest in the historical circumstances of the origin of a text or in its original author. I have tried to show that such disinterest in the origin of a text is not, and indeed should not be, sustained consistently.

We all, I believe, accept that the language of a text should be understood in terms of its original historical context. The Greek of the New Testament should be interpreted as first-century Greek, not classical Greek. Words and phrases should be interpreted in terms of their original meaning, not in terms of what the same words might have meant in a different age and context.

All texts need a context before they can be interpreted, as we have seen (see the discussion in ch. 3 above). Yet even the approach of Childs' canonical criticism, which tries to replace the original historical context of a text by its context in a canon of Scripture, allows the historical context to creep back in again at various levels.

So too, a highly 'literary' approach to the parables, say, will probably have to give more than a fleeting glance at historical criticism. If such an approach to the parables is to claim any authority beyond the relatively limited circle of literary critics, if it is to appeal to the person of Jesus in any way for authorization, then historical criticism will probably have to be brought to bear to justify that appeal. Historical criticism, with all its uncertainties and ambiguities, is, I believe, an essential part of almost every attempt to interpret the New Testament.

What a text meant in its original context is of course only part of the answer to questions put by many people when interpreting the New Testament. We started this book by referring to the tremendous popularity of the Bible, both in scholarly and non-scholarly circles. Especially for the non-scholar, what is perhaps more important about the biblical text is not so much what it meant originally, but what it means for us today. The New Testament forms part of canonical Scripture for the Christian Church and as such is thought by many to speak to the present as well as to the past.

We have touched on this issue several times by implication during the course of this book. It is probably true to say that, just as there are several methods of interpreting the New Testament text, there are also several ways in which the New Testament can be conceived of as normative for the present.[1]

I tried in the first chapter to outline one possible model in such a way as to take full account of historical criticism. Canonical criticism (as defined here) perhaps represents another way, trying in some sense to bypass historical criticism. A 'literary' approach represents yet another way of seeking to lift the texts out of their context in the past and make them speak to the present.

If my argument above has any validity, then we cannot make a total divorce between 'what a text meant' and 'what it means'. This is not to say that we can simply identify the two *tout court*.[2] I tried to argue at the end of the last chapter that a 'literary' approach to the parables might, in some circumstances, be justified. Hence what a parable 'means' in the present might not be absolutely identical with what it 'meant' in its 'original' historical context. Nevertheless, we cannot jettison the historical approach completely.

Especially if we wish to retain some sense of normativeness for the New Testament texts in a context of Christian faith, we shall have to recognize the historical nature of the texts. We shall have to recognize that the centre of the Christian faith is the historical person of Jesus of Nazareth, not just the literary figure created by the New Testament Gospels. We shall have to recognize that the language of all the New Testament texts is primarily referential, referring to entities beyond the contours of the text itself, and not purely 'literary'.

One does not have to be a Christian to interpret the New Testament. As we saw in ch. 1, the New Testament texts can be interpreted with all integrity simply as products of a particular chunk of ancient history. Further, we can quite happily accept the normative status which the New Testament has for others without necessarily subscribing to it ourselves. However, for many students starting academic study of the New Testament, personal faith and critical scholarship are closely intertwined. An underlying aim of this book has been to suggest that such intertwining is not only something to be endured, but that it can also be very fruitful.

If, as I have tried to argue, a historical approach to the New Testament is fundamental, then the New Testament lets us see various historical figures battling within their own historical situation about the values and the truth of their new religious commitment, sorting out what was essential from what was peripheral, seeking above all to live their lives in conformity with the will of the God whom they served. Those who struggle to do the same today can only gain by entering more deeply and sympathetically into the struggles of the past. That for many will remain the enduring fascination of studying the New Testament.

Notes

1. See Kelsey, *Uses of Scripture, passim*.
2. ibid., n. 18 on pp. 202–3.

Suggestions for Further Reading

The books listed here are by no means intended to constitute a definitive bibliography for the subjects concerned. They simply represent some of the books which I have found valuable in writing this book. Only books in English are cited here; books in translated form are designated by their translated titles, and the place and date are of the translated version in each case. I have appended an occasional comment to some of the titles; those with no comment attached are not intended to be down-graded: in many instances (especially with some of the articles cited), the titles are self-explanatory.

General

Barton, J. *Reading the Old Testament. Method in Biblical Study* (London 1984). A very good survey of methods, mostly with the Old Testament in mind. Especially valuable on modern literary approaches and canonical criticism.

Beck, B. E. *Reading the New Testament Today* (Guildford & London 1977). A general, and very readable, survey.

Collins, R. F. *Introduction to the New Testament* (London 1983). Very full descriptions of traditional methods, and structuralism, from an avowedly Catholic viewpoint.

Hayes, J. H. & Holladay, C. R. *Biblical Exegesis. A Beginners' Handbook* (London 1983). Fairly brief, and trying to cover both testaments.

Marshall, I. H. (ed.) *New Testament Introduction* (Exeter 1977). A collection of essays on many of the subjects discussed in this book.

1 Scripture and Canon

Aland, K. *The Problem of the New Testament Canon* (London 1962).

Barr, J. *The Bible in the Modern World* (London 1973). A very fine survey of many relevant points.

——*Explorations in Theology 7* (London 1980). A collection of useful essays.

——*Holy Scripture. Canon, Authority, Criticism* (Oxford 1983).

Best, E. 'Scripture, Tradition and the Canon of the New Testament', *BJRL* 61 (1979), pp. 258–79.

von Campenhausen, H. *The Formation of the Christian Bible* (London 1972). A standard work on the history concerned.

Dungan, D. L. 'The New Testament Canon in Recent Study', *Interpretation* 29 (1975), pp. 339–51.

Evans, C. F. *Is 'Holy Scripture' Christian?* (London 1971).

Kelsey, D. H. *The Uses of Scripture in Recent Theology* (London 1975). A valuable discussion of the ways in which Scripture has been used in contemporary theology.

Ogden, S. M. 'The Authority of Scripture for Theology', *Interpretation* 30 (1976), pp. 242–61.

2 Textual Criticism

Birdsall, J. N. 'The New Testament Text', in P. R. Ackroyd & C. F. Evans (eds.), *The Cambridge History of the Bible* vol. 1 (Cambridge 1970), pp. 308–77.

Colwell, E. C. *Studies in Methodology in Textual Criticism of the New Testament* (Leiden 1969). Contains several very important articles on methodological questions.

Elliott, J. K. 'Can We Recover the Original New Testament?', *Theology* 77 (1974), pp. 338–53.

Epp, E. J. 'The Twentieth Century Interlude in New Testament Textual Criticism', *JBL* 93 (1974), pp. 386–414. A valuable survey of modern research.

——'The Eclectic Method in New Testament Textual Criticism: Solution or Symptom?', *HTR* 69 (1976), pp. 211–57.

Fee, G. D. 'Rigorous or Reasoned Eclecticism – Which?', in J. K. Elliott (ed.), *Studies in New Testament Language and Text.* Essays in Honour of G. D. Kilpatrick. (Leiden 1976), pp. 174–97.

Kilpatrick, G. D. 'The Greek New Testament of Today and the *Textus Receptus*', in H. Anderson & W. Barclay (eds.), *The New Testament in Historical and Contemporary Perspective. In Memory of G. H. C. MacGregor* (Oxford 1965), pp. 189–208. An example of Kilpatrick's 'eclectic' approach.

Lake, K. *The Text of the New Testament* (London 1928). A standard work.

Metzger, B. M. *The Text of the New Testament: Its Transmission, Corruption and Restoration* (Oxford 1964). A good discussion of all the problems with many examples.

——*A Textual Commentary on the Greek New Testament* (London 1971). A detailed discussion of all the variant readings noted in the UBS text.

3 and 4 Problems of Introduction

A large number of Introductions are available. The following provide a good range.

Fuller, R. H. *A Critical Introduction to the New Testament* (London 1966). Short and concise, but very readable.

Guthrie, D. *New Testament Introduction* (London 1970). A fairly 'conservative' treatment.

Koester, H. *Introduction to the New Testament* (Philadelphia 1982). A slightly different approach: full discussion of the background material coupled with a refusal to respect the limits of the canon. For justification, see Koester's article cited below.

Kümmel, W. G. *Introduction to the New Testament* (London 1975). A standard reference work with very full bibliographies.

Martin, R. P. *New Testament Foundations* 2 vols (Grand Rapids 1975). A slightly different format, but covering very much of the same material. Very readable.

Marxsen, W. *Introduction to the New Testament. An Approach to its Problems* (Oxford 1968). Concise and with a more 'radical' approach.

Moule, C. F. D. *The Birth of the New Testament* (London [3]1981). Not in the form of a standard Introduction, but an extremely valuable and readable account of how the New Testament texts came to be written.

See also:
Koester, H. 'New Testament Introduction: A Critique of a Discipline', in J. Neusner (ed.), *Christianity, Judaism and Other Greco–Roman Cults. Studies for Morton Smith at Sixty* Part 1 (Leiden 1975), pp. 1–20.

5 Genre

Aune, D. E. 'The Problem of the Genre of the Gospels', in R. T. France & D. Wenham (eds.), *Gospel Perspectives II* (Sheffield 1981), pp. 9–60. A powerful critique of Talbert.

Doty, W. G. 'The Classification of Epistolary Literature', *CBQ* 31 (1969), pp. 181–99.

——*Letters in Primitive Christianity* (Philadelphia 1973). A good survey of ancient letters in the light of the Hellenistic world.

Guelich, R. A. 'The Gospel Genre', in P. Stuhlmacher (ed.), *Das Evangelium und die Evangelien* (Tübingen 1983), pp. 183–219. A valuable survey of the problem.

Shuler, P. *A Genre for the Gospels* (Philadelphia 1982).

Talbert, C. H. *What is a Gospel?* (Philadelphia 1977).

Wellek, R. & Warren, A. *Theory of Literature* (Harmondsworth 1963). A standard work of literary criticism.

6 Source Criticism

Beardslee, W. *Literary Criticism of the New Testament* (Philadelphia ^{5}1981).

Farmer, W. R. *The Synoptic Problem* (London ^{2}1976). A recent attack on the 2DH.

Fitzmyer, J. A. 'The Priority of Mark and the "Q" source in Luke', in D. G. Buttrick, *Jesus and Man's Hope* vol. 1 (Pittsburgh 1970), pp. 131–70. A valuable modern defence of the 2DH.

Palmer, N. H. *The Logic of Gospel Criticism* (London 1968). A survey of arguments used from the point of view of a philosopher.

Sanders, E. P. *The Tendencies of the Synoptic Tradition* (Cambridge 1969). A critical survey of the alleged 'laws' of development of the tradition.

Streeter, B. H. *The Four Gospels* (London 1924). The standard English work on the Synoptic problem.

Styler, G. M. 'The Priority of Mark', Excursus IV in C. F. D. Moule, *The Birth of the New Testament* (London ^{3}1981), pp. 285–316. A good modern defence of the 2DH.

Tuckett, C. M. *The Revival of the Griesbach Hypothesis* (Cambridge 1983). A critical survey of one of the 2DH's main rivals today.

7 Form Criticism

Barbour, R. S. *Traditio–Historical Criticism of the Gospels* (London 1972). Very short but manages to cover a vast amount.

Bultmann, R. *The History of the Synoptic Tradition* (Oxford 1968). A standard reference work.

——& Kundsin, K. *Form Criticism* (New York 1934). Bultmann's essay here presents his views in more easily digestible form.

Dibelius, M. *From Tradition to Gospel* (London 1934). A standard work.

Doty, W. G. 'The Discipline and Literature of New Testament Form Criticism', *ATR* 51 (1969), pp. 257–319. A useful survey article with a very full bibliography.

Ellis, E. E. 'New Directions in Form Criticism', in G. Strecker (ed.), *Jesus Christus in Historie und Theologie* (FS for H. Conzelmann. Tübingen 1975), pp. 299–315; reprinted in E. E. Ellis, *Prophecy and Hermeneutic* (Tübingen 1978), pp. 237–53.

Gerhardsson, B. *Memory and Manuscript* (Uppsala 1961).

——*The Origins of the Gospel Traditions* (London 1979). A much shorter restatement of Gerhardsson's views, taking note of earlier criticisms.

Hooker, M. D. 'Christology and Methodology', *NTS* 17 (1971), pp. 480–7. Good discussion of the dissimilarity criterion.

McKnight, E. V. *What is Form Criticism?* (Philadelphia 1969). A short and very readable summary. Relatively uncritical.

Perrin, N. *Rediscovering the Teaching of Jesus* (London 1967). Includes a good discussion of methods used.

Riesenfeld, H. *The Gospel Tradition and Its Beginnings. A Study in the Limits of 'Formgeschichte'* (London 1957). A short, programmatic study.

Stanton, G. N. 'Form Criticism Revisited', in M. D. Hooker & C. J. A. Hickling (eds.), *What About the New Testament?* (London 1975), pp. 13–27.

Taylor, V. *The Formation of the Gospel Tradition* (London 1933).

Walker, W. O. 'The Quest for the Historical Jesus. A Discussion of Methodology', *ATR* 51 (1969), pp. 38–56. A valuable survey of criteria used.

8 Redaction Criticism

Individual redaction–critical studies of the Gospels are not noted here.

Hooker, M. D. 'In His Own Image?', in M. D. Hooker & C. J. A. Hickling (eds.), *What About the New Testament?* (London 1975), pp. 28–44.

Perrin, N. *What is Redaction Criticism?* (London 1970). Short and readable, though slightly extravagant in some of its claims.

Petersen, N. R. *Literary Criticism for New Testament Critics* (Philadelphia 1978). Like Perrin, short and readable, though inclined to exaggerate methodological differences.

Rohde, J. *Rediscovering the Teaching of the Evangelists* (London 1968). A good survey with summaries of the theories of many early redaction critics.

Stein, R. H. 'What is Redaktionsgeschichte?', *JBL* 88 (1969), pp. 45–56.

——'The Proper Methodology for Ascertaining a Markan Redaction History', *NovT* 13 (1971), pp. 181–98.

9 The New Testament and Sociology

Best, T. F. 'The Sociological Study of the New Testament: Promise and Peril of a New Discipline', *SJT* 36 (1983), pp. 181–94.

Elliott, J. H. *A Home for the Homeless. A Sociological Exegesis of 1 Peter, its Situation and Strategy* (London 1982). A specialized study of one New Testament text with some important observations about the whole approach.

Gager, J. G. *Kingdom and Community. The Social World of Early Christianity* (Engelwood Cliffs 1975). A relatively early collection of essays.

——'Shall We Marry Our Enemies? Sociology and the New Testament', *Interpretation* 36 (1982), pp. 256–65. A useful survey article.

Harrington, D. J. 'Sociological Concepts in the Early Church. A Decade of Research', *TS* 41 (1980), pp. 181–90.

Kee, H. C. *Christian Origins in Sociological Perspective* (London 1980). A good introduction.

Meeks, W. 'The Man from Heaven in Johannine Sectarianism', *JBL* 91 (1972), pp. 44–72.

——*The First Urban Christians* (New Haven & London 1983). A very valuable study of the social world of Pauline Christianity.

Malherbe, A. J. *Social Aspects of Early Christianity* (Philadelphia 1983).

Rodd, C. S. 'On Applying a Sociological Theory to Biblical Studies', *JSOT* 19 (1981), pp. 95–106. Contains an important discussion about the possibility of applying sociological theories to historical texts.

Scroggs, R. 'The Sociological Interpretation of the New Testament. The Present State of Research', *NTS* 26 (1980), pp. 164–79. A useful survey article.

Theissen, G. *The First Followers of Jesus* (London 1978).

——*The Social Setting of Pauline Christianity* (Edinburgh 1982). Contains many of Theissen's best-known articles on 1 Corinthians; there is also a good introduction by J. H. Schütz.

Tidball, D. *An Introduction to the Sociology of the New Testament* (Exeter 1983).

10 The New Testament and Structuralism

Barton, J. *Reading the Old Testament* (see General section above).

Culler, J. *Structuralist Poetics* (London 1975). An important discussion of Barthes, Greimas and others, though not specifically related to the Bible.

Greenwood, D. C. *Structuralism and the Biblical Text* (New York &

Amsterdam 1985). A good critical survey of different structuralist methods applied to the biblical texts.

Johnson, A. M. (ed.) *The New Testament and Structuralism* (Pittsburgh 1976). A collection of essays.

Patte, D. *What is Structural Exegesis?* (Philadelphia 1976) A relatively short introduction by an enthusiast.

Patte, D. & A. *Structural Exegesis. From Theory to Practice* (Philadelphia 1978).

Polzin, R. M. *Biblical Structuralism* (Philadelphia 1977).

Robey, D. (ed.) *Structuralism: An Introduction* (Oxford 1973). A useful collection of essays by scholars from a number of disciplines.

Rogerson, J. 'Recent Literary Structuralism Approaches to Biblical Interpretation', *The Churchman* 90 (1976), pp. 165–77.

Thiselton, A. C. 'Structuralism and Biblical Studies: Method or Ideology?', *ExpT* 89 (1978), pp. 329–35.

11 Other Approaches

Barr, J. *Holy Scripture* (see section for ch. 1 above).

——'Reading the Bible as Literature', *BJRL* 56 (1973), pp. 10–33.

Barton, J. *Reading the Old Testament* (see General section above).

Brown, R. *The Critical Meaning of the Bible* (New York 1981). A collection of essays, including an important one entitled 'What the Biblical Word Meant and What it Means', pp. 23–44.

Childs, B. S. *The New Testament as Canon: An Introduction* (London 1984).

Dunn, J. D. G. 'Levels of Canonical Authority', *HorBibTheol* 4 (1982), pp. 13–60.

Hirsch, E. D. *Validity in Interpretation* (New Haven 1967). A strong exposition of the theory that the meaning of a text is the author's intended meaning.

——*The Aims of Interpretation* (Chicago & London 1976). Further essays on the theory of the study of literature.

Perrin, N. *Jesus and the Language of the Kingdom* (London 1976). Surveys modern interpretations of the parables.

Spina, F. W. 'Canonical Criticism: Childs versus Sanders', in W. McCown & J. E. Massey (eds.), *Interpreting God's Word for Today: An Inquiry into Hermeneutics from a Biblical Theological Perspective* (Anderson, Ind. 1982), pp. 165–94.

Via, D. *The Parables: Their Literary and Existential Dimension* (Philadelphia 1967). A 'literary' interpretation of the parables.

Wellek, R. & Warren, A. *Theory of Literature* (see section for chapter 5 above).

Index